Wisdom in the Ancient W

A diviner examining a liver.

WISDOM

in the

ANCIENT WORLD

Trevor Curnow

DUCKWORTH

First published in 2010 by
Gerald Duckworth & Co. Ltd.
90-93 Cowcross Street, London EC1M 6BF
Tel: 020 7490 7300
Fax: 020 7490 0080
info@duckworth-publishers.co.uk
www.ducknet.co.uk

A catalogue record for this book is available
from the British Library

ISBN 978-0-7156-3504-9

Illustration sources

Frontispiece: image from the back of an Etruscan mirror, Vatican Museums;
pp. 23 & 24: paintings from the Tomb of Queen Nefertari; p. 45: from Jamieson
B. Hurry, *Imhotep, the Vizier and Physician of King Zoser* (1928); p. 55: Egyptian
Museum, Cairo; p. 89: National Museum, Athens; p. 101: Metropolitan Museum,
New York; p. 114: National Museum, Cairo; p. 123: Uffizi, Florence; p. 126
(above): Municipal Museum of Piacenza, Palazzo Farnese; p. 126 (below):
British Museum; p. 127: Capitoline Museums, Rome.

Typeset by Ray Davies
Printed and bound in Great Britain by
CPI Antony Rowe, Chippenham and Eastbourne

Contents

Preface   vii
Maps   xii
Timeline   xviii

1. The Nature of Wisdom   1

1. Introduction   1
2. Four Hypotheses   3
3. The Seven Sages   6

2. Wisdom in Religion   12

1. Introduction   12
2. Wise Gods and Goddesses   14
   (a) Mesopotamia   14
   (b) Egypt   17
   (c) Mystery Cults   25
   (d) Greece and Rome   27
   (e) Zoroastrianism   30
3. Wisdom and Monotheism   31
4. Conclusion   37

3. Wisdom in Myth and Legend   39

1. Introduction   39
2. Mesopotamia   39
3. Israel   42
4. Egypt   45
5. Greece and Rome   46
6. Conclusion   50

4. Wisdom in History   52

1. Introduction   52
2. Egypt   52
3. Ugarit and Ebla   55
4. Mesopotamia   56
5. Israel and Judaism   60
6. The Teacher of Righteousness   66
7. Jesus of Nazareth   67
8. Solon and the Lawgivers   69

9. Seers, Shamans and Saints 73
10. The Early Philosophers 80
11. Pythagoras and Pythagoreanism 82
12. Heraclitus and Parmenides 85
13. Democritus and Anaxagoras 86
14. Socrates and the Sophists 87
15. Plato, Aristotle and the Schools 91
16. Zeno and Epicurus 96
17. Diogenes and Pyrrho 101
18. Plotinus and Iamblichus 104
19. Some Wise Men of Rome 106
20. Conclusion 107

5. Wisdom in Practice 108
1. Introduction 108
2. Ruling, Judging and Lawgiving 108
3. The Scribe 113
4. Diviners and Divination 118
5. Counsellors and Advisors 130
6. Architects and Planners 132
7. Scientists and Science 137
8. Healers and Healing 138
9. Magic and Magicians 141
10. Conclusion 143

6. Wisdom Literature 145
1. Introduction 145
2. Mesopotamia 146
3. Egypt 149
4. Israel 156
5. Apocalyptic 162
6. A Sapiential Selection 166
7. Hermetica 169
8. The *Chaldaean Oracles* 173
9. Conclusion 175

7. Conclusion 177
Bibliography 183
Index of Places 193
Index of Personal Names 195
Index of Modern Authors 201

Preface

I first became interested in the subject of wisdom when I was doing research on the theory of moral philosophy known as ethical intuitionism. While looking for anything helpful that philosophers might have said on the subject of intuition, I came to see a connection between intuition and wisdom. The result was that wisdom developed into a significant topic within my research and came to occupy a prominent place in the book that emerged from it, *Wisdom, Intuition and Ethics* (Curnow 1999). However, because the central focus of that work remained ethical intuitionism, many of the materials I had collected on wisdom had to be left out.

The longest chapter in *Wisdom, Intuition and Ethics* was ambitiously entitled 'The History of Wisdom', and sought to trace thinking about wisdom from the earliest times up to the present day. In constructing that history, it became clear that the history of wisdom in some ways over-lapped quite neatly with the history of philosophy, and that there were what might be termed ancient, medieval and modern ways of thinking about wisdom. However, there were also two important differences. First, if we accept the convention that the history of (Western) philosophy begins in the late seventh or early sixth century BC with Thales of Miletus, then it is apparent that the history of wisdom begins much earlier. Secondly, the modern age has been characterized by a distinct lack of interest in wisdom, such that it has been largely and routinely neglected by philosophers (and, indeed, most other people) altogether. This book is concerned with the ancient period of the history of wisdom, beginning in the third millennium BC and extending up to approximately the end of the sixth century AD. I believe that the medieval period is sufficiently different to merit separate treatment. However, even if that is accepted, it can be argued that the medieval period begins well before the onset of the seventh century AD. That particular end-date has been chosen for two reasons. First, the year 641 is that at which the last volume of the *Prosopography of the Later Roman Empire* (Martindale 1992) ends, and secondly, the emperor Justinian is said to have closed down the surviving philosophical schools in Athens in AD 529. While 'the end of antiquity' was a long drawn-out process rather than an event, if an end-date has to be chosen for practical purposes, then the beginning of the seventh century, although arbitrary, falls between earlier and later options that are less arbitrary. With regard to dates more generally, it should be noted that many of the earlier ones that appear throughout the text are a matter of considerable dispute. Fortunately, for present purposes little of substance turns on them, and the approach taken is generally not a chronological one. However, a timeline has been produced in order to provide a broad historical context, and in that I have generally followed the more rather than the less conventional dates.

As with my books on *The Oracles of the Ancient World* (Curnow 2004) and *The Philosophers of the Ancient World* (Curnow 2006b), with which the present volume forms a very loose trilogy, I have also had to impose geographical restrictions on the area covered. The earlier books generally restricted themselves to the territory covered by the Roman Empire at its greatest extent. This book adopts broadly the same principle, although there is some straying beyond those boundaries from time to time. It is not the argument of this book that the area contained within its geographical limits forms a tidy and coherent cultural entity with a single self-contained unified history. Whether for the purposes of trade, exploration or conquest, it is apparent that travel was by no means a rarity in the ancient world, and that there was a frequent exposure of one culture to another. Nevertheless, it can be argued that the Indian subcontinent and China carved out significantly different cultural histories from those of Europe and west Asia, even if none developed in isolation. As with the end-date, even if no watertight theoretical argument can be constructed for the geographical limits, pragmatism demands that some are employed.

When I set the topic of wisdom aside for some time after *Wisdom, Intuition and Ethics*, it was my hope that when I returned to it I would be faced with the relatively straightforward task of tying up a number of loose ends and bringing various disparate elements into some kind of tidy arrangement. Once I actually did return to it, I soon came to see that the task was far more challenging than I had anticipated. Not only do there now appear to be more, rather than fewer, loose ends than there were before, but a number of the loose ends themselves have become increasingly frayed. It was always my intention to display the great variety to be found in ways of thinking about wisdom in the ancient world, but the variety has turned out to be even greater than I had anticipated. That makes the challenge of imposing some kind of order on it even greater too. Any aspirations to provide a completely comprehensive coverage of the subject have had to be reined in, and a more realistic aim substituted for an over-ambitious one. Consequently, what appears here might perhaps be looked upon as a kind of mosaic, reflecting many different aspects of wisdom in the ancient world. Many other aspects have had to be left out. The culture of Ugarit, for example, gets only a brief mention [4.3], and the Hittites do not get even that. And there is far more that could be said about those cultures that do get a mention. There will also be relatively little here about how the different aspects fit together. Addressing those issues is a task for other books and other days. What is presented here might perhaps be described as a substantial introduction to a very substantial topic. However, even as it stands in its imperfect state I believe it is the first attempt to produce a monograph on the subject.

Wisdom in the ancient world is not only a substantial topic, but also an important one. The fact that wisdom was prized across so many cultures and centuries is adequate testimony to that. Perhaps it even helped to bind the ancient world together. Consequently, I believe a study of wisdom can contribute to a wider understanding of ancient culture in general, and (more narrowly) classical culture in particular, as the Graeco-Roman world assimilated and blended many different and disparate influences. From the specific vantage point of the history of philosophy, it can also contribute to a wider understanding of how philosophy emerged and developed against a background of competing claims to wisdom.

Because of the inherent untidiness of the materials, pragmatic decisions have sometimes had to be taken as to which chapter or section they should appear in. Sometimes it is simply a matter of ignorance. It is not always clear where legend ends and history begins. On many occasions it is a matter of geography, with materials from the same region clustered together, even when widely separated in time. Often it is simply a matter of convenience. The same materials could reasonably be expected to turn up in more than one place but I have sought to keep repetition to a minimum and so one place has had to be chosen over another. To make things easier for the reader, I have liberally sprinkled cross-references throughout the text: they take the form [4.2] where the first number refers to the chapter and the second to a section within it. The indexes and contents pages should also be used as navigational aids.

Seeking to bring together materials from a wide historical and geographical range inevitably brings with it the problem of translation. Although such words as the Greek *sophia* and the Hebrew *hokma* are routinely translated as 'wisdom', anyone who knows anything about translation knows that it is as much art as science. Languages do not neatly map onto each other, and it cannot be simply assumed that the domains of 'wisdom', '*sophia*' and '*hokma*' are coterminous. Furthermore, the meanings of words change over time and what serves as an adequate translation at one time may be unacceptable at another. For example, it is apparent that within Greek culture turf wars were fought over *sophia* from time to time, with different people, professions and disciplines fighting for supremacy, or at least recognition. However, having uttered a word of caution, it is necessary to balance it with pragmatism. Despite the difficulties, translation is not an impossible exercise and the case is not a hopeless one. This may be an appropriate moment at which to make the point that while I have some knowledge of some of the languages of antiquity, I am an expert in none and in a state of complete ignorance with regard to many. For translations, as for many other things, I am massively indebted to the scholarship of others, as the bibliography will make plain.

Unfortunately, there is no simple scholarly solution to the problem of transliteration. This is evident above all with regard to the names of people and places where a number of variants often exist. The fact that a place may be called by different names at different times, or by different names by different people at the same time, makes for even greater confusion. I do not believe that there is an ideal solution, so I have not sought one. On the other hand, I do not go as far as T.E. Lawrence did: responding to a proofreader's queries as to why he had used both 'Ruwalla' and 'Rualla' for a proper name, he replied, 'Should also have used Ruwala and Ruala.' His reason? 'I spell my names anyhow, to show what rot the systems [of transliteration of Arabic] are' (Lawrence 1962, p. 19)! At the very least I have sought internal consistency, although this inevitably means that some names appear differently in the body of the text from how they appear in the titles of works cited in the bibliography. I have also sought simplicity, eliminating diacriticals wherever possible, and running the elements of a name together rather than separating them with hyphens. Names that are too well-known in their English forms to change without creating unnecessary confusion (e.g. Athens) have been left as they are. Better known alternatives are generally preferred over lesser known ones, although such a criterion is not without its subjective element. Where it is not immediately obvious that alternative names in circulation refer to the same place (e.g. Akkad and Agade), I have tried to make this clear when the name first appears. Thereafter only the chosen alternative is used. The maps use the chosen alternatives. In the end, and despite the apparent theoretical chaos, I think it unlikely that any readers will be misled in practice.

Work on this book had to be fitted in between a range of other commitments over a considerable period of time. I am extremely grateful to Deborah Blake of Duckworth who showed faith in the project at an early stage and has been enormously patient in putting up with the many delays that have occurred along the way. As with my earlier works with Duckworth (Curnow 2004, Curnow 2006b), she has also produced the maps that accompany the text. Finally, special thanks are due to Nicky Metcalfe Meer who always manages to persuade me that I am doing something worthwhile whenever I begin to believe that I am not.

For Anne, Annie and Janet

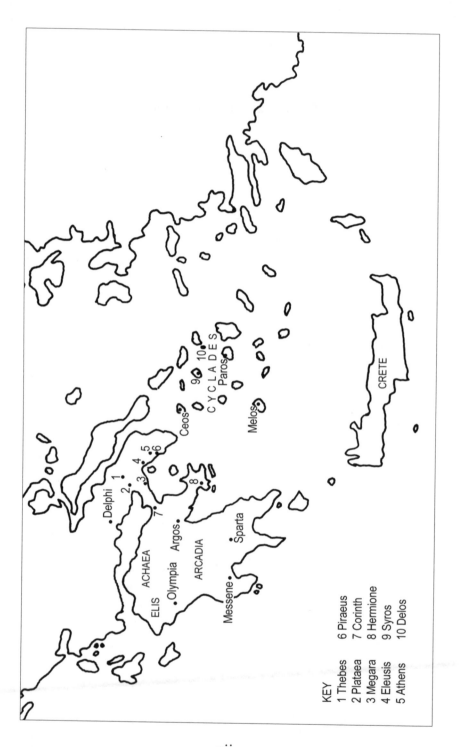

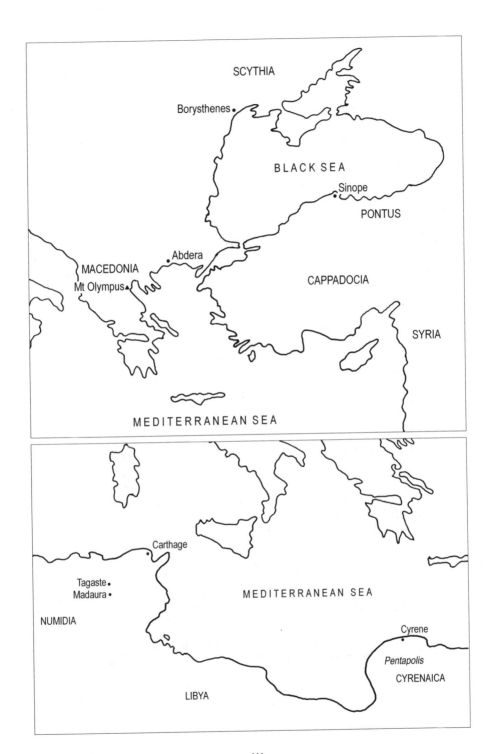

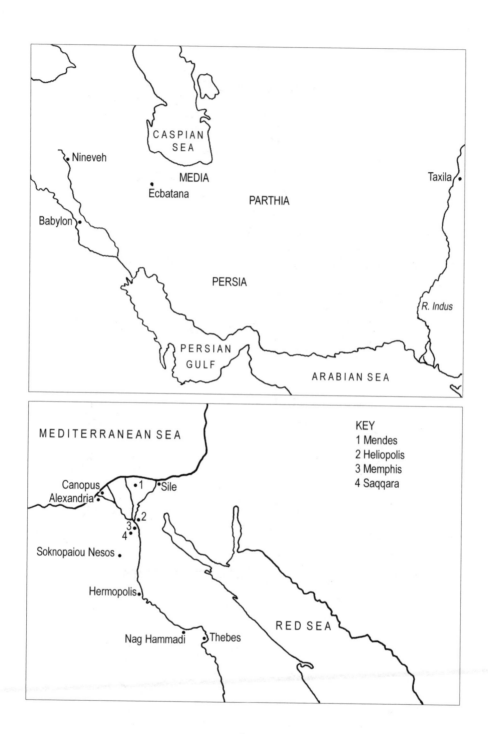

THRACE

Byzantium
•Chalcedon

Proconnesus

BITHYNIA

•Lampsacus

•Troy

MYSIA

•Pergamum

ASIA

MINOR

LESBOS 1

•Smyrna
Clazomenae

•Ephesus

2 •Priene

3
4

CARIA

5

Cos•

RHODES

KEY
1 Mytilene
2 Samos
3 Miletus
4 Didyma
5 Telmessus

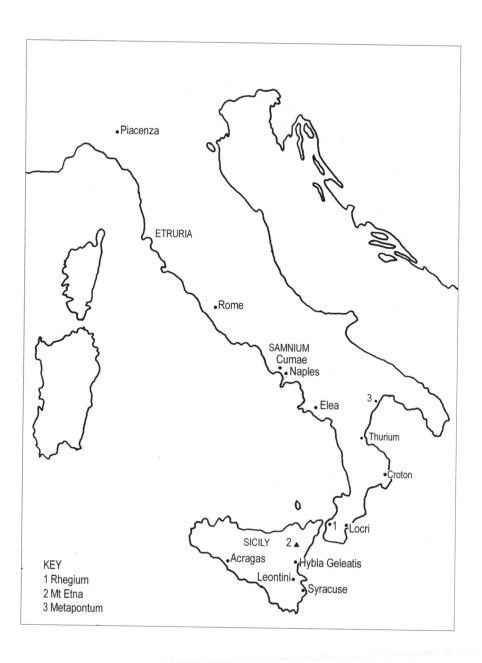

Piacenza

ETRURIA

Rome

SAMNIUM
Cumae
Naples

Elea

3.

Thurium

Croton

1 Locri

SICILY 2 ▲

Acragas

Hybla Geleatis

Leontini

Syracuse

KEY
1 Rhegium
2 Mt Etna
3 Metapontum

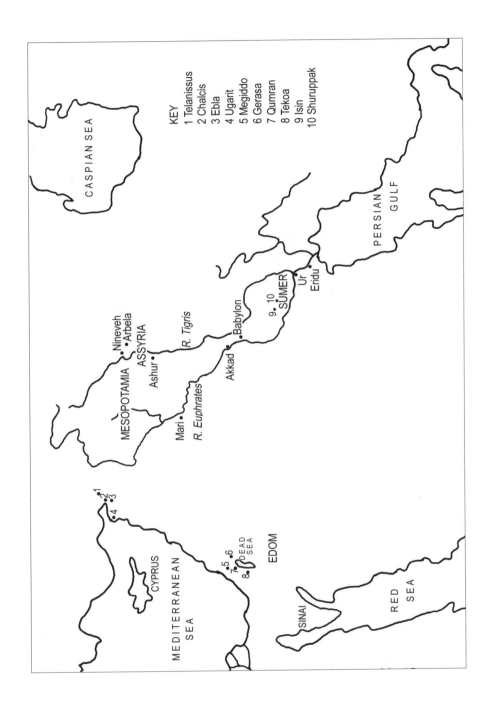

KEY
1 Telanissus
2 Chalcis
3 Ebla
4 Ugarit
5 Megiddo
6 Gerasa
7 Qumran
8 Tekoa
9 Isin
10 Shuruppak

CASPIAN SEA

MEDITERRANEAN SEA

CYPRUS

MESOPOTAMIA

ASSYRIA

Nineveh
Arbela
Ashur
Mari
R. Euphrates
R. Tigris
Akkad
Babylon
SUMER
9 10
Ur
Eridu

PERSIAN GULF

DEAD SEA

EDOM

SINAI

RED SEA

	3000	2500	2000 BC
MESO-POTAMIA	*The Sumerian Job?*	AKKADIAN PERIOD **Sargon the Great** (2334-2279) **Sharrishtakal** (Akkad)	**Shulgi** (Ur) (2094-2047)
EGYPT		OLD KINGDOM (2686-2181) **Djoser** (2667-2648) **Snefru** (2613-2598) **Khufu** (2589-2566) **Djedkare-Isesi** (2414-2375) Imhotep Hardjedef *Ptahhotep*	FIRST INTERMEDIATE PERIOD (2181-2055) **Merikare** *The Dispute of a Man with his Soul*
GREECE AND ROME			
OTHER		Ishmaia (Ebla) Azi (Ebla)	

Hammurabi
(1792-1750)

Ludlul bel nemeqi

MIDDLE KINGDOM	SECOND	NEW KINGDOM
(2055-1782)	INTER-	(1570-1069)
Mentuhotep IV	MEDIATE	**Tuthmosis III**
(1992-1985)	PERIOD	(1479-1425)
Amenemhet I		**Amenhotep III**
(1985-1955)		(1390-1352)
Senusret II		**Ramesses II**
(1880-1874)		(1279-1213)
The Complaints		Ramose
of Khakheperre-sonb		Amenhotep, son of Hapu
The Prophecies of Neferti		*Instruction of Amenemope?*
		Admonitions of Ipuwer?

Trojan War?

Saul   **Solomon**
Ilumalku   Siptinarum
Poem of Aqhat   *Counsels of Shube'awilum*

BC	1000	500	0
MESO-POTAMIA	NEO-ASSYRIAN PERIOD (1000-605) **Sennacherib** (704-681) **Esarhaddon** (680-669) **Ashurbanipal** (668-627) *Ahikar?*	**Nabonidus** (556-539) PERSIAN PERIOD (539-331)	SELEUCIDS (323-126) **Antiochus IV** (175-164)
EGYPT	THIRD INTERMEDIATE PERIOD **Osorkon II** (874-850)	PERSIAN PERIOD (525-323)	PTOLEMAIC PERIOD (305-30) *Instructions of Ankhsheshonqy?*

Alexander the Great (356-323)

GREECE AND ROME	1000	500	0
	Homer **Romulus?** **Numa?**	Thales Solon Pythagoras Heraclitus Anaxagoras Parmenides Hippocrates Democritus	Socrates Sophists Plato Aristotle Zeno Epicurus Pyrrho Diogenes Cato the Censor
OTHER		*Ecclesiastes*	Teacher of Righteousness *Ben Sira*

AD   0   500

PARTHIAN   SASANIANS   637: Arab conquest
PERIOD   of Mesopotamia

ROMAN PERIOD   642: Arab conquest
Philo of   of Egypt
Alexandria   Antony of Egypt
                  Athanasius of Alexandria
                  Plotinus

                  Proclus
                  Iamblichus

Apollonius of Tyana   529: Justinian closes
                         philosophical schools
                         in Athens.
Chaldaean Oracles
                  Augustine

Jesus of Nazareth

AD   0   500

The Nature of Wisdom

Introduction

'But where shall wisdom be found?' asked Job (Job 28:12), and from across the ancient world came many different replies. Some conceived of wisdom in supernatural personified form and answered the question in appropriate terms. In 1 Enoch (42:1-2), for example, we read that:

> Wisdom could not find a place in which she could dwell;
> but a place was found (for her) in the heavens.
> Then Wisdom went out to dwell with the children of the people,
> but she found no dwelling place.
> (So) Wisdom returned to her place
> and she settled permanently among the angels.
>
> (Charlesworth 1983, p. 33)

For others, wisdom was something far more human, manifested in a number of different possible ways. In the opinion of the author of the Fourth Book of Maccabees (15-19), for example:

> Wisdom, I submit, is knowledge of things divine and human, and of their causes. And this wisdom, I assume, is the culture we acquire from the Law, through which we can learn the things of God reverently and the things of men to our worldly advantage. The forms of wisdom consist of prudence, justice, courage and temperance.
>
> (Charlesworth 1985, p. 545)

For the philosopher Seneca, on the other hand, it was simply the highest human intellectual attainment possible: 'Wisdom is the human mind's good brought to perfection' (Long and Sedley 1987, p. 160).

And 'What is the fruit of wisdom?' asked Aristeas, in a letter to his brother Philocrates, before promptly answering his own question: 'A clear conscience of no evil done, and of living one's life in truth' (Charlesworth 1985, p. 30). Others answered differently. In the 'Sentences of Sextus' (167) it is said that 'Wisdom leads a soul to God' (Edwards and Wild 1981, p. 37), and in the 'Sentences of the Syrian Menander' (31) that it is 'bright eyes and an excellent tongue' (Charlesworth 1985, p. 593). According to Aristobolus, the philosophical heirs of Aristotle believed that 'wisdom holds the place of a lantern; for as long as they follow it unremittingly, they will be calm throughout their whole life' (Charlesworth 1985, p. 841). In one of the oldest preserved statements on the subject, attributed to King Shuruppak, 'The gift of wisdom [is like] the stars (of heaven)' (Alster 1974, p. 51). Writing perhaps three thousand years later, Augustine of Hippo said that 'To wisdom belongs the intellectual cognition of eternal things' (Augustine 2002, p. 102).

Shuruppak and Augustine were not only separated by a long period of time, they were also separated by a large geographical distance. Whether he belongs to history or legend, Shuruppak was associated with the modest ancient Mesopotamian city of the same name. Also known now as Fara (or Farah), the remains of the city lie in southern Iraq, 125 miles south-east of Baghdad. Augustine came from Tagaste, near what is now the town of Souk Ahras in north-eastern Algeria, about 2,500 miles away. There is no reason to believe that Augustine had ever heard of Shuruppak, but there is considerable evidence of cultural exchanges bearing on wisdom across the ancient world. One of the most interesting examples is the text known as 'Wisdom of Ahiqar' [6.2]. Set in Assyria and written in Aramaic, a copy was found in Egypt on the site of a former Jewish colony, and it was known to the author of the book of Tobit, who claims to have been Ahiqar's uncle.

Evidence of a different kind comes from the many stories told of those who travelled from place to place across the ancient world seeking or dispensing wisdom. An example that survives intact is the life of Apollonius of Tyana [4.9] as related by Philostratus (1970), which has its hero appearing as far west as Cadiz, as far east as Taxila, and in a host of other locations across Asia, Africa and Europe. Whatever the work's historical accuracy, it is predicated on the assumption that wisdom can be carried, recognized and acquired across political, cultural and historical boundaries. Apollonius is portrayed as a Pythagorean, but one who believes that Pythagoras based his own teachings on 'the doctrine of the Naked Philosophers of Egypt and the Wise Men of India' (Philostratus 1970, p. 224).

A different kind of evidence again is apparent with regard to divinatory techniques, which also travelled around the ancient world. It was widely believed that divination by means of the inspection of the entrails of sacrificial animals had its origins in Mesopotamia, and astrology was also closely associated with the Babylonians. Both subsequently found favour in many different places. There was also the tendency to assimilate the gods of one culture with those of another. An extreme case was Isis, who became identified with perhaps as many as thirty other goddesses [2.2]. These two phenomena are connected both with wisdom and with each other. Isis was one of the deities most closely associated with wisdom, divination was a practice associated with wisdom, and seeking to understand, or at least glimpse, the thinking of the divine was one of the purposes of divination.

All this evidence seems to me to point towards a simple basic fact, that whether or not it was ever actually articulated, there was some kind of shared sense of wisdom that permeated the ancient world. My aim in this book is to put some aspects of that shared sense of wisdom on display.

2. Four Hypotheses

It is unfortunate that much of the agenda for the study of wisdom in the ancient world has been set by biblical scholars. The negative consequences of this have been an overwhelming concentration on wisdom literature, and the adoption of certain biblical works as paradigmatic forms of that literature, however early or late they may be. Although this might be understandable if we knew nothing about the literature and culture of other ancient civilizations, that is not the case, and becomes even less so with every ancient document or inscription that is found, deciphered and translated. This heavily literary bias has led to many interesting studies of proverbs, in particular. However, while Alexander Pope may have been correct to observe in 'An Essay on Criticism' that:

> True wit is nature to advantage dressed,
> What oft was thought, but ne'er so well expressed.

it is nevertheless important to maintain some distance between the thought and the expression. What is profound may be expressed badly, what is banal may be expressed elegantly. A lot of what has been written about the *form* of the proverb strikes me as being entirely beside the point.

A focus on proverbs has also been unhelpful when questions about the origins and transmission of wisdom are raised. It is by no means clear whether proverbs have their origins in a literary or folk context (Westermann 1995). However, the idea that similar societies might generate similar pieces of folk wisdom that are subsequently polished up into similar literary gems is on the face of it entirely plausible. In the absence of the hardest evidence of direct copying, coincidence will always be a possibility. However, if the question about transmission or coincidence is asked not about proverbs but about the practice of examining the entrails of sacrificed animals in order to read the will of the gods, a rather different level of plausibility is encountered.

This leads to what may be regarded as the first hypothesis of this book, namely that wisdom in the ancient world was a multi-faceted affair. Far from being confined to a particular literary genre, it was rooted in the cultures of the ancient world in many different ways. However, this hypothesis brings with it its own problems. There seem to be so many dimensions to wisdom that it is often difficult to see where it ends. Writing in the specific and limited context of Akkadian literature, Ronald F.G. Sweet has identified seven different words in that language meaning 'wise man', ten meaning 'wise', twenty meaning 'wisdom' and one meaning 'to be wise' (Sweet 1990a, pp. 47-50). And the kinds of people to whom the

Akkadian vocabulary of wisdom was applied included kings, diviners, craftsmen of various kinds, soldiers, cult officials, exorcists, architects, builders and musicians. Multiply this phenomenon by the number of cultures and/or languages of the ancient world, and the result is frightening. In addressing this problem, I have been guided by two basic principles. First, as far as possible, I have tried to let the ancients speak for themselves. Rather than be too prescriptive and rule out any number of claims to wisdom that do not fit tidily within a preconceived notion, I have tried to let the variety of claims come through as much as possible. If a particular culture *called* something wisdom then it must be presumed that that is what they thought it was, even if the reasons for their doing so remain opaque to us. On the other hand, I think it is possible to articulate a general, if imperfect, understanding of how wisdom was widely perceived in the ancient world, and this brings me to my second hypothesis.

Although I would not claim that as it stands it fits all the facts (and neither do I claim to know all the facts), I would suggest that the pre-eminent value in the ancient world was order, and that the pre-eminent virtue linked with it was wisdom. 'Virtue' is often used as a translation for the ancient Greek *arete*, although many translators now prefer the term 'excellence', and that is the sense of 'virtue' here. There are many different excellences, and therefore many different kinds of people who might claim to excel in different areas. However, and extremely tentatively, I am inclined to think that the most important kinds of excellence in the ancient world related in some way or other to different understandings or manifestations of order. I would also suggest that there was a close perceived connection between order and what might for want of a better term be called 'civilization'. Whether on the cosmic or on the political level, the establishment and preservation of order was the foundation upon which all else rested. On top of this general and indispensable foundation was constructed the specific culture in question. Those credited with inventing the primary constituents of the culture (such as writing, kingship or pottery) were the figures of legendary wisdom. Sometimes they were thought to be gods, sometimes they were thought to have been sent by the gods, sometimes they were simply regarded as human beings of exceptional talent and accomplishment.

This leads to the third hypothesis, which I shall call the Hermetic one after the famous Hermetic saying: 'That which is above is like to that which is below, and that which is below is like to that which is above' (Holmyard 1957, p. 97). In the context of wisdom it might be rephrased along the lines that 'That which is above is like to that which is below, only more so.' Beliefs about divine wisdom seem to me to reflect beliefs about human wisdom, but extrapolated to a higher level, up to and including that of perfection. The gods are as wise as humans would wish to be. The belief that there was a divine wisdom beyond human capacity was of great significance as it underpinned the practice of divination that pervaded the

4

ancient world in so many different forms. Divination was a way of being fed the scraps from the table of divine wisdom for those who could never hope to participate in the full meal. Where there was monotheism, wisdom tended to be or become an aspect of the divine. Where there was polytheism, one or more gods tended to have a particular association with wisdom. It took a bold person, let alone a whole culture, to dismiss divine wisdom as unnecessary or irrelevant. Rather, there was a contrary tendency to credit the gods with what were in fact human inventions and achievements, thereby artificially widening the gap between human and divine wisdom.

Finally, a fourth hypothesis has been employed in order to guide the way in which the materials have been selected and presented. I believe that wisdom was manifested primarily in certain people, secondarily in certain practices, and only lastly in a certain kind of literature. We do well to remember the suspicion with which the written word was regarded by some in the ancient world. Among philosophers, Pythagoras and Socrates were particularly celebrated for never writing anything, and they were far from alone in this. The reason is perhaps not too hard to find. The written word may become a frozen thing, increasingly estranged by time from the context in which it was produced. While it may be that wisdom literature was the product of wise people, reading wisdom literature does not of itself make anyone wise. Furthermore, the widely evidenced ancient practice of falsely attributing works of wisdom literature to people with a reputation for wisdom might suggest where the ancient world itself felt the primary emphasis lay. I have argued elsewhere (Curnow 2006a) that the founders of ancient philosophical schools were regarded as the embodiments and epitomes of their schools' values, and that the way they lived their lives was in many ways as important as their teachings. The same seems to me to be true in the case of wisdom, and this is scarcely coincidental. It might be argued that philosophy emerged as the pre-eminent facet of wisdom in the ancient world, publicly staking its claim to that pre-eminence by explicitly calling itself 'the love of wisdom'.

I should point out that although I have talked of four 'hypotheses', this book has not been written in order to subject them to rigorous scientific testing. Rather, these hypotheses have been employed to give some sense and structure to the discussion, and I hope that the discussion will, in turn, shed further light on the hypotheses. In the end, the hypotheses should make sense to the extent that the book as a whole makes sense.

The remainder of the book proceeds as follows. In Chapter 2 I consider wisdom in religion. Here the primary focus is on deities from across the ancient world who were considered to have a special connection with wisdom. However, the ancient world was not always and everywhere polytheistic. Consequently the place of wisdom within monotheism is also considered. Chapter 3 looks at wisdom in myth and legend, figures from that intermediate zone that lies between the human and the divine who peopled many of the stories of antiquity. In Chapter 4, we are fully in the world of the human, and a variety of characters from the pages of history, their reputations for and contributions to wisdom, are considered. In Chapter 5 I seek to fill in some of the gaps that are left by studying individuals alone. We know that a number of professions and practices were often connected with wisdom in antiquity, even though we have few if any names to attach to them. In Chapter 6, wisdom literature is the focus, and it is given a wide interpretation. Chapter 7 seeks to draw the various threads together.

The last section of this chapter will be devoted to the 'Seven Sages' of ancient Greece. As an apparently disparate set of individuals, all of whom were associated with wisdom, they provide a convenient concrete case study to illustrate the points that have been made here. A consideration of them may also serve as a transition to the more detailed and systematic discussions to follow.

3. The Seven Sages

No one knows for certain when the idea of ancient Greece having Seven Sages first appeared and took root. A comment made by Diogenes Laertius (I.22) points to the year 582 BC, which is not impossible but also not without its problems (O'Grady 2002, pp. 268-80). The earliest surviving list can be found in Plato's *Protagoras* (written in around 400 BC), but it is not the only one, and over twenty names appear on one list or another. Before mentioning any specific names, it may be noted that the number seven remained a constant: there was never a single list of Twenty (or more) Sages, only different lists of seven. It is possible that the number was chosen in conscious imitation of the seven *apkallu* of Mesopotamia, supernatural beings who brought knowledge to humanity and served as counsellors to the antediluvian kings [3.2]. On the other hand, there were also independent Greek reasons for an attachment to the number seven. Seven was, among other things, the number of the planets, the number of the gates of Thebes, and the number of the vowels in the Greek language. All these may have helped to give the number a certain 'sacred' quality (Levin 1994, p. 74).

The list as given by Plato in *Protagoras* (343A) is: Thales, Pittacus, Bias, Solon, Cleobolus, Myson and Chilon; and 'their wisdom may be recognized as ... consisting of pithy and memorable dicta uttered by each' (Plato 1956, p. 77). On the face of it, this is a tidy picture: a single list, and a single criterion for appearing on it. However, a very different picture emerges from the pages of Diogenes Laertius (I.42), writing hundreds of years later, but drawing on a wide variety of earlier sources (Diogenes Laertius 1972). Citing Hermippus of Smyrna, a third-century BC writer, he gives a total of seventeen different names that had appeared in various lists of seven. The seventeen, in alphabetical order, were: Acusilaus, Anacharsis,

The Seven Sages, from the Nuremberg Chronicle, 1493.

Anaxagoras, Aristodemus, Bias, Chilon, Cleobulus, Epimenides, Lasus, Leophantus, Myson, Periander, Pherecydes, Pittacus, Pythagoras, Solon and Thales. But that is not the end of it. Citing another source, Hippobotus, he then adds the names of Orpheus, Linus and Epicharmus to the mixture, bringing the total to twenty. Yet another name, that of Pamphilus, is also mentioned (on the authority of Dicaearchus of Messene, a pupil of Aristotle), making twenty-one, and there may have been more. Because not all of these names are familiar, and because most of them will not appear again, it may be helpful to say a little about each. I shall take them in alphabetical order.

Acusilaus (sixth century BC) came from Argos. He was the author of a number of works, the most famous being a collection of legends that traced the genealogies of the gods. Anacharsis (seventh/sixth century BC?) was not a Greek but a Scythian prince, credited by some with the invention of the potter's wheel. The stories that have survived about him bear the imprint of legend, and some have doubted his historicity. Some writings of a Cynic persuasion were attributed to him centuries after when he (might have) lived. Anaxagoras (fifth century BC) came from Clazomenae in Asia

7

Minor and may have been the first philosopher to live in Athens. However, the Athenians strongly disapproved of his views that the sun and moon were simply physical objects, and he had to flee. He seems to have embraced and advocated an early form of atomism. Aristodemus (sixth century BC) was a Spartan. It is said that he refused to accept a prize presented to him for being the wisest of the Greeks and suggested it should be given to Chilon instead. Bias (sixth century BC) came from Priene in Asia Minor. He achieved a reputation as a persuasive speaker who championed the causes of those who had been wronged. He also wrote a number of poems. He apparently possessed a certain degree of cunning: when Priene was being besieged he persuaded the attackers that the city had plenty of food left by scattering a thin layer of corn over a large pile of sand. Chilon (sixth century BC) was another Spartan. He was held in high esteem as a man of integrity whose words and deeds were always consistent with each other. He held public office and was seen as a source of sound advice. He also wrote a number of poems. Cleobolus (seventh/sixth century BC) came from the island of Rhodes. He was a strong, handsome man who composed a number of poems and epigrams. Epicharmus (sixth/fifth century BC) was originally from Cos, but moved to Sicily when young. He wrote comedies, and some credited him with inventing the genre, although it is more likely that he was only responsible for a number of innovations. A number of philosophical works of a Pythagorean nature were attributed to him, and he is said to have studied with Pythagoras himself. Epimenides (seventh/sixth century BC) was a Cretan, credited with mystical powers, and said to have once slept for 57 years. He was also a poet and composed an early version of the story of Jason and the Argonauts. Lasus (sixth century BC) was another poet. He came from Hermione in the Peloponnese and was the teacher of the poet Pindar. Nothing is known for certain of Leophantus (sixth century BC?). He may have come from Ephesus. Linus (seventh century BC?) probably came from Thebes, but the stories about him are very confused and he is a mystical, almost mythical figure. A few surviving verses, suggesting an acquaintance with Pythagoreanism, are attributed to him. Myson (seventh/sixth century BC) was probably another Spartan. He seems to have lived a simple life. The oracle of Apollo at Delphi, in response to an enquiry from Anacharsis, is said to have declared Myson the wisest man of his time.

The position of Orpheus in legend is well known; he is the paradigmatic poet and musician whose songs could soothe the most savage of beasts. However, the historical basis of the legend is much more problematic, although it is indisputable that a religious cult developed around the figure of Orpheus, practising, amongst other things, vegetarianism. His name became attached to a number of poems related to the activities of the mystery cults. Pamphilus is another very obscure figure. It is possible the reference is to the celebrated fourth century BC painter of that name, or a supposed teacher of Aristotle. Periander (seventh/sixth century BC) is

8

in many ways the most puzzling figure to appear on any list, although in fairness the testimony about him is somewhat confused. However, the usual and dominant reading is that he ruled Corinth with a rod of iron for years and was responsible for the death of his wife. Although a number of pithy sayings are attributed to him, his name appears on only two lists of the Seven Sages that have survived. Pherecydes (sixth century BC) came from Syros, an island in the Cyclades. He was regarded as a seer and is said to have taught Pythagoras. He wrote about how the gods and the world came to be. Pittacus (seventh/sixth century BC) may have been a teacher of Pherecydes. He came from Mytilene, on Lesbos. He was chosen by the community to take charge and proceeded to govern wisely before retiring from office. He reformed the constitution and was an advocate of the rule of law. Pythagoras (sixth century BC) is both well known and hardly known at all. He came from the island of Samos, but later moved to southern Italy where he founded his own community. Because he wrote nothing, and his sect was secretive, there is considerable confusion (and a large measure of ignorance) concerning precisely what he taught. However, it seems safe to assume as a very minimum that the community practised strict dietary laws, and that number played a key role in the Pythagorean understanding of the world. Solon (seventh/sixth century BC) enjoyed a reputation as both a legislator and a poet in his native Athens. His legal reforms brought about, among other things, the abolition of debt bondage. Last, and certainly not least, comes Thales (seventh/sixth century BC). From Miletus in Asia Minor, he is often regarded as the first philosopher in the Western tradition. His achievements appear to have been many and various, but lay in particular in the direction of the sciences. The first firm date in the history of Western philosophy is generally taken to be 585 BC, the year when Thales predicted an eclipse of the sun.

These, in brief, are those who appear in one list of the Seven Sages or another according to Diogenes Laertius. The first observation that might fairly be made about them is that there appears to be nothing that they all have in common. More surprisingly, perhaps, the same might be said about the small sub-group comprising Bias, Pittacus, Solon and Thales, the only four names to appear on all known lists of the Seven. Bearing in mind Plato's observation that 'their wisdom may be recognized as ... consisting of pithy and memorable dicta uttered by each', it is true that Diogenes Laertius attributes to various Sages a variety of pithy sayings. However, he notes (I.40) that, 'Their utterances are variously reported, and are attributed now to one now to the other' (Diogenes Laertius 1972, p. 43), and some appear to have none attributed to them at all. The impression is that various wise sayings have become attached to people renowned for their wisdom, but without (in most cases at least) any real evidence to suggest that they were actually responsible for them. It is therefore difficult to believe that these utterances were the real basis for the attribution of wisdom to them.

9

Diogenes also reveals that people disagreed over the criteria whereby people had been selected for one list or another. For example (I.40), 'Anaximenes remarks that they all applied themselves to poetry; Dicaearchus that they were neither sages nor philosophers, but merely shrewd men with a turn for legislation' (Diogenes Laertius 1972, pp. 41, 43). Although there is no evidence that they all did, it is apparent that at least a respectable number of those who appeared in the lists produced poetry of one kind or another. The precise significance of this is unclear as it is said that Pherecydes was the first Greek to write in prose. Nevertheless, it remains a fact that there is a significant sub-group of Sages who had a reasonably strong connection with poetry. Similarly, a number of them also seem to have been involved in some way or another with government or legal reform or both. In his life of Solon (3), Plutarch observed that all of the Sages except Thales 'gained their reputation for wisdom from their prowess as statesmen' (Plutarch 1960, p. 46). This certainly seems to be the basis for Periander's inclusion. Although some have argued for two separate Perianders, the tyrant and another one who was the Sage, the fact that Periander managed to rule Corinth for forty years must say something about his political abilities. If poets and politicians form two sub-groups, another might be made up of philosophers or, more broadly, scholars of various kinds, those who move in the world of knowledge and learning. And perhaps yet further and smaller sub-groups might be identified. It is tempting to look at the Sages in the same way that Ludwig Wittgenstein looked at games: 'if you look at them you will not see something that is common to *all*, but similarities, relationships, and a whole series of them at that' (Wittgenstein 1972, p. 31e).

One obvious question to ask is whether the different criteria for inclusion in the group were competing or complementary, consecutive or contemporaneous. Without knowing a lot more than we do now (and perhaps a lot more than we are ever likely to know) about exactly who produced the various lists, and when and why, any answer to this question is going to remain tentative. But on the basis of the hypotheses outlined earlier [1.2], I think it is possible to advance such a tentative answer. If wisdom is genuinely multi-faceted, then it is not only possible but even expected that it should appear in a variety of guises and forms. If that is so, then the different suggested criteria for selection of the Seven Sages are not competing but complementary. Just because some are selected for their facility for poetry does not mean that politicians and philosophers are thereby excluded from consideration. And shrewdness of action might be considered as much a manifestation of wisdom as elegance of expression. Perhaps one of the points behind drawing up the original list was to illustrate the many different ways in which wisdom might manifest itself while still remaining wisdom? This is not to say that anything at all might count, only that there seems no obvious or compelling reason to insist that there was only a single simple criterion. However, just as there must be *some* limit to what can be called a game (otherwise the concept is meaningless), so there must also be some limit to what can come under the rubric of wisdom. Furthermore, just because different vehicles for wisdom *could* co-exist does not mean that they *did* co-exist. Concepts have their own life-histories and the paradigm of the sage is unlikely to have stood still for centuries. Indeed, we know that it did not. Some new vehicles for wisdom emerged (philosophy amongst them), some older ones became regarded as outmoded. But to what extent was there a persistent underlying core concept of wisdom?

This is where the second hypothesis might be expected to have a role to play. To what extent could the underlying core concept involve the notion of order? I believe a case for this can be made, although I would not claim that it is as robust in all particulars as I might wish. Taking the three professions of poet, politician and philosopher, it might be argued that the poet creates (or reproduces) order with words, the politician imposes order on the social world, and the philosopher (and especially the philosopher of nature such as Thales) seeks to understand or reveal the order that underlies the world. Although the poet might perhaps be thought to have the weakest connection with order, it is generally true to say that the ancient world perceived a far closer connection between language and reality than the modern world does, such that the arrangement of words might offer genuine insights into the arrangement of the world. I would not want to push the argument too far, but I believe that the notion of order can help to make some sense of an apparently very disparate set of facts.

I have also suggested a fourth hypothesis, whereby people are the primary manifestation of wisdom, and the idea of the Seven Sages seems to bear this out. The list is always a list of specific *people*, often very different ones. Because they are always individuals, the precise way in which they manifest wisdom will often be difficult to pin down with precision. Although the Seven Sages may share certain similarities, it is difficult to argue that they constitute a *type*. Yet for those who compiled the lists, those who appeared on them must clearly have shared *something*, even if that something may have been different for different people at different times, and even if that something appears entirely opaque to us. This is part of the challenge of studying wisdom in the ancient world.

This brief examination of the Seven Sages of ancient Greece has been intended to serve as an introductory case study, designed to illustrate in a more concrete way some of the points made in a more abstract way earlier in the chapter, and to convey something of the flavour of what is to come. In the next chapter I shall look at wisdom in religion and the different ways in which wisdom has been associated with the divine

2

Wisdom in Religion

1. Introduction

In his *Apology* (23A-B), Plato puts these words into the mouth of Socrates:

> But the truth of the matter, gentlemen, is pretty certainly this: that real
> wisdom is the property of God, and this oracle is his way of telling us that
> human wisdom has little or no value. It seems to me that he is not
> referring literally to Socrates, but has merely taken my name as an
> example, as if he would say to us, 'The wisest of you men is he who has
> realised, like Socrates, that in respect of wisdom he is really worthless.
> (Plato 1969, p. 52)

The idea that wisdom was in some way associated with the divine was
widely entertained in the ancient world. However, it was interpreted in a
number of different ways with different implications. In this section I shall
be considering those interpretations and implications in broad terms,
mapping out the general terrain as a preparation for a more detailed
examination of aspects of it in subsequent sections.

At its most extreme, the idea that 'real wisdom is the property of God'
divorces wisdom from the human realm altogether. If wisdom exists only
in the dimension of the divine, then from the human perspective it remains
an inaccessible object of speculation, and 'human wisdom' is either a
total illusion or a vastly inferior counterpart of the real thing. The
notion of wisdom being 'the property of God' tends to be interpreted in
one of two different ways. Either wisdom is in some sense a *possession*
of the divine (or of a particular god), or else it is an *aspect* of the divine.
When it is the latter, then there is often a tendency towards some kind
of divine *personification* of wisdom. When this occurred within monotheism, it could create something of an internal strain that could prove
difficult to contain.

If divine wisdom is so far removed from the human realm as to be
impenetrable, then there is little left to do except believe in it. However,
as the words attributed to Socrates illustrate, divine wisdom did not need
to be something totally remote from human experience. It was widely
believed in the ancient world that even if divine wisdom could not strictly
speaking be understood by humans, nevertheless it was still possible for
them in one way or another to gain a limited access to it. Socrates cites the
pronouncement of the oracle of Apollo at Delphi, but this is just a single

example of the highly varied and widespread phenomenon of divination. Divination, however practised, offered the prospect of learning from the divine. To put the matter in the terms of a legal analogy, if the actual reasoning of the divine judges could not be fathomed, it might nevertheless be possible to gain knowledge of the verdicts they passed. If divine wisdom as such was not something that humans could aspire to, at least it might be possible, if the gods so willed, to receive some fragmentary insights into aspects of it.

Once the possibility of communication between the human and the divine was accepted, then its mechanics and limits had to be established. At one extreme lay spontaneous revelation, with the human party playing an essentially passive role. At the other extreme lay forms of theurgy and magic where it almost appeared as if the divine could be compelled to communicate. In between lay a range of options, impressive both for their variety and their inventiveness. In principle, almost anything could be interpreted as containing a message from the gods, if only it were within the wit of humankind to read it. Sometimes the communication was carried by messengers sent by the gods.

Within polytheism, as the case of Apollo illustrates, there was the possibility of one or more gods having a special connection with wisdom. Although this did not have to happen, it frequently did. The number and nature of gods specially associated with wisdom seem to reflect, as did the different lists of the Seven Sages, the multi-faceted nature of wisdom in the ancient world. However, just as it is possible to identify groups of Sages with certain characteristics in common, the same is true of the gods. One such group comprises what might be termed the 'professional' gods, that is to say, those gods who were particularly associated with a particular skill or activity. Of these, an important sub-group may be mentioned here: a number of gods were specifically associated with the skill of writing and, more broadly, with the profession of the scribe. It is difficult to decide whether crediting the gods with the invention of writing is an act of collective human modesty or an act of collective human amnesia. Such a projection of 'human wisdom' upon the gods would be in line with the third hypothesis set out earlier [1.2]. More cynically, it might be suggested that members of the scribal class, where such a class existed, had much to gain and little to lose from associating themselves with wisdom and beings of a higher order.

This introductory section has been concerned with generalities and so has mainly proceeded at a rather abstract level. The following sections and sub-sections of this chapter will look at a number of specifics to illustrate and fill out the points that have been made. A beginning will be made by looking at a number of gods from across the ancient world who were regarded as having a special connection with wisdom.

2. Wise Gods and Goddesses

(a) Mesopotamia

I shall begin in Mesopotamia. Although it is apparent from the surviving evidence that Mesopotamian religion underwent some changes during the course of its long history, these changes took place within a shared framework. Indeed, insofar as it makes sense to talk of a shared Mesopotamian worldview, it is largely because of a shared religion and shared body of legends. It is no coincidence that the changes Mesopotamian religion underwent over the centuries reflected political changes. To give perhaps the most obvious example, Marduk achieved a position of pre-eminence amongst the gods of Mesopotamia at the same time as Babylon achieved a position of pre-eminence amongst the cities of Mesopotamia. Babylon was the place with which Marduk was particularly associated and where his greatest temple, the Esagila, was located. Given the Mesopotamian outlook, in which the affairs of the world were ruled by the decrees of the gods, it would naturally be assumed that the pre-eminence of Babylon was a consequence and manifestation of the pre-eminence of Marduk rather than vice versa. In many ways the worlds of humans and gods were very similar, and just as Mesopotamian societies had rulers, so rulership was the primary function of the gods, as well as being regarded as one of the greatest gifts of the gods to humanity. And just as kings might jostle each other in order to achieve a position of dominance, so might the gods. There was certainly plenty of scope for competition for the Sumerians alone seem to have had thousands of gods. However, over time a modicum of order was established, and as part of this process a number of originally different gods were identified with each other. In due course, Mesopotamian religion became dominated by a comparatively small number of major gods, and of these only relatively few had a particular interest in or connection with wisdom. Of these, the most important were Ea (also known by his Sumerian name of Enki) and Marduk.

The stories of Ea and Marduk, father and son, are closely intertwined and both gods feature prominently in the epic known as the *Enuma Elish* (Dalley 2000, pp. 232-74) which sets out the Babylonian creation myth. It may be noted that an alternative Assyrian version of the epic exists that makes the Assyrian god Ashur (or Assur) its hero, rather than the Babylonian Marduk. The date of composition of *Enuma Elish* is unknown and wildly different estimates have been advanced. It tells of the two primeval gods Apsu (or Abzu: male, fresh water) and Tiamat (female, sea water) and their offspring. Ea was their great-great-grandson. The opening lines of the work lay a great deal of emphasis on the importance of naming things in the work of creation. The processes of naming and bringing into being were clearly perceived as closely related, if not identical. After a prolonged power struggle, Marduk eventually became the supreme god and the

Ea (Enki).

human race was created from the blood of one of the defeated gods. This was by no means the only story that was told to explain the origin of the human race, but they all generally follow the same line, namely that the human race was created for the benefit of the gods, with the intention that humans would work so that the gods might rest. The destiny of humanity was one of collective slavery in service to the gods. Given that their worldview placed them in a very lowly position, it is perhaps scarcely surprising that the Mesopotamians credited the gods with the origins of all knowledge.

The connections of Ea and Marduk with wisdom are complex. Both Ea and Marduk were sometimes spoken of in such a way as to suggest that they functioned as advisors or counsellors to the other gods. So, for example, a work sometimes known as 'Advice to a Prince' dating from perhaps the early first millennium BC describes Marduk at line 26 as 'the sage of the gods, the prince, the counsellor' (Lambert 1996, p. 113). The idea that one would want a wise person as a counsellor hardly seems controversial. The association of Marduk with wisdom can also be found in another text (perhaps dating to the twelfth century BC?), usually known by its opening words (in Akkadian 'Ludlul bel nemeqi', in English, 'I will praise the Lord of wisdom'), where Marduk is explicitly identified as the lord of wisdom in line 3 (Pritchard 1969, p. 596). If I read Bottéro correctly (Bottéro 1992, p. 249), the phrase 'the sage of the gods' is a formula that originally attached to Ea, and the word used for 'sage' in 'Advice to a Prince' is *'apkallu'*. Technically *'apkallu'* simply seems to mean 'wisest', and that would clearly be an acceptable alternative translation to 'sage' in the line cited above. *Apkallu* (or *abgal*) was also the name given to creatures credited with bringing civilization to humanity [3.2].

Ea's name means 'House of the Water', the water in question being the fresh water of Apsu. 'Apsu' is also the name of the house that Ea built for himself. Consequently, it is not always clear what is the gift of Ea and what the gift of water. The idea that water is not only a source of life but also in some way a source of wisdom seems to be present in a number of elements of Mesopotamian thought, including in the legend of the *apkallu*. Over the course of Mesopotamian history, Ea became associated with many different things, and his cult was merged with many others, making the true picture difficult to decipher. At one time or another he seems to have been connected with fertility, various crafts, destiny, sorcery and more. Although it is not always clear what the Mesopotamian understanding of wisdom included or excluded, it is at least clear that Ea and Marduk were the deities most closely associated with it.

Although to some extent Marduk simply replaced Ea in a number of ways in the wake of Babylonian supremacy, differences always remained between them. In particular, Marduk seems to have embodied rulership to a greater degree than Ea ever did. Ea, on the other hand, had a rather deeper association with the notion of order. In a work somewhat cumbersomely known as 'Enki and the World Order: The Organization of the Earth and its Cultural Processes' (Kramer 1963, pp. 174-83), that association is made very plain. In it, Ea (Enki) tells how he decided which city was to have which resources, established borders, filled the river beds with water and the water with fish, provided nomads with cattle, and so on. But before doing so, he says something about himself. Among other things:

> I am the record keeper of heaven and earth ...
> I am he who decrees the fates with Enlil in the 'mountain of wisdom' ...
> (Kramer 1963, p. 175)

The god of wisdom is also clearly the god of order. Enlil (or Ellil), another Mesopotamian god, stands here for power.

Ea and Marduk were by no means the only gods associated with wisdom in Mesopotamia. Nisaba (or Nidaba) was originally a Sumerian goddess of grasses, including reeds. When, with the development of cuneiform, the reed became the instrument of writing, she became associated with the scribal profession. Her cult reached its peak during the second millennium BC, but was eventually overshadowed by that of Nabu. The mythologists hit upon the happy expedient of marrying Nisaba and Nabu off to each other, although he already had a consort called Tashmit. Nabu's cult reached its peak in the first millennium BC, when he became recognised as a son of Marduk, just as Marduk had earlier become recognised as a son of Ea despite having quite independent origins. During the Hellenistic period in Mesopotamia (331-126 BC), when the land was ruled by the Seleucids and there was pressure to merge Babylonian and Greek cults, Nabu was sometimes identified with Apollo. His cult lasted until the

16

second century AD. In the form of Nebo, his name appears in the Bible (Isaiah 46:1) and perhaps something of his popularity can be seen in the fact that a number of Babylonian personal names incorporated his own (such as Nebuchadnezzar and Nabonidus). Like Nisaba, he was also a god of scribes and writing. However, because the Mesopotamian form of writing was cuneiform, it would perhaps be more accurate to say that they were divinities associated with cuneiform in particular rather than writing in general. It is not clear that they had any connection with wisdom other than through their association with scribes and writing, but this association appears to have been regarded as sufficient to establish that connection.

Many Mesopotamian gods were connected with divination in one way or another. For example, there was Nanshe, a goddess associated with fishing and justice as well as divination, and Ningal, the wife of the moon god, whose cult specialized in the interpretation of dreams. However, from the beginning of the second millennium onwards, two gods in particular became particularly associated with it. These were Shamash and Adad (or Hadad). Exactly why and how Adad became associated with divination is unclear. He was in origin a sky god, a god of wind, rain and storm. During the first half of the second millennium, Shamash became the supreme god of divination. He was a sun god, but also a god of justice. These two aspects appear to have been connected by the belief that the sun god sees all, and so is best placed to judge all. As a sky god, Adad may have been associated with divination for the same reason. The temple of Shamash in Babylon was called the 'House of the Judge of the World'. Because divination was understood in Mesopotamia as seeking the judgment of the gods, it becomes understandable why the supreme judge amongst the gods became the principal deity associated with divination. In the tidy way in which mythology sometimes works, a place was found for Adad as his assistant.

(b) Egypt

As in Mesopotamia, in Egypt there was also a close and complex relationship between religion and politics (as we would distinguish them). Although for much of antiquity Egypt was a unified country ruled by native dynasties, the centre of power shifted from time to time and this could have theological and mythological consequences because some gods were very clearly connected in a special way with particular cities ands regions. As a result, as in Mesopotamia, there was more than one account of creation and more than one account of the relationships between the different gods: there was no single understanding of these matters shared by all Egyptians at all times.

Because, compared with the Mesopotamians, the Egyptians appear to have had a very underdeveloped vocabulary of wisdom, it is necessary to take a rather more interpretive line in identifying connections with wisdom.

Thoth (left) officially recording the crowning of the king by Amon.

The first deity associated with wisdom was Thoth, and his connection with wisdom was relatively straightforward.

> I am Thoth the skilled scribe whose hands are pure, a possessor of purity, who drives away evil, who writes what is true, who detests falsehood, whose pen defends the Lord of All ... I am Thoth who foretells the morrow and foresees the future ... (Faulkner 1985, p. 181)

So says *The Book of the Dead*. Although originally a moon god, Thoth became the god of writing and learning. Indeed, he was said to have been the inventor of writing, and his iconography often shows him engaged in it. It was natural that he should be closely associated with scribes, and he seems to have been regarded as the scribe of the gods. As such, he also seems to have been regarded as a kind of advisor to the gods, due to his great learning, which covered many areas. Magic and the esoteric both came within his purview. The Greeks later came to identify him with Hermes and so Thoth stands behind the later Hermetic tradition [6.7]. And because of his position as scribe to the gods, it was he who was the recorder of history. As the quotation above illustrates, the god of knowledge and the recorder of history was credited with knowing the whole course of history, past, present and future.

As in Mesopotamia, the Egyptians attributed power to words and one of their creation myths attributed the origins of the world to the god Ptah who brought it into being 'through his heart and through his tongue' (Wilkinson 2003, p. 18). What this seems to mean is that Ptah first conceived of the world and then created it through the act of speech whereby pronouncing the name of something caused it to exist. The main centre of Ptah's cult was Memphis, and the inscription recording this account of creation is normally referred to as 'The Memphite Theology'. However, there is another dimension to Ptah's character which suggests a different kind of creation. He was associated with the crafts, and in particular sculpture, one of his titles being translated as 'sculptor of the earth'. As such he was credited with the creation of the world in a more 'hands on' way as well. Not surprisingly, the practitioners of crafts of all sorts seem to have felt a special affinity for him, and the Greeks came to identify him with Hephaestus, their god or artisans. Ptah also seems to have been widely regarded as one of the gods most receptive to human prayers and acquired the epithet of 'the ear which hears'.

Despite all this, surprisingly there is little to explicitly link Ptah with Egyptian discussions of wisdom, or, better, to link him with discussions within the explicit Egyptian vocabulary of wisdom. The same might be said of Maat, a complex figure with a number of different aspects. Because of this, modern understandings of Maat have tended to change and be revised over time. It is probably the case that none of the understandings are actually wrong, in the sense of lacking any foundation, but some may be better than others in their ability to capture Maat's complexity. There was not only a goddess Maat but also a principle of *maat*, and it is not always clear where one ends and the other begins. It may be simplest to see the goddess as a personification of the principle, and the complexity of one naturally matches that of the other. As a principle, Assmann sees *maat* as bringing together theology, science, philosophy, society, the state, the cosmos and religion (Assmann 1989, p. 412). But perhaps the feature of Maat/*maat* that is emphasized most strongly in the contemporary literature is that of order. In a mythological sense, Maat stands for the forces of order against the forces of disorder, but the order represented by Maat is not simply the absence of disorder, for she is also associated with justice and therefore with the moral sense of order as well as the physical one. Indeed, living in accordance with *maat* operated as a moral principle in Egyptian society. How to do so was a major theme of Egyptian wisdom literature [6.3]. Those who wished to advertise their virtue might do so not only by claiming their general observance of *maat* but also by listing a number of specific occasions when they had done so. For example, the priest Neferseshemre (twenty-fourth century BC), after proclaiming his adherence to *maat*, proceeds to go into some detail as to how he achieved this:

> I judged between two persons in order to reconcile them. I rescued the oppressed from one more powerful than he as far as I was able. I gave bread to the starving and clothing (to the naked), a means of landing to him without a boat. I buried him who had no son. I made a ferry-boat for him who had none. I was respectful to my father, kind to my mother, and I brought up their children. (Williams 1990a, p. 30)

19

Self-justification in terms of *maat* may have been prompted by or itself prompted the idea of justification before Maat, and the goddess came to play a leading role in beliefs concerning the judgment of the dead. It is no coincidence that the passage just cited comes from a tomb inscription. Although Neferseshemre is concerned with saying what he *did*, it became more common to make a posthumous 'negative confession'. For example:

> I have not mistreated cattle.
> I have not blasphemed a god.
> I have not killed.
> I have not had sexual relations with a boy.
> I have not built a dam against running water.

> (Pritchard 1969, p. 34)

And so on in very similar vein. Although the *point* being made is a general one, that the deceased has lived in accordance with *maat*, the way in which it is made is by listing a long line of specific deeds of which he is innocent.

It is clear that *maat* could be manifested in various ways; *maat*, it might be said, is present both in the ordered cosmos and in the ordered life. Importantly, *maat* was also present in the ordered society, and the ordered society was closely associated with effective rulership. In the Old Kingdom at least, the pharaoh seems to have been seen as the incarnation of Maat, the source and fount of order in the social world. An important aspect of social order was a system of laws, and from the little that is known about ancient Egyptian law, it seems clear that this too was based on the principle of *maat* (Shaw and Nicholson 2003, p. 159). However, while effective rulership might provide the foundations of social order, and while the power wielded by the pharaoh was considerable, the pharaoh's ability to become involved in everyday affairs was clearly limited, and a number of powers were delegated or shared, and it is possible that the figure of Maat served as a kind of badge of office for the senior magistrates who assisted the pharaoh in the administration of justice.

But in the ordinary course of events, much of what goes on in everyday life falls below the threshold of consciousness of the organs of state. Here the principle of *maat* also had a role to play. An eighteenth-century BC inscription sets out a kind of definition of *maat*, although it is subject to more than one interpretation (Assmann 1989, p. 40). It suggests that the true meaning of *maat* is that (good) deeds are rewarded by the (good) deeds of others. It is possible to see in this an Egyptian version of the so-called golden rule of 'do unto others'. It is also possible to see in it an Egyptian statement of the principle that actions have consequences. More prosaically, it could be interpreted as a declaration of the benefits of cooperation, or simply of work. If the first interpretation is contentious (although possible), the second two can certainly be supported with evidence from elsewhere. The idea that actions have consequences is a staple of Egyptian wisdom literature [6.3]. The virtues of work and the identification of

20

laziness as a vice (especially for servants!) can also be found there (Jasnow 1992, p. 26). The importance of cooperation to the survival of a society seems self-evident and can be construed as simply one aspect of social order, perhaps a bottom-up aspect of social order as opposed to the top-down kind represented by central political power. In the end, it is possible to understand *maat* not only as cooperation but also as everything that holds a society together. This again may be evidenced from wisdom literature: nothing, no aspect of everyday life, is too trivial to be considered since the order of *maat* was all-embracing, all pervasive. In the end, what holds a society together is its entire pattern of personal relations, every-thing people do to each other (Dunand and Zivie-Coche 2004, p. 145). It is this universality of *maat* that sets the concept at the heart of the Egyptian outlook on the world and makes it the key to understanding it (Assmann 1989, p. 12).

For a goddess and principle associated with order, a time of disorder clearly presents a challenge, and there is evidence that during the time known as the First Intermediate Period there was some rethinking of *maat*. Some of the literature from that time strikes a note of despair at the absence of *maat*, which is demonstrated by the presence of disorder and injustice. Consequently, while the idea of *maat* was never abandoned by the Egyptians, the ways in which they thought about it may have changed over time. Assmann (1989, pp. 136-7) suggests that during the first millennium BC Maat became increasingly sidelined in the Egyptian view of things, and he associates this with a decline in fatalism and a growing belief in events being dictated by the will of the gods (possibly showing evidence of some Mesopotamian influence?). Despite the fact that Maat was a personal goddess, there was a clear sense in which the order of *maat* was an impersonal one. Wilkinson (2003, pp. 150-1) notes that hardly any temples to Maat existed, suggesting that very little point was seen in appealing to her to change the order of things. This absence of a significant personal cult would also tend to reinforce the view that Maat was more personification than person. However, because *maat* was associated with ethics as well as physics, with how things ought to be as well as with how things are, Maat remained as a judge in the afterlife even if her impor-tance in this life diminished, and even if the actual order of this world was subject to modification through petitions to other gods, *maat* remained the standard to which the world should aspire.

This discussion of Maat may usefully illustrate two points. First, that what begins as a discussion of one aspect or dimension of wisdom easily crosses over into being the discussion of another. Secondly, although (as with Ptah) there is little *formal* linkage between Maat and the vocabulary of wisdom, this may reflect deficiencies in either the vocabulary itself or in our understanding of it. To exclude Maat from the discussion would be to lose sight of an important dimension of Egyptian thought. This leads to a further point. I suspect the discussion of wisdom with reference to Egypt has been shaped to a large extent by what has come to be regarded as Egyptian wisdom literature [6.3] in which neither Maat nor Ptah has a significant explicit role to play. However, when attention is shifted towards the kinds of people who were regarded as wise, and the kinds of things that wisdom was thought to bring about, then it seems clear that behind them can be seen Ptah and Maat. Ptah and Maat therefore appear courtesy of my second and fourth hypotheses. This is particularly significant because wisdom as such receives relatively few mentions in Egyptian wisdom literature, whereas the wise person receives considerably more. It might also be pointed out that there is *some* explicit association of Maat with wisdom: the Berlin Papyrus records a prayer to Osiris which asks that 'the divine entities reward you with Maat, for they know her wisdom' (Lamy 1981, p. 51).

A less contentious case is that of Isis, for unlike Ptah and Maat, her association with wisdom was both indisputable and international. She provides as good an example as any of how a cult can grow, absorb and spread. Wilkinson (2003, p. 146), focusing on Egypt, notes that she 'merged with many other goddesses including Astarte, Bastet, Nut, Renetutet and Sothis' as well as Hathor. Ferguson (1970, p. 218), drawing on a variety of sources, produces an enormous list of further identifications, including Cybele, Juno, Terra, Demeter, Minerva, Venus, Diana, Proserpina, Ceres, Belona, Hecate, Nemesis, Hera, Aphrodite, Hestia, Athena, Praxidike, Wisdom, Leto, Kore, Dictynnis, Themis, Helen and Atargatis. And those are apparently not all. Apart from the fact that all the identifications are with female deities, there is little or no obvious pattern to them, but it is evident that through becoming identified with various deities with various associations of their own, Isis came to be seen as connected in one way or another with many different areas of life. When one goddess was believed to have such widespread influence, it is scarcely surprising that she became a major object of popular devotion. But she became even more than that as her cult developed both an oracular and a mystery dimension.

For one whose cult attained such significant proportions, the origins of Isis are very vague. She emerges onto the historical record around the middle of the third millennium BC, but with no obvious attachment to any particular place. She appears as the sister, wife and queen of Osiris. When her husband is killed by his enemies, they dismember him and scatter the parts of his body. Isis reassembles him, magically brings him back to life and becomes pregnant by him. This association of Isis with magic was an early and persistent one. For obvious reasons, there were also strong associations with life and suffering. For reasons that are less obvious, she was also associated with navigation and the sea, and the spread of her cult doubtless owed much to seafarers. For example, it is known that her cult was established in the port of Piraeus by Egyptian merchants before the end of the fourth century BC. Eventually, temples to Isis could be found across the whole length and breadth of the Roman

Maat.

Empire, most of them in ports or near the sea. Because of the close connection between the cults of Isis and Sarapis (or Serapis), where one went, the other often tended to go.

As the cult expanded, so did the areas for which Isis claimed responsibility. In a document generally referred to as the 'Isis Aretalogy of Kyme-Memphis', dated to the first or second century BC, the goddess proclaims her prowess:

> I am Isis, the sovereign of every land; and I was educated by Hermes [Thoth] and with Hermes [Thoth] I invented letters, both sacred and common ...
> I separated earth from heaven ...

Isis (right) and Queen Nefertari.

2. Wisdom in Religion

I invented seafaring ...
I demonstrated mysteries to mortals ...
I am mistress of warfare ...
I am she who is in the rays of the sun ...
I am she who is called the lawgiver ...
Fate obeys me ...

(Valantasis 2000, pp. 373-5)

Quite why she claimed to have had a share in the invention of writing, given that there was a longstanding and strong tradition giving sole credit to Thoth, is not clear. It is possible that this connection developed at the same time as Isis became more associated with creation, given the affinity between the word and the thing in the Egyptian view of the world. There was also a tradition that Isis had been the discoverer of the true name of the god Re, providing another link with the power of the word. In any event, the cults of Isis and Thoth seem to have become increasingly close over the centuries, and the Thoth/Hermes/Isis cluster of deities seen as an important source of wisdom.

It is tempting to see in Isis herself a divine personification of wisdom, and the different goddesses with whom she became identified as representing so many different aspects of wisdom. However, that is probably too tidy an interpretation of the facts. There is no evidence that *all* of the goddesses with whom she was identified had a *specific* connection with a *recognized* aspect of wisdom. On the other hand, Isis seems to have become a focal point about which various aspects of wisdom came to cluster in such a way that she seems to have come to represent wisdom more than perhaps any other deity in the ancient world ever did. During the Ptolemaic period her cult became linked with that of Sarapis. While the two cults never actually merged, they were frequently found in close proximity. Many, perhaps most, of their temples provided two functions that were much in demand. Sarapis and Isis were both oracular gods and healing gods. As oracular gods they shared some of the benefits of their divine wisdom with those who sought it. As healing gods, they practised an art that was often seen as a repository of wisdom in its own right [5.8].

(c) Mystery Cults

There was a further dimension of the cult of Isis that was relatively rare. Hers was one of the few mystery cults of the ancient world. Our knowledge of these cults is limited as they were surrounded by secrecy, although it would be an exaggeration to say that we know nothing about them at all. The principal ones seem to have been those of Demeter, Isis, Cybele, Dionysus and Mithras. All were of considerable antiquity, although their early histories and movements are not easy to trace. What they all had in common was a personal spiritual dimension that was generally lacking from religion in the ancient world. The fact that these particular cults had

Mithras.

mysteries attached to them does not appear to have been coincidental. 'Like Demeter and Isis, Cybele was initially the goddess of the earth and of fertility, and like them came to be regarded as the inventor of agriculture and of legal order' (Tripolitis 2002, p. 31). Dionysus was also a nature god, associated in particular with the vine. In the case of Mithras, it is presumably significant that his iconography routinely depicts him in the act of slaying a bull, from whose collapsing frame ears of corn are often sprouting. Each deity therefore has a connection with the natural cycle of life and death. From what is known, each mystery cult seems to have given its adherents some kind of profound personal experience that had the effect of convincing them that they could look forward to another life after death. This was transmitted through a process of initiation, which was often spread across a number of stages. At Eleusis, the most famous centre of the mysteries of Demeter, there seems to have been a strong visual element to the experience of initiation.

In the case of the cult of Isis, there survives what is usually regarded as a reliable eyewitness statement, although it appears in a work of fiction, *The Golden Ass*, or *The Transformations*, by Apuleius of Madaura (Apuleius 1950). Warning the reader that he can only say so much, and that it will probably not mean very much, he writes:

> I approached the very gates of death and set one foot on Proserpina's threshold, yet was permitted to return, rapt through all the elements. At midnight I saw the sun shining as if it were noon; I entered the presence of the gods of the under-world and the gods of the upper-world, stood near and worshipped them. (Apuleius 1950, p. 286)

26

2. Wisdom in Religion

In their own different ways, the mysteries seem to work by means of a process or act of revelation whereby initiates receive a profound insight, and this insight seems to be communicated through some kind of powerful experience. But whatever the differences between them, ultimately they all seem to offer the same thing: 'What is involved in the actually religious part of these mysteries is always immortality, and thus, in the broadest sense, "redemption" ...' (Reitzenstein 1978, p. 11). Because immortality was the distinguishing feature of the divine, the mysteries offered the opportunity to become if not gods then at least godlike. As such, the mysteries seem to have offered a glimpse of divine wisdom while promising greater things to come.

(d) Greece and Rome

The mystery cults had their origins in very different parts of the ancient world. Isis came from Egypt, Mithras from Persia, Cybele from Anatolia, and Dionysus may have come from Thrace. Demeter's origins are obscure, but she may have come from the place where she was best known, Greece. Another god whose cult travelled and spread widely, and who had a close connection with wisdom, was Apollo. The origins of his cult are obscure and disputed. Both Asian and northern European ancestry have been argued for, but the Greeks were firmly of the opinion that he was born on the island of Delos. Whereas many Greek and Roman deities became identified with each other, the Romans never produced their own equivalent of Apollo and simply adopted him as one of their own.

Although, like most of the gods, he had many aspects and interests, Apollo was the god most closely identified with oracles. It was certainly not the case that he was the only god who presided over oracular sites, but some of the most famous were associated with him. Delphi achieved a particularly high and widespread reputation, but there were at least forty others (Curnow 2004). Although the historical basis for the story might best be described as shaky, a strong tradition developed during Roman times linking Apollo with the books known as the Sibylline oracles. The term 'Sibyl' seems to have originated as the proper name of a prophetess of uncertain place and time. In due course it became a title given to a small number of prophetesses, including one from Cumae near Naples. She was said to have been the mouthpiece of Apollo there, and the Sibylline oracles were her collected pronouncements. Books of Sibylline oracles were being consulted in Rome as early as 496 BC, and they were kept in the temple of Jupiter Optimus Maximus. When the temple was destroyed by fire in 83 BC, so were the books. New ones, or copies of old ones, were acquired and were suitably deposited in the temple of Apollo in 12 BC.

Although many Greek oracles had a strong connection in one way or another with the ground and what lay beneath it, Apollo was a sun god, like Shamash. He was also a healer, although over time his healing functions were progressively taken over by his 'son' Asclepius. The sanctuaries of Asclepius were also oracular, with incubation being the normal practice. This involved those seeking cures spending the night in a special room where they hoped to receive messages from the god in a dream. However, although the cult of Asclepius became of increasing significance in the sphere of healing from around 500 BC onwards, Apollo continued to exercise an influence in this field. The first temple dedicated to Apollo in Rome was built on the Palatine between 433 and 431 BC as a response to an outbreak of plague in the city. (It was in this temple that the Sibylline books were later stored.) Asclepius only arrived there in 293 BC when another plague struck the city's inhabitants. The Hippocratic Oath sworn by physicians continues to put 'Apollo the healer' ahead of Asclepius.

Asclepius himself is a complex character about whom the stories are complex and contradictory. Although generally regarded as a god, he first appears in Homer's *Iliad* as a very human healer, and some stories suggest that he was a human who became a god. His cult seems to have come into prominence at the same time as the emergence of Hippocratic medicine, and one of the most important sanctuaries dedicated to Asclepius was established on the island of Cos, the home of Hippocrates. It was founded on the site of an earlier one dedicated to Apollo. The emergence of Hippocratic medicine during the fifth century BC was also the emergence of a new profession, or, if one prefers, the emergence of a new approach to an old profession. Hippocratic medicine might be regarded as an attempt to make the wisdom of healing fully human [5.8]. However, it was never the only form of healing available.

The kind of healing associated with Apollo was primarily that of a world where disease was caused by pollution and the cure involved purification. The kind of approach associated with Hippocrates, on the other hand, was scientific and systematic. And it is interesting to note that, according to Isidore of Seville, some regarded Hippocratic medicine as a *rediscovery* of the medical knowledge of Asclepius that had been lost for 500 years (Edelstein and Edelstein 1975, I, p. 185). Indeed, it is tempting to see the figure of Asclepius as a kind of Hippocratic ideal-type, a relatively obscure character from mythology upon whom was projected the image of the healer, blown up to divine proportions in line with the third hypothesis I advanced earlier [1.2] The kind of healing associated with Apollo remained, but seems to have largely retreated away from the areas where Hippocrates operated. Where medicine could heal, there was no need of purification. Asclepius addressed himself primarily to those physical health problems that the followers of Hippocrates could do nothing for.

It may be noted that Apollo came to be identified with a number of healing deities in Gaul, indicating that the healing dimension of his cult retained its potency for many centuries after the emergence of Asclepius and Hippocrates. However, it may also be noted that the Gallic deities in question (for example, Grannus) were all associated with water in some way or other (usually springs), and that water was the pre-eminent medium of purification in the ancient world. Therapeutic springs straddled the boundary between the old and the new approaches to healing. Their mineral contents often provided a scientific basis for their beneficial effects, while the traditional association with purification remained strong.

In principle, any god might have an oracle, and it might be visited for any purpose. In practice, few had more than one and many had none. Of those of which there is knowledge, Apollo, Asclepius, Isis and Sarapis had far more than any other deities did, and Zeus was probably the only other god to have more than half a dozen (Curnow 2004). The fact that the largest number of all belonged to Asclepius is indicative of the extent to which what was sought was healing.

In addition to Isis, two other goddesses became closely associated with wisdom, Minerva and Athena. Often identified with each other, some have suspected that the cult of Minerva had its origins in that of Athena. In any event, there were a number of similarities between them and both seem at an early stage to have had a special connection with crafts of various kinds, being credited in some cases with their invention. There was a tradition that Athena invented the potter's wheel, although there was also a tradition that Anacharsis, one of the Seven Sages, should take the credit [1.3]. One of the epithets borne by Athena was *'ergane'*, designating a worker or maker. The idea of crafts and their origins being associated with gods was widespread in the ancient world, and examples have already been seen in the cases of Ea and Ptah. What is interesting to note is that neither Greece nor Rome appears to have had any particular interest in attributing the discovery of writing to a god, let alone to a major one. This may reflect the fact that the Greeks and Romans developed alphabetical systems of writing that were considerably simpler and easier to learn than the hieroglyphs of the Egyptians or the cuneiform of the Mesopotamians. While learning to write might be an achievement in Greece and Rome (and still is), it did not set people apart in the way it did in Egypt and Mesopotamia. While literacy may not have been universal, neither was it sufficiently uncommon to identify an elite.

Athena seems to have had a general connection with the arts, literature and philosophy, although it is not always easy to identify precisely what the connection consisted of or what it actually meant in practice. Because of her martial qualities she was often depicted fully armed, but she also acquired a reputation for peace and the resolution of conflict, as a restorer and preserver of order. Epithets attached to her included *'pronoia'* (having foresight) and *'boulaia'* (counsellor), both of which have connections with wisdom. Divine foresight underpinned much of the practice of divination [5.4], while the idea that a counsellor should be associated with wisdom was, for understandable reasons, widespread throughout the ancient world [5.5]. Although there is some haziness of detail in certain areas, it seems reasonably clear that she was associated with wisdom in a variety of ways, and that many of her qualities were those that humans might also manifest.

The cult of Minerva, insofar as it existed in its own right, was relatively underdeveloped. Some think it may have come into existence as an Etruscan transformation of the cult of Athena. She is virtually absent from Roman legend, and the principal aspect of her cult that seems to be genuinely independent is her role as a healer. The temple of Minerva Medica on the Esquiline in Rome celebrated her as the patroness of the medical profession. For reasons that are obscure, both Athena and Minerva were associated with the owl, which stood as a symbol for both and for wisdom. It has been suggested (Becker 1994, p. 223) that the connection is to be found in the owl's ability to see at night, thus symbolizing 'wisdom penetrating the darkness of ignorance'.

In sum, all across the ancient world, gods were given credit for human inventions, patronized human professions and responded to human petitions. They were repositories of wisdom, sources of wisdom and exemplars of wisdom, responsible for everything from inventing the potter's wheel to maintaining the order of the cosmos.

(e) Zoroastrianism

So far in this chapter the focus has been on polytheism. In the next section I shall consider wisdom in the context of monotheism. As a transition I shall consider wisdom in the context of a religion that is often seen as dualistic. Although its centre of gravity was on the very eastern edges of the geographical area covered by this book, its influence spread far beyond there. According to Mary Boyce:

> Zoroaster was ... the first to teach the doctrines of an individual judgment, Heaven and Hell, the future resurrection of the body, the general Last Judgment, and life everlasting for the reunited soul and body. These doctrines were to become familiar articles of faith to much of mankind, through borrowings by Judaism, Christianity and Islam ... (Boyce 1984, p. 29)

Consequently, far from being a remote and unfamiliar religion, Zoroastrianism can look surprisingly familiar in parts. At the heart of it is the figure known as Ahura Mazda, meaning 'Lord Wisdom'. In the beginning, according to Zoroastrian thought, there was Ahura Mazda, the one uncreated god, by nature good wise and just, and the creator of all that is good in the universe. Ahura Mazda was also associated with the principle of *asha*, and *asha* bears many resemblances to the Egyptian principle of *maat*. The principle of *asha* was intrinsically connected with order, and in particular moral order, so, like *maat*, it can also mean truth and righteousness. However, experience soon reveals that *asha* does not rule uncontested and Zoroastrianism opposed to it a contrary principle known as *druj*, embodied in Angra Mainyu, the spirit of evil and destruction. Angra Mainyu is a primeval *being*, but not a primeval *god*. History is the playing out of the struggle between *asha* and *druj*, between Ahura Mazda and Angra Mainyu. But in the end, and in every way, Ahura Mazda will prove superior and his ultimate victory is assured. Ahura Mazda and Angra Mainyu are sometimes known by later forms of their names, Ohrmazd and Ahriman.

To help him in his work, both in creating the ordered world and in overcoming Angra Mainyu, Ahura Mazda created six benevolent deities known as the Holy Immortals. These were Ameretat (immortality), Armaiti (devotion), Asha Vahista (*asha*), Haurvatat (integrity), Kshatra Varya (dominion) and Vohu Manah (good thought). To these are sometimes added a seventh, Spenta Mainyu, which is Ahura Mazda's own holy spirit. It seems that in its original form Zoroastrianism may have opposed Angra Mainyu to Spenta Mainyu, as two spirits separate from Ahura Mazda, but that later Spenta Mainyu became identified with Ahura Mazda. On the other hand, all seven Holy Immortals can be understood as different aspects of Ahura Mazda. Because good and evil were understood to be choices open to all, those who chose good were literally fighting alongside Ahura Mazda and the Holy Immortals against Angra Mainyu. The observance of *asha* in its moral sense is part of the battle against *druj*.

Even from this very short sketch of Zoroastrianism, it is apparent that wisdom and order are at the heart of its outlook on the world: 'Wisdom is in the Zoroastrian system a power in the mental and physical war against evil' (Russell 1990a, p. 82), and the war against evil is at the same time the war against disorder. As a religion with a long history, Zoroastrianism went through a number of changes, but its fundamental dualism was a constant, as was the supremacy of wisdom in its worldview.

3. Wisdom and Monotheism

Although there were various movements *towards* monotheism in the ancient world, this section will concern itself only with Judaism and Christianity, along with what is sometimes seen as a deviant form of Christianity, Gnosticism. Before embarking on the discussion of the substantive subject matter, some words of introduction may be helpful.

First, it may be pointed out that while the works of wisdom literature contained within what came to be called the Old Testament and the Apocrypha arose within a specifically Judaic context (although never in one that was immune to outside influences), they were all accepted into the Christian canon in one way or another. Consequently, there is a certain continuity between the two religions in this respect although obviously not in all. For the sake of convenience, I shall generally talk about the Old Testament, Apocrypha and New Testament, even though these terms cannot strictly speaking do service when discussing Judaism. Secondly, the presence here of Gnosticism requires some explanation.

There has long been a lively debate as to whether Gnosticism had its origins before or after Christianity, and which influenced which in its development. That the two existed alongside each other for some time and interacted is indisputable. Most other things can and have been disputed. I do not propose to go further into these disputes here,

Some may find it surprising to find any discussion of Gnosticism in a section of the book dealing with monotheism. On the face of it, Gnosticism can sometimes appear anything but monotheistic, and it is often talked of in terms of dualism. However, it may be argued that ultimately all the baffling array of beings that inhabit the Gnostic universes come from and are manifestations of a single god. The dualism that is undoubtedly present in Gnosticism is primarily a metaphysical opposition between spirit and matter. In the end, Gnosticism seems to fit best here, even if the fit is not perfect.

Although, as I have already indicated [1.2], I believe that wisdom literature is not the best place to begin in an examination of the meaning of wisdom in the ancient world, in this section there is little to work with apart from a particular body of literature. It has become common practice to identify Job, Proverbs and Ecclesiastes as the wisdom books of the Bible, with Wisdom of Solomon and Ben Sira (also known as Sirach or Ecclesiasticus) from the Apocrypha added to them. Beyond these, scholars have detected 'wisdom influence' in many more (Dell 2000, pp. 64-95). 'Wisdom influence' is a matter for later [6.4]. Furthermore, not all the contents of all the wisdom books are relevant here. The idea that, within monotheism, God is regarded as wise is unexceptional, unlikely to be disputed, and requires no further examination. There are also substantial portions of the wisdom books that could be regarded as secular texts with no theological implications of any kind. Again, this will be a topic for later discussion [6.4]. As I indicated earlier [2.1], the understanding of wisdom can sometimes set up an internal strain within monotheism, and that is my primary interest in this section.

Unsurprisingly, 'wisdom' is mentioned many times in wisdom literature. However, the problem is less with what is said than with what is meant. There are a number of passages in the wisdom books of the Bible where it would appear that what is being discussed is not 'wisdom' but 'Wisdom', not a virtue but a being:

> Wisdom cried aloud in the street;
> in the markets she raises her voice;
> on the top of the walls she cries out;
> at the entrance of the city gates she speaks...
>
> (Proverbs 1:20-1)

This might be read metaphorically or allegorically, with 'Wisdom' simply being a poetic personification of 'wisdom'. However, such an interpretation becomes considerably more difficult when Wisdom actually does speak, and in the first person:

The Lord created me at the beginning of his work,
the first of his acts of old ...
When he established the heavens, I was there ...
when he marked out the foundations of the earth,
then I was beside him like a master workman ...

(Proverbs 8:22, 27, 29-30)

It may be noted that this account of the creation has no obvious echoes at all in Genesis, although some have sought to interpret Genesis 1:26, 'Let us make man in our image', as evidence that God had some help in at least the later stages of the process. On the other hand, there are rather clearer similarities to the Isis aretalogy discussed earlier [2.2b]. However, the key question is not how much these words resemble those found elsewhere, but what they imply here. More specifically, the question is whether the figure of Wisdom is to be regarded as tantamount to a goddess, in which case monotheism is undermined, or as something else. And if Wisdom is something else, what kind of thing is that something else? Does Wisdom constitute some kind of rupture in the unity of the Godhead, or can it be dismissed as some kind of lesser entity?

There is no simple answer to this question because Wisdom has a history. As a collection of collections, the dating of Proverbs is highly problematic, but what is clear, if nothing else is, is that it is considerably earlier than either Ben Sira or Wisdom of Solomon, works in which Wisdom also clearly appears as a being rather than as a concept. It is generally agreed that Ben Sira was written in the second century BC. In it, Wisdom describes herself thus:

I came forth from the mouth of the Most High,
and covered the earth like a mist.
I dwelt in high places,
and my throne was in a pillar of cloud.
Alone I have made the circuit of the vault of heaven
and have walked in the depths of the abyss.

(Ben Sira 24:3-5)

The dating of Wisdom of Solomon is more controversial, but many estimates converge on the period between 50 BC and AD 50 (Crabbe 2003, pp. 87-90). Wisdom does not speak in the first person in this book, and some of its passages about her might easily be given an allegorical interpretation:

I loved her and sought her from my youth,
And I desired to take her for my bride,
And I became enamoured of her beauty.

(Wisdom of Solomon 8:2)

In some other passages, however, this does not appear to be a credible option:

For she is an initiate in the knowledge of God,
And an associate in his works.

(Wisdom of Solomon 8:4)

It is not difficult to see resemblances between the portrayal of Wisdom and what has already emerged in the discussion of Maat and Isis. Scholars have also argued for other influences, such as the cults of the Canaanite goddess Asherah and the Syrian goddess Astarte. The fact that these two goddesses are often taken as one, and in turn identified with the Babylonian Ishtar, and that Astarte was one of the many goddesses who came to be identified with Isis, simply underlines the fluidity of the context in which thinking about Wisdom developed. Even Persian influences have not been discounted. With the benefit of hindsight it is possible to point out that Judaism retained its strongly monotheistic character and did not find room within it for a secondary deity. However, that is not to say that there were not in it at some stage of its historical development certain polytheistic tendencies or hangovers, or to deny that from time to time some might have gone down a less strictly monotheistic path than others, even if those paths historically turned out to be dead ends.

Some have sought to see in Wisdom not a goddess but some kind of hypostasis. According to this view 'she is God's Wisdom acting as a separate entity ultimately identical with Yahweh' (Scott 1992, p. 75). The notion of an hypostasis stretches monotheism to its limits, affording it some of the benefits of polytheism, permitting separate identifiable persons, separate independent realities, to exist within a single godhead. Not surprisingly it has been a subject of both confusion and contention. However, at the very least, to describe Wisdom as an hypostasis is to assert that Wisdom is not an illusion, that there is something objectively there. Exactly what is objectively there is another matter, as is the notion of *ultimate* identity. What does seem to be clear, however, is that the notion of an hypostasis has been employed in this context to deal with the internal strain set up within monotheism by a notion of Wisdom that seems to have acquired considerable strength and threatened to break free.

Others have seen in Wisdom 'a full-blown expression of God in female terminology' (Scott 1992, p. 81). The 'female' element is significant. 'Wisdom' has been used as a translation of both the Hebrew '*hokma*' and the Greek '*sophia*', and when the books of the Old Testament were translated from Hebrew into Greek, '*sophia*' was used to translate '*hokma*'. While one is not a perfect translation of the other, and 'wisdom' is not a perfect translation of either, they have become established in their usage. However, there is an important difference in that while 'wisdom' has no connotations of gender in English, both '*hokma*' and '*sophia*' are feminine in their respective languages, as are their cognates in other related languages. The use of such terms naturally suggests feminine imagery,

34

which in some cases verges on the erotic when employed by masculine writers.

Perhaps the simplest way to sum up this part of the discussion is this. Although Wisdom never *formally* became regarded as an independent goddess within Judaism, on more than one occasion she came as close to being so regarded as it was possible to do without monotheism being fatally compromised. Moreover, the feminine gender of '*hokma*' and the obvious similarities between Wisdom and Isis and Maat (amongst others) meant that the discussion of Wisdom/wisdom easily absorbed and attracted terminology and ideas that pushed monotheism to its limits.

So far this discussion of Wisdom has limited itself to sources from Judaism. However, as these became taken up in turn by Christianity, they informed and influenced Christian thinking. Indeed, according to Scott:

> There can be little doubt that one of the earliest significant images used by the Christian Church to help define the relationship of Jesus to God was the Jewish figure of Wisdom. (Scott 1992, p. 83)

The problem with this is that the Jewish figure of Wisdom had become articulated within a totally, and sometimes extremely, feminine vocabulary, and this was scarcely a matter of detail that could easily or conveniently be overlooked. To drastically oversimplify a long and complicated history, the relationship of Jesus to God also became articulated in terms of *logos*, a term traditionally translated in St John's gospel as 'the Word', but having a variety of meanings, including 'reason'. As a masculine term, the application of *logos* to Jesus was less problematic. More than that, there had been something of a merging, or at least confusing, of *sophia* and *logos* by this time, a development sometimes linked with the works of the Jewish philosopher Philo of Alexandria (13 BC-AD 45), although the extent to which he was a leader in this or simply a follower is difficult to establish. This at least partial reconciliation of *sophia* and *logos* seems to have made it less difficult to project the feminine image of Wisdom onto the masculine image of Jesus. However, as Christian theology developed in a trinitarian direction (with the aid of the concept of the hypostasis), and the figure of the Holy Spirit emerged alongside God the father and God the Son (Jesus as Christ), some aspects of *sophia* seem to have transferred to, or at least been duplicated by, the Holy Spirit. Indeed, some early writers, for example Irenaeus, seem to have identified the Holy Spirit with Wisdom. (It may be noted that while *sophia* became absorbed into the Trinity, the cult of Mary the Mother of God absorbed many features of Isis, both in terms of epithets and in terms of iconography.)

It would be going much too far to say that Christian trinitarianism was the result of the Judaic doctrine of Wisdom, but I do not think it is going too far to say that the latter in some way prepared the ground for the former. What might be called the semi-independence of Wisdom within a monotheistic structure certainly made it no harder for trinitarianism to emerge, and the identification to a greater or lesser extent of Jesus with Wisdom is clear evidence of genuine continuity. What is evident is that both Judaism and Christianity sought to find a place for Wisdom at the very highest level, and in seeking to find an accommodation for Wisdom, both Judaism and Christianity took monotheism to its very limits. The same, I think, is true of Gnosticism.

There is no one Gnosticism, but many different versions of it. There are differences of opinion as to what it is, where it came from, and why. Because the term 'Gnosticism' is a modern one, its application to ancient theories is sometimes a matter of dispute. On the other hand, *'gnosis'* was a word in common circulation in antiquity, and certainly some people either called themselves or were called by others 'Gnostics'. For many early Christians 'Gnostic' and 'heretic' often amounted to the same thing. The term *'gnosis'*, however generally had either neutral or positive connotations, referring to knowledge, but often in an esoteric sense, intuitive rather than rational, experienced rather than read about. In the context of Gnosticism, the *gnosis* in question related to the human condition. In the Gnostic view of the world, human beings were lost souls and *gnosis* was the key to salvation. Gnostic writings frequently addressed themselves to explaining how this had come about, and in doing so set out in detail a baffling array of cosmogonies. The overall Gnostic view of the universe was what has been aptly described as 'dualism on a monistic background' (Rudolph 1983, p. 58). There is no one single simple narrative that permeates all Gnostic writings, and doubtless the Gnostic sects disagreed as much with each other as they did with those who were not Gnostics. Furthermore, the Gnostics seem to have taken a relatively flexible view of things and 'valued change and creativity' (Davies 2006, p. xiii). As a result, even on the limited evidence of the few Gnostic texts that have survived, it is apparent that alternative versions of important texts developed and were tolerated. However, this summary provided by Richard Valantasis gives a reasonably representative account of the Gnostic view of things.

> In Gnostic tradition, Sophia was one of the spiritual beings that emanated from God. But whereas in Genesis God was the creator of the world, in Gnostic mythology Wisdom took the initiative and attempted to create the world without God's approval. Sophia's attempt was a failure – instead of a world, she created the demiurge, a hypostatization (a materialization) of her arrogant desire. The demiurge in turn created a world – our world – almost completely devoid of spirit and soul. Our only hope for redemption lies in the small divine spark from Sophia that found its way in. (Valantasis 2006, p. 21).

Gnostic writings often contrive to appear both familiar and unfamiliar at the same time; they take familiar elements, but weave them together in an unfamiliar way. Here God, Wisdom and creation are brought together, as they were in Proverbs, but the world that we know was not created by God or Sophia. Indeed, this is one of the points on which Christianity and Gnosticism stood most opposed. The Christian God is the God of the Bible, whereas for the Gnostics the God of the Bible is the demiurge. This is part of the *gnosis* of the Gnostics. Apart from 'the small divine spark', the world created by the demiurge is worthless. This is also part of the *gnosis*. The monistic background is that there is ultimately only one God, of which the small divine spark is ultimately part. The dualistic foreground is the sharp contrast between that small divine spark and the creation of the demiurge. However, ultimately everything comes from God:

> There is no evil realm of matter in Gnosticism; there are only erroneous worldviews that regard the world of matter as a realm independent of the mind of God. (Davies 2006, p. xv)

As with Judaism and Christianity, Gnosticism finds an important place for Wisdom at or close to the highest level. However, where Judaism and Christianity saw Wisdom in a wholly positive light, in Gnosticism the figure of Sophia is at best ambiguous.

4. Conclusion

This chapter has sought to explore ancient thinking about wisdom in the context of the divine. In the specific context of monotheism, it is apparent that the figure of Wisdom, whether understood as personification, hypostasis or something else, came to occupy a significant place in Judaism, Christianity and Gnosticism. Because it preceded and influenced the other two, it is the understanding of Wisdom within Judaism that is primary. Within his summary of what he presents as 'the broad consensus regarding the concept of wisdom in early Judaism', James H. Charlesworth makes two points of particular importance here.

> Wisdom does not command but persuades, especially in Proverbs. She brings into human society the divine voice. Wisdom is sometimes depicted as the one who is sent by God to humans ... Wisdom existed before creation and was with God and is therefore in some ways involved in the act of creating before time. (Charlesworth 2003, pp. 94, 95)

The association of Wisdom with creation is undeniably strong, and can also be found outside the monotheistic religions, most clearly, perhaps, in the cult of Isis. If the act of creation is interpreted on a more modest level, as invention, then again there are strong associations with wisdom. Minerva and Athena were credited with the invention of various crafts, Thoth invented writing, and so on. And this in turn links with the idea of Wisdom as 'the one who is sent by God to humans'. The gods did not invent things and then just keep them to themselves. They shared their inventions, they provided instruction, they communicated with mortals. Wise gods and goddesses are the teachers of humanity, the bringers of civilization. This was apparently a very widely held belief:

> It is a common idea in world religions that the skills employed by men are so mysterious and wonderful that only the gods could have devised them. It follows from this that at some time in the past the gods must have instructed men in such arts as the use of fire, metals, seeds, tools and weapons. (Colless 1970, p. 118)

Just as was seen in the case of the Seven Sages [1.3], so it is also possible within the various polytheistic religions of the ancient world to see various clusters of competences. Some wise gods and goddesses are counsellors, some are inventors, some are scribes, some are healers, and so on. And many are several at the same time. The economy of divine wisdom bears a remarkable resemblance to what goes on on the mortal plane, as might be expected on the basis of my third hypothesis [1.2]. In the next chapter I shall consider wisdom on the plane that lies between the human and the divine.

Wisdom in Myth and Legend

1. Introduction

In this chapter I shall be concerned with wise characters from myth and legend. I would not wish to pretend that the dividing line between myth, legend and history can be established with any certainty, and it may be that some of the characters who appear here have been unfairly removed from the historical record. On the other hand, some cases do appear to be clear cut. In the end, if some characters find themselves in the wrong places, no harm is done as everyone who needs to appear somewhere *will* appear somewhere. Where it is appropriate and available, I have used the distinction between antediluvian and postdiluvian to mark the boundary between legend and history.

2. Mesopotamia

I shall begin again in Mesopotamia with the enigmatic figures known as the *apkallu*. As has been noted [2.2], technically '*apkallu*' simply seems to mean 'wisest' or 'sage'. However, in Mesopotamian mythology, the term is also applied to a strange and complex group of individuals. Unfortunately, the legends about them survive in only a fragmentary and not entirely coherent form, although the fundamental core of the stories told about them is fairly clear. In the days between the creation of mankind and the great flood that destroyed nearly all of it, Ea sent seven sages, the *apkallu*, for the instruction of mankind. There was a tradition that each was a counsellor to an early king, but it is unclear whether this was an original feature of the myth or a later addition. Central to the myth is the idea that they brought the skills and knowledge necessary for civilization. The first of the *apkallu* was Adapa, a name that itself meant wise (Bottéro 1992, p. 248). He was also known as Uan, perhaps a pun on the word *ummanu* meaning 'craftsman' (Dalley 2000, p. 328). According to the principal source for this, the ancient historian Berossus:

> he gave them an insight into letters and sciences, and every kind of art. He taught them to construct houses, to found temples, to compile laws, and explained to them the principles of geometrical knowledge. He made them distinguish the seeds of the earth, and showed them how to collect fruits. In short he instructed them in everything which could tend to

softenmanners and humanise mankind. From that time, so universal were his instructions, nothing material has been added by way of improvement. (Hodges 1876, p. 57)

These gifts to mankind are sometimes referred to by the Sumerian word '*me*', and comprised all that was required for civilization. They were perceived as much as rules for correct living as knowledge, and behind these rules stood the gods as enforcing agents. In the complex concept of *me* can be seen, perhaps, a fundamental principle of human social order backed up by divine sanction. Soden (1994, p. 177) suggests that the order associated with *me* extended far beyond the human and encompassed the entire cosmos. In any event, the story of Adapa clearly suggests that the wise bring what is required for civilization to exist.

After this, the story begins to become more confused. According to the legend preserved in a surviving fragmentary text (Dalley 2000, pp. 184-7), Adapa was the priest of Ea in his temple at Eridu. Eridu was regarded as one of the most ancient cities of Mesopotamia and the place where kingship first appeared as a gift from the gods. Although the narrative is not without its lacunae and ambiguities, it seems that Ea chose to make Adapa omniscient and wise, but not immortal. As such, he is an heroic figure, but nothing more. However, another very different story is told of Uan by Berossus (Hodges 1876, p. 57). According to this one, Uan emerged from the sea with the body of a fish, although added to this were a human head and human feet. At night, this amphibious creature returned to the sea to rest. All the *apkallu* took this form. As they were created and/or sent by Ea, who was closely associated with the fresh water of his great-great-grandfather Apsu, there is a certain logic in the *apkallu* having something in common with freshwater fish. Iconographical evidence indicates the *apkallu* could also be portrayed with the heads of birds, or with wings, or both. The one thing they were certainly not, according to this version of the myth, is human beings who were made wise. They were supernatural creatures, not gods, but bearing gifts from the gods.

So far only Adapa/Uan has been mentioned by name. For the sake of completeness, something can be said about the other *apkallu*, although little can be said with any certainty. They are known by various names, and different lists are not entirely consistent with each other. Berossus, writing in Greek in the third century BC, calls them Annedotus, Euedocus, Eneugamus, Eneubolus, Anementus and Anodaphus (Hodges 1876, pp. 53-4), while a much older Sumerian king list calls them Uanduga, Enmeduga, Enmegalamma, Anenlilda, Enmebulugga and Utuabzu (Wilson 1977, p. 150). Although the myth relating to Adapa might generously be described as sketchy, virtually nothing is known of the others at all apart from their names, the names of the kings they served as counsellors, and the city-states in which they discharged this function. Collectively it is said that they angered the gods and were

An *apkallu*.

banished back to the waters whence they came (Dalley 2000, p. 182). And other sources relating to the myth suggest that it was not Ea who sent them but Marduk, or Nabu or Ishtar.

There is a further myth that bears on the subject of wisdom, and this one concerns the individual variously known as Atrahasis, Utnapishtim and Ziusudra. With him we perhaps begin to approach the ill-defined threshold that divides invented myth from mythologized fact. If the name of Atrahasis (meaning 'extra-wise') is unfamiliar, his story is less so. The surviving text (Dalley 2000, pp. 9-35), which includes its own creation myth, tells of the gods sending a great flood to destroy humanity, but thanks to a warning from Ea, Atrahasis builds a boat and so is saved. It is this flood that ends the period when the *apkallu* walked upon the earth, and the distinction between the antediluvian and the postdiluvian seems to have remained firmly established in the Mesopotamian mindset. That parts of Mesopotamia suffered serious flooding from time to time is hardly implausible, but what, if any basis, the story of a great flood bears to real events remains a matter for speculation.

Atrahasis is an interesting figure. By surviving the flood he and his wife became the living links between the antediluvian and postdiluvian ages. They also seem to have been the only human beings to have been made immortal (Leick 2001, p. 83). More than once the narrative presents Atrahasis as talking to Ea, the god of wisdom, and this is perhaps the basis for his own reputation for wisdom. On one occasion he is clearly asking the god to explain a dream to him. However, it is also said that his father was called Shuruppak, who was the last king of the city-state of Shuruppak before the great flood. (Excavations at Shuruppak have uncovered evidence of very substantial flooding there in around 2750 BC.) The names of both Shuruppak (the king) and Atrahasis (as Ziusudra) appear in a Sumerian work known as 'The Instructions of Shuruppak to his Son Ziusudra'. The earliest surviving fragments of this have been dated to around 2500 BC. The work includes a variety of proverbs, aphorisms and observations within a framework indicating that this is Shuruppak's advice to his son. Just before the final flourish in which Shuruppak pays his valedictory respects to Nisaba comes line 278, which could either be regarded as a final aphorism, or as a summation of the entire text: 'The gift of wisdom [is like] the stars (of heaven)' (Alster 1974, p. 51). Atrahasis is therefore the beneficiary of both the divine wisdom of Ea and the human wisdom of Shuruppak, and most fittingly called 'extra-wise'.

3. Israel

While there are few believers in Thoth or Marduk in the world today, the idea that anything that appears in the Bible should be treated as mythology will doubtless seem objectionable to some, but there is no obvious reason why Atrahasis should be treated as mythological while Noah is treated as historical. Indeed Dalley (2000, p. 2) sees in 'Noah' a possible derivation from 'Utnapishtim', the Akkadian name of the survivor of the Mesopotamian flood. For present purposes the most important antediluvian figure in the Bible is without doubt Enoch, although in fact the Bible says very little about him and what it does say is vague and confused. Genesis (4, 5) seems to draw on two different and conflicting genealogies, one of which makes Enoch the son of Cain, the other makes him the son of Jared, a seventh-generation descendant of Adam through the line of Seth. In an enigmatic phrase it is said that 'God took him' (Genesis 5:24), and this came to be understood to mean that he ascended into heaven. Towards the end of the first millennium BC a literature began to grow around Enoch and there survive three books concerning him, sometimes known as the Ethiopic (1), Slavonic (2) and Hebrew (3) Enochs after the languages in which they have been preserved. Debates concerning the dating of these texts have been as long as they have been inconclusive, and some have argued for 2 Enoch and 3 Enoch to be from the late first millennium AD, and so outside the scope of this work. Fortunately, it is 1 Enoch that is of most interest here, and for that an earlier date is agreed. It is a composite work and seems to have taken shape during the last few centuries BC. Consequently, although it is sometimes regarded as a Christian text, some or all of it is pre-Christian in origin.

1 Enoch uses the character of Enoch as a container into which to pour a vast amount of learning of all kinds. Although the work is generally characterized as an apocalypse, and it is in the sense that the book talks about what was *revealed* to Enoch in one way or another, in some ways putting it into the category of apocalyptic literature is misleading. For example, a section of the book (chapters 72 to 82) is essentially an astronomical treatise (of Babylonian origin?) that takes the form of an 'instruction' in which Enoch passes on his learning to his son Methuselah (82:2-3):

> I have given wisdom to you, to your children and to those who shall become your children in order that they may pass it on (in turn) to their own children and to the generations that are discerning. All the wise ones shall give praise, and wisdom shall dwell upon your consciousness; they shall not slumber but be thinking; they shall cause their ears to listen in order that they may learn this wisdom ... (Charlesworth 1983, p. 60)

As Philip S. Alexander notes (Alexander 1998, pp. 95-6), part of what seems to be going on in 1 Enoch is an attribution of various areas of human learning to divine revelation, much in the manner that the Mesopotamians believed that the *apkallu* had brought all important knowledge to humanity and the Egyptians credited Thoth with the invention of writing. Enoch is presented as an example of the omniscient sage. His knowledge also extends to the future, and in these sections of 1 Enoch the book becomes more conventionally 'apocalyptic'.

It may also be noted that a connection developed between Enoch and Hermeticism [6.7]. The connection with Hermeticism may be explained, or encapsulated, in part by a reference to Enoch in the book of Jubilees (second century BC) that says (4:17):

> This one was the first who learned writing and knowledge and wisdom, from (among) the sons of men, from (among) those who were born upon earth. (Charlesworth 1985, p. 62).

Bearing in mind that Hermes became identified with Thoth, and that Thoth was credited with the invention of writing, this seems to credit Enoch with the invention of writing, so permitting his identification with Thoth and Hermes.

Two other Old Testament figures may be briefly mentioned, Job and Daniel. It is interesting to note that there is scarcely any mention of either in the Bible outside of the books that bear their names. However, the book of Ezekiel (ch. 14) twice refers to Noah, Daniel and Job together. The implication seems to be that all three are epitomes of righteousness. With regards to Job, because the book that bears his name is universally regarded as a work of wisdom literature, and because nothing is known of him except what appears in that work, he will be considered elsewhere [6.4]. The case of Daniel is a more interesting one. The biblical book that bears his name is set in historical times, during the seventh and sixth centuries BC. However, although part of the book is written in the first person, its composition in its present form is reliably dated to around 165 BC. A later author has appropriated the identity of a much earlier figure. According to a widely (although not universally) accepted theory, the figure of Daniel was at least in part derived from that of Danel, the father of the eponymous hero of the 'Poem of Aqhat', a Ugaritic work dated to the fourteenth century BC. It is apparent from the poem that Danel was renowned for his wisdom, and the message of the poem seems to be that human beings need to know their place in the order of things, and in particular to be constantly mindful that they are very different from gods (Mack-Fisher 1990a, p. 72). If the reference in Ezekiel is taken to be to Noah, *Danel* and Job, and if Noah can be identified with Atrahasis, then the three appear to have been grouped together because of the reputation they all had for being wise, rather than (or in addition to) being righteous.

Whatever his historicity or ancestry, the hero of the book of Daniel is clearly marked out as a man of exceptional talents. Along with three others, Hananiah, Mishael and Azariah, he was picked out because he was 'skilful in all wisdom, endowed with knowledge, understanding, learning' (1:4). In addition to the talents he shared with the others, 'Daniel had understanding in all visions and dreams' (1:17), and in this he excelled. However, his interpretations are clearly based on what God reveals to him, rather than on any kind of science. The second part of the book of Daniel is a series of prophecies (made by the author of the book with the substantial benefit of hindsight), an early example of apocalyptic writing [6.5]. Daniel is an attractive figure to whom to attribute such prophecies because of his reputation for being able to interpret dreams. Although he is credited with various kinds of wisdom, it is his talent for dreams that sets him above others.

To categorise as 'legendary' characters whose skulls supposedly sit in Cologne cathedral might seem peculiar, but there is little that can be said with certainty about the 'Three Wise Men' who appear in the New Testament nativity narrative. In fact, they appear only in Matthew's gospel, and while he mentions a plurality of wise men, he gives no actual number. Later writers took it upon themselves to fill in the many gaps. The term used by Matthew refers not to wise men, let alone kings, but to 'magi'. The term may originally have applied to a sub-group of the Medes who became a Zoroastrian priestly caste. In time the term came more broadly to be used for those who practised various kinds of divination, and in particular astrology. This seems to lie behind Matthew's use of the term in connection with people who were alerted to important events by a celestial sign. Given

Imhotep depicted as God of Medicine.

that in the ancient world divination was associated with wisdom [5.4], the translation of 'magi' by 'wise men' in this context is not an unreasonable one. Whatever later tradition, or the narrative of Matthew, may owe to history, the general underlying point, that those who read the stars were credited with wisdom, has a strong basis in fact.

4. Egypt

Ancient Egypt was surprisingly lacking in legendary figures. However, two important historical figures managed to achieve legendary status and so it may be appropriate to deal with them here. The first was Imhotep, vizier to the pharaoh Djoser (2667-2648 BC) and the man credited with designing the so-called step pyramid at Saqqara. A surviving fragment of a larger inscription records some of his titles and attainments:

> The Treasurer of the King of Lower Egypt, the First after the King of Upper Egypt, Administrator of the Great Palace, Hereditary Lord, the High Priest of Heliopolis, Imhotep the builder, the sculptor, the maker of stone vases ... (Clayton 1994, pp. 33-4)

References to a number of works attributed to him survive, but the works themselves do not. At some point during the first millennium BC he became regarded as a god and a number of temples were dedicated to him. At least some of these became centres of healing, and the Greeks identified him with Asclepius, and he probably had a significant reputation as a healer while alive. He was also associated with writing and wisdom.

A somewhat similar figure was Amenhotep, son of Hapu, who lived over a thousand years later (*c.* 1430-1350 BC). He served the pharaoh Amenhotep III as chief architect and was granted the exceptional privilege of building a mortuary temple for himself among those of the pharaohs. Centuries after his death he became regarded as a god in recognition of his wisdom and healing powers (although there is no evidence that he laid claim to any such powers during his own lifetime). Inscribed statues of him survive in which he is depicted as a scribe. The cults of Imhotep and Amenhotep were sometimes found in close proximity to each other, as in the temple of Hatshepsut on the west bank of the Nile opposite Thebes where in the second century BC Ptolemy VIII built a chapel dedicated to them. There is no doubt at all that each was the leading architect of his age, and that they were also both scribes can be taken as a given, since learning to write was the foundation of Egyptian education, and no one could rise to the ranks they did without being highly educated [5.3].

5. Greece and Rome

In turning to the world of Greece there is again no convenient antediluvian/postdiluvian position to begin from. For the sake of convenience, I shall assume that the period up to and including the Trojan War is legendary. With regard to wisdom, one of the most interesting characters of the Trojan War is probably also one of the least well-known, Palamedes.

> Tradition credited Palamedes with a great number of inventions, including one or more letters of the alphabet, the order of the alphabet, the invention of numbers, the use of coinage, the calculation of the lengths of months according to the movement of the stars, the game of draughts, the game of dice and the game of five stones. (Grimal 1991, p. 320)

Quite why he was credited with so many inventions is unclear and it is difficult to tell how early or how late these various inventions were attributed to him, or what, if any, factual basis there might be for the reputation he came to enjoy. A similar kind of character can be found in Daedalus, hero of an early experiment in human flight. A number of different inventions were credited to him (including animated statues) and the original Labyrinth was built to his design. His nephew Talos was also an inventor reckoned to be variously responsible for the saw, the compass and the potter's wheel. Some have seen in Daedalus a transformed version of the Canaanite Kothar (Price and Kearns 2003, p. 144), a god normally associated with metalworking.

A different kind of wisdom is represented by Tiresias, the most outstanding seer of Greek legend, uniquely credited with having lived as both a man and, for a time, as a woman. Struck blind by Hera, he received the gift of prophecy from Zeus by way of compensation. As with Daniel, his special talents were very much god-given rather than the result of human endeavour. He was the founder of a soothsaying dynasty with his daughter Manto and her son Mopsus. This was not the only such dynasty. The seer Amphiaraus passed on his gift to his son Amphilochus, whose nephew (also called Amphilochus) also possessed them. All three of them probably had their own posthumous oracles (Curnow 2004, p. 47), as did Tiresias and Mopsus. Cassandra, the daughter of King Priam of Troy, was another who received the gift of prophecy from a god (in this case Apollo), but with the spiteful twist that she would not be believed. Another outstanding seer was Melampus, said to have acquired the power to understand animals after snakes had licked his ears. This came in very useful when he heard worms discussing the strength of a beam holding up the ceiling of a cell in which he was being held. Because of this special knowledge, he was in a position to secure a transfer before it fell in.

Mopsus is an enigmatic figure who features in stories about both the Trojan War and the voyage of the Argo. Tradition credited him with the foundation of a number of cities, including one named after him, Mopsuestia ('The Hearth of Mopsus'). According to Apollonius of Rhodes (IV.1502ff.), he died in Africa after being bitten by a snake. An inscription dating from the eighth century BC discovered at Karatepe seems to refer to a 'house of Mopsus', but if it does it, it might simply be an example of a powerful family claiming a legendary founder for itself. Given that the most elastic interpretation of all the materials appears unable to reconcile them all into one coherent narrative, even when the considerable licence of legend is employed, some have argued for more than one figure bearing this name, while others have gone further and argued for Mopsus being the name of a family of seers (Price and Kearns 2003, p. 358), presumably stretching over several generations. It would appear that with Mopsus we stand on the indistinct borderline between myth and history.

A different kind of wisdom again was embodied in Nestor. An old man, he appears in the stories about the Trojan War as the voice of experience, a wise counsellor, a peacemaker and mediator. Curiously, given his more common associations with cunning, Odysseus also appears in the *Iliad* [2.166-210] as a purveyor of wisdom and diplomacy. When the coalition of forces fighting the Trojans threatens to break up, it is Odysseus to whom Athena turns to persuade, cajole, encourage them to stay united, which he does, and they do. It is also in the *Iliad* that Machaon and Podalirius appear, the sons of Asclepius, the purveyors of the wisdom of healing. There is also the character of Mentor, whose very name has become synonymous with advice and counsel. Not only is he the one to whom Odysseus turns to take care of his affairs and his family while he is away from his home, he is also the one whose form Athena chooses to take on at one point.

All these characters may have their basis, more or less, in one way or another, in history. A very different kind of figure is Prometheus, whose name is usually interpreted to mean 'foresight'. In one sense, Prometheus is out of place here as he should appear amongst the gods. However, in one of the most famous myths associated with him, he attends a meal being shared by both gods and humans and seems to occupy something of an intermediate position between the two. Stealing fire from the gods, as he is said to have done, does not require being a god if gods and humans can sit down at the same table. On the other hand, there was a tradition that he had actually formed the first human beings out of clay, which clearly and radically sets him aside from humanity. Although there is no clear indication that Prometheus was explicitly regarded as wise, his creation of humanity and bringing of the gift of fire puts him on a par with others elsewhere who certainly were. Like the *apkallu* [3.2] he is a vehicle through which humanity acquires elements of civilization.

Whether there is any historical basis for the stories about Rhadamanthus is an entirely open question. That he became a figure of legend is beyond dispute. Said to be the son of Zeus and the brother of Minos, a paragon of wisdom and justice, he was credited with providing Crete with its first laws. Such was his pre-eminence in this field that he later became one of the judges in the underworld. As a character explicitly identified as a judge and lawgiver, Rhadamanthus is the first of this type to be encountered here, and it may be appropriate to say something about the difference between the two skills he embodies, as both will resurface on a number of occasions in the course of this book.

> The mediator, or arbitrator, was a man of wisdom, but he had only his own wits to call on for a decision, and no power to enforce it. (Lewis 2007, p. 28)

Although these observations are made in the specific context of the world of Homer (and the example of Nestor in the *Iliad* is used to illustrate them), they have a far wider resonance and application. In the absence of an actual legal *system*, the authority of a judge is primarily personal. In some, indeed many, cases that authority might be based on political power, since the right (if not the duty) to judge generally accompanies rulership. However, even those without such power might nevertheless be chosen to act as judges because of their reputations for wisdom. It is their personal reputation rather than any public office that gives their judgment authority. Lawgivers, on the other hand, have an eye more on the future than on the present. They seek to provide a firm foundation on the basis of which others may judge. As such, they are systematic thinkers in a way that judges are not. In *Politics* (1273b25-35), Aristotle makes a further distinction between those who make *laws* and those who make *constitutions*. Lawmakers reform only the law, whereas those who make constitutions reform society. In the category of those who produced both laws and constitutions, he places Solon and Lycurgus (Aristotle 1998, p. 61). Solon has already been met as one of the Seven Sages [1.3], and he will be met with again [4.8]. Here I want to take a closer look at Lycurgus.

As with Imhotep and Amenhotep, there is little doubt that Lycurgus was an historical figure. But there is also little doubt that history became encrusted with and distorted by legend to such an extent that it has become obliterated for all practical purposes. Consequently, I shall discuss Lycurgus here, rather than in the next chapter. Cartledge (2002, p. 58) suggests the possibility that Lycurgus might be Apollo in human guise. On the other hand:

> Lycurgus may have been a myth, in our sense, but it was for the laws that he had supposedly given them that the Spartans who perished at Thermopylae gave their lives so willingly. (Cartledge 2002, p. 28)

The legends about Lycurgus abound and conflict, but they are constant in one thing, namely that he reformed Spartan society from top to bottom. More than simply a set of laws, more than merely a constitution, he gave the Spartans both an identity and an ideology. While in modern terms Spartan society may appear distinctly unappealing in a variety of ways, in ancient times it was respected for its stability, order, and apparent immunity to tyranny. It had many admirers, and Plato drew far more on Sparta than he did on his native Athens in constructing his ideal state in *Republic*. Aristotle is less complimentary. In *Politics* he compares Sparta unfavourably with Crete, while observing that the Spartan constitution seems to have been substantially based on the Cretan one (1271b20-5). However, given the high esteem in which the Cretan system was held (a fact closely connected with the reputation of Rhadamanthus), this is not the most damning of criticisms. How radical the reforms of Lycurgus were is difficult to assess without knowing precisely how he found things, and how many of the reforms attributed to him alone were implemented over a longer period by others is also impossible to assess. The legend at least, is clearer. According to this, Lycurgus left behind him a society that in many ways prioritized the collective over the individual, that discouraged the accumulation of wealth, that incorporated a system of political checks and balances, and that above all manifested the values of order and stability.

In compiling and composing his series of parallel lives from the histories of Greece and Rome, Plutarch set Lycurgus alongside Numa. Traditionally, Numa was the second king of Rome, succeeding Romulus and ruling from 715 to 673 BC. It seems entirely likely that there is some historical basis to the legends surrounding Numa, but the legends are so numerous that he seems to sit more comfortably in this chapter than in the next. If Romulus was the political founder of Rome, Numa was its religious founder, amongst other things. If Romulus represented 'the terrible side of kingship', Numa 'stood for the god-fearing, law-giving, wise and intellectual side' (Dumézil 1996b, p. 523). Later traditions even made him a follower of Pythagoras, but with no historical basis whatsoever. The achievements ascribed to him include reforming the calendar, establishing the city's boundaries, reorganizing the social structure, introducing a programme of religious ceremonies, and setting up a new priesthood:

> But the grandest achievement of his reign was, that throughout its course, he remained the jealous guardian of peace even more than of power. (Livy 1.22, 1960, p. 40)

Numa is said to have founded Rome's temple of Janus, whose doors were only closed during peacetime. While he ruled, they were never open. After he died, they were rarely closed. In a variety of ways, Numa bestowed order on Rome and provided secure foundations for its future stability. The comparison with Lycurgus is not unreasonable. Whatever the truth of the matter in either case, both were credited with radically transforming their own societies, putting them on new and firmer footings, leaving them more enlightened places than they found them.

6. Conclusion

This chapter has been concerned with the intermediate zone that lies between the world of gods and the world of humans. Some of its occupants may once have been gods who were later thought of as human, some may once have been historical figures who acquired legendary status. Like Janus, many of them face in two directions at the same time. While certain of them, most notably the *apkallu* are clearly of a different stamp, most of them are in one way or another recognizably human, even if they have become humanity writ large.

In many cases, wisdom has been seen to be closely associated with knowledge. However, it does not appear to be associated with just any kind of knowledge but rather with what might be termed 'civilizing knowledge'. In the case of the *apkallu*, it is the very basis of civilization itself that they bring. The same, in a more limited way, might be said of Prometheus and

Palamedes. Numa and Lycurgus, on the other hand, serve an important function on a more modest scale. They are not associated with the civilization of humanity as such, but with putting their own individual societies on wiser footings. In the case of Enoch, the kind of knowledge with which he is associated is encyclopaedic, reflecting a belief held by the Stoics [4.16], among others, that wisdom involves omniscience. While not omniscient, the achievements of Imhotep and Amenhotep, son of Hapu, clearly elevate them well above the human norm. The impression is that many ancient cultures could not quite believe that humanity could achieve what it had. Either credit for the requirements of civilization was given directly to the gods or their emissaries, or the human beings associated with them were retrospectively divinized. As will be seen [4.16], even the founder of a philosophical school could be regarded as a god by his followers. And if Roman emperors such as Claudius and Titus could be deified, it is scarcely surprising that an elevated position could also be found for the inventor of writing or the potter's wheel.

As I indicated earlier [1.2], it is my belief that wisdom is best studied in all its variety in its embodiments in various wise people. To some extent this chapter and Chapter 2 have been designed to prepare and pave the way for the next one, in which the wise people of the ancient world finally take centre stage.

Wisdom in History

1. Introduction

The aim of this chapter is to look at a variety of individuals from the ancient world who were in one way or another regarded as wise. Put that way, the chapter may appear to be over-ambitious and under-focussed, and indeed there lies a danger in both directions. It has been noted [1.2] that in Akkadian alone there are many words that may point to someone being wise and many professions with which wisdom was associated. And yet, as I hope will emerge during this chapter, the picture is not completely chaotic and there are recurrent themes. Although some regarded as wise may be highly individual, there are also a number of types. In particular, a number of professions were particularly associated with wisdom, for example those of the scribe and the diviner. More will be said about these and other professions in Chapter 5. Because of the overlap between the two chapters it is difficult to avoid repetition entirely, but I have sought to keep it to a minimum.

2. Egypt

I shall begin in Egypt. The final section of Papyrus Chester Beatty, dated to around 1300 BC, reads:

> Is there anyone here like Hardjedef? Is there another like Imhotep? None has appeared among our relatives like Neferti or Khety, that foremost of them. I cause thee to know the names of Ptahemdjedhuti and Khakheperre-sonb. Is there another like Ptahhotep, or Kairis as well? These learned men who foretold what was to come, that which issued from their mouths happened, being found as a state written in their books. Thus the children of other people are given to them to be heirs, as though they were their own children. Though they concealed their magic from everyone else, it may be read in a book of wisdom. (Pritchard 1969, p. 432, slightly amended)

The text as a whole is a eulogy to the scribal profession, in which the praises of the written word are sung and the memory of great scribes of the past evoked. Of the names mentioned in the list, most are well-known and the writings of some of them (or at least the writings attributed to some of them) survive in whole or in part. It is clear that the profession of scribe enjoyed a considerable prestige in ancient Egypt and was probably hereditary to a large extent. Many texts that have survived have done so because they were frequently copied as part of the process of training a scribe.

The name of Imhotep is already familiar [3.4] and nothing further needs to be said about him here. Hardjedef was a son of the pharaoh Khufu (2589-2566 BC), the builder of the great pyramid at Giza. Some lines of a work attributed to Hardjedef survive, but it is thought to be the work of another, and later, hand. Although the subject will be discussed at greater length later [6.3], it may be appropriate to say a brief word here concerning the 'instruction' sub-genre of Egyptian wisdom literature. Both Imhotep and Hardjedef are credited with works of this kind that set out instructions for living (and succeeding) in the world. They are generally presented in the form of a father passing on his acquired wisdom to his son. Ptahhotep, another name mentioned in the list above, is also credited with such a work. Like Imhotep, he seems to have been a vizier, in this case to the pharaoh Djedkare-Isesi (2414-2375 BC). Surviving works are also attributed to Khety, Neferti and Khakheperre-sonb, but they belong to different genres. The so-called 'Satire on the Trades' attributed to Khety is another hymn of praise to the scribal life and disparages many other professions: he proclaims, 'Behold there is no profession free of a boss – except for the scribe: he is the boss' (Pritchard 1969, p. 434). Neferti appears in a work known as 'The Prophecies of Neferti' in which the pharaoh Snefru (2613-2589 BC) is given the benefit of his wisdom and learning. The work is actually thought to have been written about 600 years later, at about the same time as 'The Complaints of Khakheperre-sonb'. The 'lament' (which can take a variety of forms) is taken by some to be another sub-genre of Egyptian wisdom literature.

It may be noted that the four works that survive or of which there is knowledge are attributed to or involve figures from around the middle of the third millennium BC: Imhotep, Hardjedef, Ptahhotep and Neferti. It is almost as if this period later came to be regarded as a kind of golden age of wisdom and learning to which people looked back with reverential awe. There was also a general respect for the past, and for what had been handed down from it: Rekhmire, vizier to Tuthmosis III (1479-1425 BC) declares, 'Every sage is one who will heed what the earlier ancestors have said' (Williams 1990a, p. 26). It may also be noted that works of the instruction sub-genre of wisdom literature are normally attributed to either scribes or pharaohs (or, in the case of Hardjedef, the son of a pharaoh), suggesting that these people were amongst the most likely to be associated with wisdom.

The author of another work, known as the 'Onomasticon of Amenope' was also a scribe, as he tells us in the opening words of the text:

Beginning of the teaching for clearing the mind, for instruction of the ignorant and for learning all things that exist: what Ptah created, what

> Thoth copied down, heaven with its affairs, earth and what is in it, what the mountains belch forth, what is watered by the flood, all things upon which Re has shone, all that is grown on the back of earth, excogitated by the scribe of the sacred books in the House of Life, Amenope, son of Amenope. (Gardiner 1947, p. 2*)

How much the work was that of Amenope himself and how much he was drawing on that of earlier writers is unknown, and all that is known of Amenope himself is what he tells us in these lines. It is thought that the work dates to around 1100 BC. Although the claim that those in possession of the work may be able to learn about 'all things that exist' is certainly an exaggeration, the aim of the text is to present the world (or rather, words that relate to things in the world) in an ordered and structured way. The classifications it uses range from Egyptian towns to beverages to types of meat and parts of oxen. The logic according to which items are arranged within the different classifications is not always easy to discern, although Egyptian towns are listed from south to north. Because of the apparently eccentric set of categories and because some items show up in more than one of them, it is a matter of dispute as to how systematic the work really is and what was intended by it. It is also unclear how innovative Amenope is being, what his own precise contribution to the exercise is. Nevertheless, if one understanding of wisdom is that it involves knowledge of everything, then this appears to be, in ambition if not in realization, an authentic book of wisdom. Indeed, Williams (1990a, p. 27) points out that the term most often used in Egyptian to designate a wise person literally means 'one who knows things'.

Exactly what a wise person might be expected to know is unclear. The name of Hardjedef, which has already been mentioned, is associated in the *Book of the Dead* (Faulkner 1985) with the discovery of a spell beneath a statue of Thoth in Hermopolis. Another spell was said to have been discovered by Khaemwaset (a son of Ramesses II) and/or written by Amenhotep, son of Hapu [3.4]. How well-founded these particular associations are is a matter of dispute, but it clearly suggests that those regarded as wise might have more than a passing acquaintance with the ways of magic.

A surviving fifteenth-century BC inscription composed by Thuty, an official at the court of Queen Hatshepsut, relates to another area of expertise associated with the wise in Egypt:

> I investigated a time and predicted what was to come, (being) one who was skilled in looking at the future, aware of yesterday and thoughtful concerning tomorrow, ingenious regarding what would happen. (Williams 1990a, p. 28)

It is not clear *how* Thuty carried out his investigations. There is nothing necessarily magical or mystical about an ability to anticipate the direction in which events are moving. Indeed, a high official who was constantly

Amenhotep, son of Hapu.

surprised by developments might well be seen as poorly qualified for the post. The passage from Papyrus Chester Beatty quoted above links the gift of foresight with a list of exceptional individuals, but perhaps in this respect they were not as exceptional as that author suggests. In another inscription another court official, this time the nineteenth-century BC royal physician Nedjemusonbe, also claims to be 'one who predicts before it comes, who sees before it happens' (Williams 1990a, p. 28). The extent to which this is bluster is clearly open to debate, but even if it does not accurately reflect an achievement, it would appear that it at least points towards something that was recognized as a legitimate aspiration.

3. Ugarit and Ebla

The picture elsewhere in the ancient world was similar in some ways, different in others. In many places the position of the scribe in society was important, central and elevated. As will be seen in greater detail later [5.3], to be a scribe and to be educated were often much the same thing, so that positions and talents that required education were by default filled from the scribal class. A surprising number of names have survived. For example, Loren Mack-Fisher (1990b) has compiled a list of over twenty major scribes who were connected with the royal court at Ugarit. One of the first known, Ilumalku (fourteenth century BC) was clearly a figure of some authority, revered by later generations. Some of his writings have survived. Some scribes functioned as counsellors, including Husanu and Yasiranu, a father and son of the fourteenth and thirteenth centuries BC who held important positions. Sapsumalku (fourteenth century BC) is expressly referred to in terms indicating that he was regarded as wise. Others, including another father and son, Karranu and Iltahmu (thirteenth century BC), and Ehlitesub (thirteenth century BC) achieved the highest office in the land. Siptinarum (twelfth century BC) was the author of the 'Counsels of Shube'awilum', a work 'in which a father advises his son who is embarking on a journey, possibly a metaphor for life itself' (Crenshaw 1998, p. 6). Naamrasap (thirteenth century BC) was also a producer of literary works. These are the names of those scribes who are known to have been held in exceptional esteem, and appear to have been regarded as particularly wise as well as well-educated. From Ebla we know the names of Azi, a civil servant, teacher and archivist and Ishmaia, a mathematician working. Both were active in the middle of the third millennium BC (Leick 1999).

4. Mesopotamia

However, the ability to write was not in itself a requirement of wisdom. It has been said that of all the Mesopotamian kings, only three claimed to be literate (Sweet 1990a, p. 65): Shulgi of Ur (ruled 2094-2047 BC), Lipit-Ishtar of Isin (ruled 1934-1896 BC) and Ashurbanipal (ruled 668-627?). Whether or not that is strictly true, it is evident that Ashurbanipal in particular was a man of considerable learning, as evidenced by the ruins of his library that have been found at Nineveh. There is also his own testimony to that effect:

> Marduk, the wisest [*apkallu*] of the gods, gave me wide understanding and extensive intelligence, and Nabu, the scribe who knows everything, granted me his wise teachings ... I learned the art of the Sage [*apkallu*], Adapa, so that now I am familiar with the secret storehouse of all scribal learning, including celestial and terrestrial portents. I can debate in an assembly of scholars [*ummanu*] and discuss with the clever oil diviners the treatise 'if the liver is a replica of the sky'. (Sweet 1990a, p. 55, slightly simplified).

In boasting of his own achievements, Ashurbanipal was following in a long royal tradition, and many inscriptions glorifying the wisdom of kings can be found. Interestingly, while staking his own claim, Nabonidus feels the need to point out that he is extremely wise despite the fact that he cannot read (Sweet 1990a, p. 57). Like Ashurbanipal, he also stakes a claim to

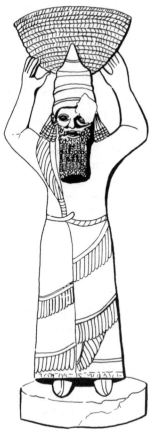

Ashurbanipal.

esoteric knowledge. However, beyond being able to advertise it as an accomplishment, it is not obvious what need or use a king had for such esoteric knowledge, especially since there existed a class of specialist practitioners in that area of learning [5.4, 5.9]. In considering what kinds of expertise a king might need more pressingly, at least three obvious examples readily spring to mind. The first, and most obvious, is the ability to rule well. The second, and related one, since the king was the fount of justice in Mesopotamian society, is to be a good judge (in the broader as well as in the narrower sense of the term). And the third, the need for which is amply demonstrated by the course of Mesopotamian history, is the ability to wage war successfully. All of these requirements pertain to the establishment and preservation of order. The successful waging of war might seem to require something resembling shrewdness rather than wisdom. However, if waging war can be regarded as a craft, then it would appear that the terms used to indicate wisdom are applicable in this context too (Sweet 1990a, pp. 52, 58). More than that, if the political order below reflected the divine order above, then the king as warrior was also the agent of the gods.

Rulership was in large part concerned with the maintenance of order, with the organization of society, and it is no coincidence that Hammurabi's claim to wisdom was announced at the beginning of his celebrated code of law. However, it is not a code of law as that term would normally be understood today. The 'code' of Hammurabi is more like a collection of judgments. Although it may be systematically arranged, it is not a set of principles, but rather a set of decisions. Indeed, Bottéro (1992, p. 183) suggests that the prologue that announces Hammurabi's wisdom is all of a piece with the 'code' as a whole since in it Hammurabi is seeking to present a testimony to his own wisdom by assembling a list of his wise decisions. In the words of Hammurabi himself, his aim is:

> to cause justice to prevail in the land,
> to destroy the wicked and the evil,
> that the strong might not oppress the weak ...

> (Pritchard 1969, p. 164)

However, although the prologue to the code is mainly concerned with listing the many excellences of Hammurabi, it ends with a modicum of modesty:

> When Marduk commissioned me to guide the people aright,
> to direct the land,
> I established law and justice in the language of the land,
> thereby promoting the welfare of the people.

> (Pritchard 1969, p. 165)

Behind the law stands Hammurabi, and behind Hammurabi stands Marduk. Hammurabi also describes himself as 'the shepherd, called by Enlil' (Pritchard 1969, p. 164). A century or two earlier, Lipit-Ishtar had also described himself as 'the humble shepherd of Nippur' who was 'called' by Enlil 'to the princeship of the land in order to establish justice' (Kramer 1963, p. 336) in the prologue to his own code of laws.

Whether or not we agree with Sweet (1990a, p. 65), that 'the king was the wise man *par excellence*', there is a logic to his position that goes beyond the simple fact that kings seem to have been the keenest to proclaim their wisdom to others. As the person with the greatest responsibility for the preservation of political and social order, he occupied a pivotal and unique position in Mesopotamian society. If the gods had established cosmic order, then the king was the source of civil order. While there may have been a substantial amount of unmerited royal bragging down the centuries, and some kings were doubtless wiser than others, I think it is fair to argue that within Mesopotamian

Hammurabi (left) and Shamash.

culture there was the perception of a natural association between rulership and wisdom.

A number of other names are known to us for one reason or another
(Leick 1999). Sharrishtakal was an Akkadian priest and politician of the
twenty-third century BC. Asqudum was a diviner in Mari in the eighteenth
century BC. Kabtiilanimarduk was a ninth-century BC Babylonian author.
Akkullannu was an Assyrian astrologer active in the seventh century BC.
Nergaletir was a Babylonian astronomer of the same period. A rough
contemporary was Nabuzuqupkena, author of many learned works. His
son, Adadshumuusur, was an author and exorcist. His son, Uradgula, also
practised exorcism as well as medicine. Balasi was a friend and teacher of
Ashurbanipal. Dunnashaamur (seventh century BC) was a prophetess
from Arbela. Ilussaamur was another prophetess of the same period, but from
Ashur. Sinqishaamur was another contemporary prophetess, an Assyrian
from Arbela. Nabuahheeriba may have been an adviser to Ashurbanipal.

59

Anuabuter (second century BC?) was a Babylonian author of astronomical works. A disproportionate number of names are known from the period of Ashurbanipal, partly because the ruins of his palace and library were discovered at Nineveh, and partly because both he and his father Esarhaddon seem to have had an efficiently functioning intelligence service in place whereby they received reports on a variety of issues from across their domains. Oracles of various kinds appear to have been of particular interest, hence the number of prophetesses who were in communication with them. The status of the prophetesses is not always clear, but most of the other names mentioned, and many more that could have been, were scribes who also practised other skills.

5. Israel and Judaism

Moses is an enigmatic character about whom much has been written. Not for the first time and not for the last time, an historical core is presumed about which a great deal of legend has accumulated. In *Preparation for the Gospel* (IX.26), Eusebius, quoting Alexander Polyhistor, says:

> But Eupolemus says that the first wise man was Moses, and that he was the first to teach the Jews letters, and from the Jews the Phoenicians received them, and from the Phoenicians the Greeks, and that Moses was the first to give written laws to the Jews. (Eusebius 2002a, p. 462)

This kind of view was not unique to Eupolemus (second/first century BC). Aristobulus (second century BC?), another source cited by Eusebius (XIII.12), believed that Pythagoras and Plato had been influenced by the works of Moses. For obvious reasons, these ideas were particularly attractive to Jewish philosophers, but they were by no means confined to them. Numenius of Apamea (second century AD) famously asked 'For what is Plato, but Moses speaking in Attic Greek?' (Eusebius 2002a, p. 442). Numenius tends to be classified as a Neopythagorean, but, like Aristobulus, is perhaps better regarded as an eclectic, and a fairly radical one at that. What is evident is that in various circles for various reasons at various times there was a strong urge to draw different traditions together into a single cultural and intellectual lineage, and the name most often selected to stand at the head of that lineage was Moses. The fact that such a position could be argued for, however good or bad the actual argument might be, is further evidence of the trans-cultural nature of wisdom in the ancient world.

A very different, and earlier, figure in the Bible is Joseph. His story is that of someone who rose to high office through his talents, and especially his ability to interpret dreams. As such, he demonstrates recognizable sapiential traits. However, if one name from the Bible had to be picked to epitomize wisdom, it would probably be that of Solomon:

60

4. Wisdom in History

> Solomon's wisdom surpassed the wisdom of all the people of the east, and all the wisdom of Egypt. For he was wiser than all other men, wiser than Ethan the Ezrahite, and Heman, Calcol and Darda, the sons of Mahol. (1 Kings 4:30-1)

The figures with whom Solomon is compared comprise an obscure group. However, it would seem to be more than a coincidence that the names Ethan, Heman, Calcol and Darda appear together in only one other place in the Bible (1 Chronicles 2:6), where they are described (along with Zimri) as sons of Zerah. Zerah was the son of Judah, who was a brother of Joseph and son of Jacob. According to tradition, Ethan the Ezrahite also wrote Psalm 89. What all this means is unclear. However, it seems surprising that a group of people whose wisdom is compared with Solomon, even though the comparison favours him rather than them, get only a fleeting mention, and a confused one at that. If they were worth mentioning for their wisdom, why do we not hear any more about them? Why do their names never appear in any of the Bible's wisdom literature?

Before proceeding further, a note of caution must be sounded. As it appears in the Old Testament, 'hokma' (and its derivatives) can have a variety of meanings. For example, Jonadab, a friend of David's son Amnon, is associated with hokma (2 Samuel 13:3), but he is described in various translations as 'subtle', 'crafty' and 'shrewd'. Given that Jonadab appears in the narrative only to help his friend seduce his own half-sister, it is easy to see why translators have avoided using the term 'wise'. Bezalel and Aholiab are also associated with hokma (Exodus 35:30-5), but in their cases they are highly skilled and knowledgeable craftsmen who design and supervise the building of the Tabernacle. There is also the 'wise woman' of Tekoa who speaks to King David (1 Samuel 14:1-20), although it is not clear in what her wisdom consists, and her final words (14:20) attribute to David himself 'wisdom like the wisdom of the angel of God to know all things that are on the earth'. The extent to which hokma was understood as a broad and undifferentiated category of competence is unclear, although I think the assumption has to be that distinctions between different kinds or manifestations of hokma were understood. Indeed, one way of reading the quotation about Solomon with which this section began is that his wisdom surpassed those of others not so much in terms of quantity as in terms of quality: his kind of wisdom was greater than the kind of wisdom to be found in the east or Egypt. On the other hand, if the architects Imhotep and Amenhotep could be deified by the Egyptians, there is no reason why Bezalel and Aholiab should not be revered by the Jews.

There are many cases in the Old Testament of people from the east, Egypt or elsewhere who are referred to in one way or another as wise, but this usually occurs in a collective way. There are the 'wise men out of Edom' (Obadiah 8) who are to be destroyed. The reference is largely obscure, and it is not clear in what their wisdom consisted. It may be that the people of Edom were particularly noted for their divinatory arts, as some peoples were. A curse on 'wise men' is to be found in Jeremiah (50:35-6):

> A sword upon the Chaldeans, says the Lord,
> and upon the inhabitants of Babylon,
> and upon her princes and her wise men!
> A sword upon the diviners,
> that they may become fools!

Who exactly the 'wise men' referred to here are is unclear, but the juxtaposition with 'princes' suggests they are perhaps counsellors, and it is possible that 'diviners' is meant to also have some connection with 'wise men'. Certainly in the book of Daniel (5:15) the 'wise men' consulted by the king seem to be diviners. The 'wise men' of Egypt mentioned in Exodus (6:11) are associated with sorcerers. The Egyptian 'wise men' mentioned by Isaiah (19:11) are mocked as stupid counsellors. The Persian king's wise men mentioned in Esther (1:13) also seem to be counsellors. Although the picture is far from clear and consistent, the implication seems to be that some of the kinds of people regarded as wise elsewhere were not so regarded in Israel. Having noted the names of various prophetesses in Mesopotamia [4.4], by way of contrast King Saul is said to have 'put the mediums and the wizards out of the land' (1 Samuel 28:3). The exact scope of 'the mediums and the wizards' is unclear, but it appears at least to cover 'all who trafficked with ghosts and spirits' as the New English Bible renders the same words.

Instead, the Old Testament presents a very different kind of prophet. One of the most famous is Elijah, an eccentric solitary figure who appears to have supernatural powers, including that of foresight, and who acts as the conscience of the nation and especially of its king, Ahab. However, we are told (1 Kings 22:6) that on one occasion Ahab summoned around four hundred prophets to meet with him, and elsewhere (1 Samuel 10:5) Saul is told that he will meet 'a band of prophets coming down from the high place with harp, tambourine, flute and lyre before them, prophesying'. Consequently, although Elijah may be paradigmatic of a particular kind of prophet, his was not the only kind. Those summoned by Ahab are called upon to give advice on whether he should go to war or not, suggesting that the prophets acted as the king's advisers. In the case of Saul, his encounter with the band of prophets is connected with the bestowal on him of the gift of prophecy. These prophets may have been priests of some kind. The prophet Gad is described as 'David's seer' (2 Samuel 24:12), the prophet Nathan has visions containing messages for David (2 Samuel 7), and the prophet Samuel introduces himself to Saul as a seer (1 Samuel 9:19). Whether as advisors or diviners of some kind, it is clear that the prophets of ancient Israel had much in common with those regarded as wise elsewhere in the ancient world. However, divination fell from favour, with a result that the attribution of wisdom to those who practised it became increasingly problematic if not impossible:

> One reason for the disappearance of the seers in Israel was the theocentric nature of the Yahweh religion; another was the fact that the function of the seers fell into disrepute because of their resemblance to analogous phenomena in Canaanite paganism. The polemics of the prophets and the laws against pagan soothsaying and divination necessarily threw an air of ignominy over the activities of the Israelite seers. Their proceedings were then regarded as illegitimate and incompatible with the true Yahweh religion. (Lindblom 1963, p. 95)

The distinguishing feature of the prophets we know by name is the messages, welcome or unwelcome, that they bring. Both their roles as prophets and the messages they receive are often unasked for. They are essentially God's vehicles, rather like the prophets who operated as the mouthpieces of Apollo at some of his oracles. As such, and perhaps like the prophetesses who reported to Ashurbanipal, they had little that could be called wisdom in their own right. On the other hand, there are also indications of something else. The 'symbolic perceptions' that Lindblom attributes to both Amos and Jeremiah (1962, pp. 138-9) might alternatively be described as interpretations of omens. Similarly, while the prophets are often portrayed as passive participants in the whole process, there is evidence that sometimes prophecies were actively sought:

> Then all the commanders of the forces, and ... all the people from the least to the greatest, came near and said to Jeremiah the prophet, 'Let our supplication come before you, and pray to the LORD your God for us ... that the LORD your God may show us the way we should go and the thing that we should do.' (Jeremiah 42:1-3)

Clearly Jeremiah (seventh/sixth century BC) is here being asked to enquire of God what should be done, and ten days later he came back with a reply. In this way he resembles diviners as they are found elsewhere in the ancient world, although his 'technique' seems to amount simply to prayer. However, while Amos (eighth century BC) is called a seer by Amaziah (Amos 7:12), he replies (7:14) that he is 'no prophet, nor a prophet's son'. The most obvious interpretation of these remarks is that Amos is distancing himself from a kind of prophetic profession normally passed down from father to son, which in turn suggests that the kind of prophecy being talked about involves a skill that can be learned (and is more easily passed on than a gift). One further person identified as a prophetess may be mentioned, namely Deborah. She holds a unique position: in the book of Judges she is the only female Judge, she is the only Judge who actually 'judges', and she is credited with prophetic gifts, which none of the other Judges are.

Judging is very much associated with Solomon, whose name effectively became a byword for wisdom. Many works were attributed to him on this basis, although there is little or no reason for believing that he wrote any of them. However, although Solomon clearly had a reputation for wisdom, the Bible is remarkably scant on evidence of it. It is said (2 Chronicles 1:7-12) that when God offered Solomon anything he wanted, Solomon chose, and received, 'wisdom and knowledge'. It is also said than when the Queen of Sheba visited him, he 'answered all her questions; there was nothing hidden from Solomon which he could not explain to her' (2 Chronicles 9:2). Elsewhere (1 Kings 4:33) he is specifically said to have had great knowledge of trees and animals of all kinds. Such encyclopaedic knowledge has already been seen to be associated with wisdom in the case of Enoch [3.3]. Most famously, however, the story is told (1 Kings 3:16-28) of his judgment when two prostitutes contested the maternity of a child. The declaration that the child should be divided into two served to reveal the identity of the true mother.

> And all Israel heard of the judgment which the king had rendered; and they stood in awe of the king, because they perceived that the wisdom of God was in him, to render justice. (1 Kings 3:28)

In the references to Solomon in 2 Chronicles, the implication is that his wisdom was one associated with great learning, although the details are left extremely vague. In the story of the two prostitutes in 1 Kings, his reputation for wisdom is not associated with knowledge but rather with his judgment and justice. It is curious that only one example of his judgment is felt to be needed in order to justify his reputation for wisdom. Many chapters are devoted to Solomon and his reign, but no other examples are given of his wise judgment. Much more is said about his reputation than about the basis for it, although if it really is true that 'He also uttered three thousand proverbs' (1 Kings 4:32), that might add something to the body of evidence. On the other hand, it might be argued that his reputation, at least in terms of his judgment, rested on quality, not on quantity. The reason for regarding this one judgment as wise seems to be its imaginative leap, Solomon's means of getting to the truth, and so being in a position to exercise justice, by saying something totally unexpected although (in one sense) completely logical. It may also be noted that as a shrewd judge and purveyor of justice, Solomon bears a strong resemblance to the wise Mesopotamian monarch. Later traditions that grew up about Solomon portrayed him in a rather different light. In the Hellenistic period, his reputation acquired a distinctly magical tinge, a fate he shared with Moses. As 'there was nothing hidden from Solomon', it became assumed that his knowledge extended to the esoteric as well as the exoteric. As a consequence, many astrological and alchemical works were attributed to him.

At some point – no one seems very clear when, although the idea can be found in Ben Sira – the idea became generally accepted that the line of prophets had come to an end. Also in Ben Sira are lines (50:1-21) in praise of Simeon the Just, or the Righteous, who is emblematic of a new kind of wise man emerging within Judaism. There is disagreement as to who this Simeon was since two high priests in Jerusalem bore that name around a century apart: Simeon I was high priest in around 300 BC, while Simeon II served from 219 to 196 BC. Whichever one it was, Simeon is seen as standing at the beginning of a line of a new kind of wise men: his is the first name in the list of Sages found in the work known as *Pirke Abot*, or 'Wisdom of the Fathers'. The first name in the list after that of Simeon is that of Antigonus of Soko. After that come a number of pairs of names, all belonging to leaders of the Pharisees: Jose ben Joezer and Jose ben Jochanan, Joshua ben Perachyah and Nittai of Arbel, Judah of Tabbai and Simeon ben Shattach, Shemaiah and Avtalyon, and finally Hillel and Shammai. The latter two are dated to the end of the first century BC, and are recognised as the first of a group known as the Tannaim. Before explaining who they were, it is necessary to provide a little background.

One of the features of Ben Sira is its identification of Wisdom with the Law, or Torah. However, there is not one Torah, but two. One is the 'written' one, contained above all in the five books attributed to Moses. The second is the 'oral' Torah. However, both terms are misleading. The distinction is not so much between what is written down and what is not as about what is fixed and what is not. The books of Moses may not be changed, but their full meaning is not immediately apparent; they need interpretation and explanation. The distinction is therefore primarily between Torah as text and Torah as exegesis, one unchanging, the other constantly developing. The idea that the oral Torah was passed on from master to pupil may help explain the genealogy presented in the *Pirke Abot*, which may not be historically watertight. A similar desire to set out tidy genealogies can be seen in the work of Diogenes Laertius, and this approach goes back at least as far as Sotion who may have written his *The Succession of Philosophers* as early as the third century BC.

Returning to the Tannaim, the term is used to refer to the rabbinical scholars who developed the oral Torah between (approximately) the first century BC and the third century AD, while the term Amoraim is used to refer to another group who continued to develop it for a further two or three hundred years. This kind of development can be seen in the *Pirke Abot*, where in addition to the twelve names mentioned before, scores of other sages also feature, adding to and developing the thoughts of others over centuries.

The issues discussed by the Jewish rabbinical Sages were primarily those that most concerned everyday life: 'The interests of the sages in man and his problems – in his person, his spirit, and his soul – is infinitely greater than in the order of nature and of the world' (Urbach 1979, p. 214). Indeed, *Pirke Abot* is sometimes translated as 'Ethics of the Fathers'. Their roles probably changed in various ways over the long period of their existence and they appear to have come from all classes and areas of society. Although in one sense they functioned as leaders, they do not normally seem to have occupied any formal high office. Rather, like the prophets before them, they generally operated independently, often on the fringes of society, taking a critical stance. Their independence sometimes led to poverty and a reliance on private patronage. Like all social critics, their position can be seen either as symbiotic or parasitic, depending on one's point of view.

This line of development in wisdom within Judaism takes us to near the end of the historical period covered by this book. But there were other lines of development that also need to be mentioned.

6. The Teacher of Righteousness

Although he is not known by name, the character normally referred to as the Teacher of Righteousness forms an interesting and useful focus for bringing together a number of themes and issues relating to developments with Judaism. Nothing is known for certain about the Teacher of Righteousness, not even whether he existed, and although he is usually referred to by this designation, some prefer a different translation such as 'true exponent of the Law' (Gaster 1964, p. vi). Some argue that this designation is not the title of one particular individual, but rather one that was passed on from one to another. Given that the Hebrew terms meaning 'righteousness' and 'wisdom' seem to have gravitated towards each other at times (Weeks 1994, p. 70), and given that Ben Sira identified wisdom with the Law, it might be suggested that the Teacher of Righteousness should also be regarded as a teacher of wisdom. This is supported by an interpretation of a set of hymns that regards them as the work of the Teacher and depict him as the recipient, through revelation, of the wisdom of God (Harrington 1996, pp. 79-80). Such an interpretation also locates the Teacher of Righteousness within a longstanding and widespread tradition, that of 'divine education' (Colless 1970, p. 139). And the idea that Wisdom herself is a teacher is expressed more than once in Proverbs (8:4-7)

> To you, O men, I call,
> And my cry is to the sons of men.
> O simple ones, learn prudence;
> O foolish men, pay attention.
> Hear, for I will speak noble things,
> And from my lips will come what is right;
> For my mouth will utter truth;
> Wickedness is an abomination to my lips.

4. Wisdom in History

The hymns some attribute to the Teacher of Righteousness are among those texts discovered at Qumran that are collectively known as the Dead Sea Scrolls. Although many disagreements about them remain, there is a widespread (but not universally held) view that they were the possessions of a group of Essenes, and that many of them were actually produced by the sect. The Essenes themselves were a movement within Judaism that probably emerged during the second century BC under the leadership of the Teacher of Righteousness. They seem to have formed themselves into a number of close-knit communities, and may have practised healing. Qumran seems to have been home to one of their communities for around two hundred years.

There is so little that is known about the Teacher of Righteousness that there is little point in piling speculation upon speculation. However, a few general points may be made that may help to put the Essenes in context. First, following Philo of Alexandria, it is widely believed that the name 'Essene' is ultimately a Greek one, coming from the same root as 'hosios', which means holy. Their beliefs appear to have been quite eclectic and a variety of influences have been suggested, including Pythagoras and Persia. They appear to have led ascetic lives, and held Moses in particularly high esteem.

The literature associated with the sect suggests that although they were in many ways orthodox in their beliefs, the Teacher of Righteousness seems to have been regarded as (or claimed to be) a prophet. Since the line of development within Judaism beginning with Simeon the Righteous was predicated on the belief that there were to be no more prophets, this presumably set the Essenes in opposition to Simeon and his successors. It would also appear that while the Essene movement itself may have been quite substantial, it was not always united and that there were factions within the larger sect.

These points are made largely to prepare the ground for the next section. The Teacher of Righteousness might be taken as an example of a charismatic figure who attracted a following of loyal supporters, who did not wholly reject the orthodoxy of the time, but who developed it in unorthodox directions, who claimed to receive revelations from God and to be a vehicle for the wisdom of God. If the Teacher of Righteousness was one example of this kind of figure, Jesus of Nazareth might be taken as another.

7. Jesus of Nazareth

Jesus has already been discussed in Christian theologians' terms in connection with the figure of Wisdom [2.3]. Here I want to consider him in what might be called pre-theological terms, as he may have appeared to the majority of his contemporaries. For someone who has been written about so much, the human figure of Jesus remains surprisingly elusive, and this has enabled many to fill in the gaps in our knowledge according to their own preconceptions. Not only that, but the basic materials from which the picture of Jesus must be constructed have changed. The discoveries at Nag Hammadi have brought to light many works lost for centuries, some of which portray Jesus in a significantly different way from how he appears in the canonical four gospels. Whether they portray him any better or more accurately is another matter. Some are Gnostic in character and seek to present an account of his life, nature and teachings in Gnostic terms. Others are harder to classify. One of the more interesting is the 'Gospel of Thomas' which is a collection of sayings of various kinds all attributed to Jesus, some familiar, some unfamiliar. As Jaroslav Pelikan points out (Pelikan 2005, p. 11), the 'most neutral and least controversial' of the titles given to Jesus in the canonical gospels is 'rabbi', identifying him as a teacher, and the rediscovered works offer a broader sense of what he might have taught. Using categories developed by Rudolf Bultmann with the canonical gospels in mind, William Stroker (1989) has classified all the sayings attributed to Jesus in non-canonical works under six headings: apophthegms, parables, prophetic and apocalyptic sayings, wisdom sayings, I-sayings, and community rules. The fact that this can be done without undue difficulty indicates the broad continuity between the canonical and the extracanonical. The presence of the category of prophetic sayings reinforces Pelikan's observation (2005, p. 12) that another title given to Jesus in the gospels is 'prophet'. Calling Jesus a teacher and a prophet puts him in familiar territory. The further titles Pelikan identifies, namely 'messiah' and 'Lord', may be noted, but have no special resonance or relevance from the point of view of wisdom.

Of all the different kinds of saying, perhaps the parables are those most often associated with Jesus within the canonical works, and they are present in the extracanonical ones as well. What is notable about the parables is their ordinary, everyday quality. They are not full of amazing revelations, they are not uttered on God's behalf, they are simply devices for making a point by drawing an analogy with the commonplace. It is perhaps in the use of the parable that Jesus best reveals himself as a teacher, as one who seeks to explain, to educate, to enlighten. Whereas the voice of the prophets is ultimately not their own, but that of God, the voice of the parables is a distinctly human one. And although it is a book of sayings rather than a book of parables, the voice of Jesus is a particularly human one in the case of the 'Gospel of Thomas':

> Jesus in the Gospel of Thomas performs no physical miracles, reveals no fulfilment of prophecy, announces no apocalyptic kingdom about to disrupt the world order, and dies for no one's sins ... And Thomas's Jesus is not born miraculously of the virgin Mary and is not the unique or incarnate son of God. (Meyer 2005, pp. 61-2, 65)

What the 'Gospel of Thomas' depicts instead is a figure who might be characterized as 'a Jewish teacher of wisdom' (Meyer 2003, p. 7) whose teachings contain clear echoes of centuries of wisdom literature.

The extent to which the *style* of Jesus' teaching was innovative or emulative has been a matter of debate. For example, a body of literature has grown up around the idea that Jesus owed a great deal to the Cynics [4.17]. Needless to say, this is a matter of keen debate and considerable disagreement. What is important point about this debate is that in it Jesus is compared with an existing category of wise person, the itinerant philosopher and teacher, and that is the first time that type has been encountered here. On the basis of my third hypothesis [1.2], it is tempting to consider whether the development of the teaching aspect of Wisdom noted in Proverbs may not have been based on a human model, and in some ways reflects the emergence of such a type. But this is speculative. However, it is worth noting that of all the philosophical 'schools' that were in existence at the time of Jesus, it was the Cynics who were the most independently minded, setting up no institutions, and committed (admittedly to differing degrees in practice) to a life of simplicity. If Qumran was genuinely the home of an Essene community, then the Essenes seem to have had something very similar to monasteries. Jesus, on the other hand, founded no such institution. The idea that Jesus can be thought of in terms of a sage, however traditional or radical a sage he might have been, is no longer in itself radical (Witherington 1994).

8. Solon and the Lawgivers

Greece, which means going back several centuries from the time of Jesus. The name of Solon was ever-present on the lists of the Seven Sages, and he is a convenient figure with whom to begin. While it cannot be denied that elements of legend may have attached themselves to him over the centuries, he nevertheless seems a much more solid individual than either Lycurgus or Rhadamanthus [3.5].

> The Athens of his time was hit especially hard by economic and social crisis and stood on the brink of violent civil strife. Apparently, two main 'factions' were opposed to each other: the wealthy and the powerful and the *demos* ... Solon was elected chief official (archon) in 594 and given full power to resolve the conflict. (Raaflaub 2005, pp. 39-40)

The scenario is somewhat formulaic, but there is no particular reason to doubt its historicity. The fact that mediators are called upon in times of crisis is scarcely controversial. However, Solon acted not only to resolve the particular conflict affecting Athenian society in 594 BC, but also to prevent future conflict from arising. He was not only a mediator but also a reformer, and this seems to be the basis for his inclusion amongst the Seven Sages. In his own words:

> I wrote laws too, equally for poor and rich,
> And made justice that is fit and straight for all.
>
> (Gagarin and Woodruff 1995, p. 27)

In this way, not only did he prevent social disorder in the short term, he also laid the foundations for a more stable order in the longer term. Aristotle distinguished between those who reformed only laws and those who (also) reformed constitutions, placing Solon in the latter category [3.5]. The point seems to be that Solon's reforms changed the distribution of power within Athenian society, thereby establishing the political community on a new footing.

In fact, he did rather more than this. Fragments of poems written by Solon survive that are rather more concerned with values or ethos than with the law as such. He makes it clear he believes that:

> bad government brings the most evils to a city;
> while good government makes everything fine and orderly,
> ... This is the source
> among human beings for all that is orderly and wise.
>
> (Gagarin and Woodruff 1995, p. 26)

It may be noted that 'good government' is a translation of '*eunomia*', which might also be translated as 'good order', and Raaflaub (2005, p. 54) sees a strong resemblance between *eunomia* and *maat*. Solon's role almost seems to be that of a teacher, one who is seeking to educate a society in the ways of good order. He does not seem to have been alone in this regard. Before the time of Lycurgus, Spartan society drew inspiration from the poems of Tyrtaeus (seventh century BC) who, like Solon, used his verses to seek to inculcate values:

> To die falling in the front lines is a noble thing
> for a brave man, fighting for his fatherland ...
> Come on, young men, fight, standing by each other,
> don't run off shamefully or give way to fear ...
>
> (Lewis 2007, pp. 53-4)

As Raaflaub observes, 'In ancient Greece, a poet was entertainer, artist, craftsman – and much more: a teacher and educator of his people' (Raaflaub 2005, p. 27). In *Lysis* (214a) Plato goes so far as to call poets 'in a manner our fathers and guides in wisdom' (Plato 1970, p. 85). According to Kerferd, the reason for this was that the poet, along with 'the seer and the sage' was 'seen as revealing visions of knowledge not granted to ordinary mortals' (Kerferd 1981, p. 24). This may help to explain the high esteem in which poets were evidently held, and it is notable that in the case of the (presumed) mythical poets Orpheus and Musaeus, oracles are attributed to them almost as if they were gods. The connections between wisdom and poetry do not end there. Many of the Seven Sages were said to have written poetry [1.3] and many early philosophers also chose to use poetry rather than prose as their preferred literary vehicle. As a kind of craftsman and artist, a poet would probably tend to be associated with Athena and wisdom in any event, whatever the content of the poetry [2.2].

In the cases of Tyrtaeus and Solon, there is surviving evidence, however fragmentary, of what they wrote. The same cannot be said of Thaletas, a poet who lived in Crete in the seventh century BC. However, his poems were said to have been influential in the development of principles of justice in Crete. Lycurgus is said to have visited him, and he may have visited Sparta in turn. In a similar way another Cretan lawgiver, Epimenides (sometimes regarded as one of the Seven Sages), and Solon supposedly met. Although the stories cannot be entirely discounted, they may have more to do with the Cretan reputation for sound laws (partly based on the reputation of Rhadamanthus) than with any historical events.

Some others with a reputation for wisdom as lawgivers can be mentioned. One of the most interesting is Zaleucus of Locri (seventh century BC?). He was meant to be both severe and scrupulous, and one story about him claims that having inadvertently broken one of his own laws he felt obliged to execute himself. Another story about him, often repeated but certainly untrue, is that he was a student of Pythagoras. Yet another is that he obtained the laws for Locri (in Italy) from an oracle. This is another somewhat formulaic scenario and suggests a desire to establish the foundations of human law in divine wisdom. In *Politics* (1274a), Aristotle recounts yet another story about him:

> Onomacritus was the first person to become an expert in legislation. Though a Locrian, he trained in Crete while on a visit connected with his craft of divination. Thales was his companion; Lycurgus and Zaleucus were pupils of Thales; and Charondas was a pupil of Zaleucus. But when they say these things they speak without regard to chronology. (Aristotle 1998, p. 62)

The chronology is indeed very confused, but the story is an interesting one. Onomacritus is a figure from sixth century BC Athens. He is said to have written some of the poems attributed to Orpheus and forged an oracle attributed to Musaeus. The connection with divination seems clear enough, and the connection between laws and Crete was something of a commonplace. The connections between Thales, Lycurgus and Zaleucus are implausible, although the fact that they are made indicates a desire to link the names for whatever reason. Charondas probably lived in the seventh century BC and is said to have written the laws of Catana in Sicily.

71

His reputation spread well beyond there, and he seems to have had an influence on the legal codes of many different places. Aristotle praises him for his precision, which presumably means that he drafted his laws with care.

Philolaus of Corinth, Phaleas of Chalcedon and Androdamus of Rhegium are also mentioned by Aristotle as legislators of note (all of uncertain date). Philolaus and Phaleas both seem to have addressed themselves to the problem of land ownership and how it might best be organized in the interest of social stability. Philolaus and Androdamus both enjoyed sufficient reputations for them to be invited to draft new laws for communities other than their own, suggesting that, like Charondas, their reputations travelled far and wide.

Aristotle also discusses the legacy of Pittacus of Mitylene, one of the names that appears on all surviving lists of the Seven Sages. The stories told about him are not entirely consistent, but it is generally agreed that he became an elected dictator after helping to overthrow an unelected one. According to Diogenes Laertius (I.75):

> He ruled for ten years and brought the constitution into order, and then laid down his office. He lived another ten years after his abdication and received from the people of Mitylene a grant of land ... Furthermore, he declined an offer of money made to him by Croesus, saying he had twice as much as he wanted ... (Diogenes Laertius 1972, p. 77)

Although some sources suggest that Pittacus may have had a less enlightened side, the sayings attributed to him by Diogenes Laertius are often pithy and full of common sense. His physical appearance was clearly unprepossessing, and he is described as fat, flat-footed and dirty. He wrote a book about law in prose, and many poems. The particular reason for him being singled out so consistently as one of the Seven Sages is not apparent. But whether or not the sayings attributed to him are genuine, it seems likely that his primary claim rested on his reputation as both a good ruler and a good lawmaker. However, that is with the benefit of hindsight. Why the people chose him as their elected dictator in the first place is unclear. A story told by Herodotus (I.95-102) perhaps points to how and why it might have happened.

In fact the story is not about Greece at all, but about the Medes, and the person who may have been their first king, Deioces. According to Herodotus,

> Deioces, who was already a man of mark in his own village, now entered wholeheartedly into the task of distinguishing himself for just dealing ... His reputation for being the only man to settle a dispute according to strict justice spread to the other villages ... As the knowledge of his impartiality increased, so the number of his clients increased ... He then announced that he had had enough of it ... It was contrary to his interest to spend all his time

settling his neighbours' quarrels to the neglect of his own affairs. The result was that robbery increased and the contempt of law throughout the country was worse than ever. [The Medes then met and decided] 'Let us appoint one of our number to rule us so that we can get on with our work under orderly government, and not lose our homes altogether in the present chaos.' (Herodotus 1965, pp. 53-4)

Deioces was the obvious candidate (which was his intention) and duly became the first king of a united people. Although there are some doubts as to the historical accuracy of this story, it seems likely that there is a core of fact (Cook 1999, pp. 5-7). Deioces seems to be the same person as Daiaukku who may well have united the Medes in around 700 BC and founded their capital city of Ecbatana. His rise to power, if the story has some truth in it, came on the back of a reputation for wisdom and justice, and because of that reputation he was trusted with power. While the specific story of Deioces makes it clear that he actively sought and planned for his rise to power, it may nevertheless reflect a more widely repeated scenario. Moreover, this was in keeping with one particular line of Greek political thought.

> Xenophon and Isocrates agree that the quality of the management is more important than the type of constitution, and that democracies, oligarchies, tyrannies and kingships are all doomed if they are not properly ruled. (Gray 2005, p. 146)

Indeed, from the political point of view it might be argued that the wise were specifically those who were best equipped to rule. In fact, this is the basic argument put forward by Plato in *Republic* (473-5): kings must be philosophers and philosophers must be kings, and 'the philosopher doesn't desire one part of wisdom rather than another, but desires the whole thing' (Plato 1992, p. 150). However, whereas Plato apparently thought that wise philosophers had to be artificially produced through a process of education, many others obviously thought that the wise were a naturally occurring phenomenon and all that had to be done was to identify them.

9. Seers, Shamans and Saints

Although divination was widely practised in ancient Greece and Rome, relatively few names are known of those who actually practised it. To a large extent, this function was exercised through established channels, such as the various oracles of Apollo scattered throughout the Greek world or the college of augurs at Rome. Augury at Rome went back to the city's very origins: according to Livy (I.18) neither Romulus nor Numa ascended to the throne without the endorsement of the appropriate omens. However, those who actually sought these omens are largely anonymous, and in any event membership of the college seems to have rapidly become an honour rather than a profession. One of the most famous was Attus Navius (seventh/sixth century BC), who defended augury against the taunts and challenge of the king Tarquin Priscus. But by the third century BC membership was being awarded to Fabius Verrucosus while he was still in his teens, and by the time of Gaius Marius (157-86 BC) it seems to have become for the most part little more than a means of flattering the powerful, even though the work of augury itself continued.

In Greece, being a seer seems to have often been more of a family business, and Herodotus (IX.33-7) tells an interesting story about how Greek diviners were involved on both sides at the battle of Plataea in 479 BC. On the Greek side was Tisamenus. Although he was with the Spartans, he was originally from Elis, and belonged to the Iamidae family, a famous soothsaying clan who claimed descent from Apollo himself. Pausanias (VI.2) tells how he saw a statue at Olympia dedicated to Thrasybulus, another member of the same family, who 'instituted a kind of prophecy from the offal of dogs which was all his own' (Pausanias 1971b, p. 288). In an unknown way, gecko lizards also appear to have been pressed into divinatory service. Herodotus also mentions the name of Antiochus, the father of Tisamenus who was presumably also a seer. On the Persian side was Hegesistratus, also from Elis, but a member of the Telliadae family, and presumably related to the Tellias Herodotus mentions (IX.27) who had been helping the Phocians with his divinatory powers. Another hereditary family of prophets were the Branchidae, the custodians of the oracle of Apollo at Didyma until they abandoned it in the fifth century BC.

The presence of figures like Tisamenus and Hegesistratus at Plataea was not anomalous. In his life of Nicias (23), Plutarch describes an incident in the Athenian campaign against Syracuse in such a way as to suggest that seers regularly accompanied armies.

> It happened that at that moment, however, that Nicias did not even have an experienced soothsayer with him. His former intimate associate, Stilbides, who had done much to hold his superstitious fears in check, had recently died. (Plutarch 1960, p. 237)

The presence of such people on military campaigns may have been the rule rather than the exception, and for much of ancient history war itself was the rule rather than the exception. This obviously gave seers considerable influence. In peace time, seers also played their part, but their position was far from unassailable. In his life of Pericles (6), Plutarch tells the tale of Lampon, a seer, who explained what the strange phenomenon of a one-horned ram meant. The philosopher Anaxagoras carried out a dissection and produced a more scientific account of the phenomenon. However, as Plutarch points out:

there was nothing to prevent both the scientist and the prophet from being right, since one correctly diagnosed the cause and the other the meaning of the prodigy. It was the business of the first to observe why something happens and how it becomes what it is, and of the second to foretell the purpose of an event and its significance. (Plutarch 1960, p. 170)

There seems no doubt that some seers had a better reputation than others. In 'Peace', Aristophanes (1970) pours scorn on Hierocles, accusing him of being a sham, yet others clearly put considerable faith in him (Nilsson 1972, p. 133). People like Hierocles and another seer, Diopeithes, were also the custodians of traditional beliefs. According to Plutarch in his life of Pericles (32), Diopeithes secured a law in Athens making atheism a crime.

While seers are one kind of sage with special powers, there is another kind that I shall call the shaman. This type also existed in the ancient Greek world, and the names of some of them have come down to us. It is evident that elements of legend have become attached to each and questionable how much of what was written about them can be believed. The first who may be mentioned is Abaris the Hyperborean, mentioned rather disparagingly by Herodotus (IV.36), who supposedly never ate and travelled around the world with a magic arrow thanks to which, according to some sources, he was able to fly. For some reason the Hyperboreans were thought to be particularly devoted to Apollo, while later traditions claimed that Abaris was not only a priest of Apollo but also a Pythagorean, and even a pupil of Pythagoras himself. From Apollo he received the gift of prophecy, and he was also credited with healing powers. Accounts of when he might have lived are not entirely consistent, but suggest the sixth century BC. How much faith is to be put in any of this is disputable. However, the stories about Abaris may at least represent some kind of Greek link with the kind of shamanism more often associated with central Asia. It is probably no coincidence that Abaris was sometimes said to come from Scythia, near the Black Sea.

Magical stories were also told by Herodotus (IV.13-15) about Aristeas of Proconnessus, variously said to be able to travel outside his body or return from the dead. His ghost is said to have turned up in Metapontum and told the residents there to set up an altar to Apollo. As Metapontum was for a time a stronghold of Pythagoreanism, he was obviously associated with that in some way or another, if only in the popular imagination. However, Herodotus obviously had access to a poem attributed to him, so there was evidently something of substance there. A similar curious case is Zalmoxis, who was said to have been the slave of Pythagoras. He was one of the Getae, a hostile tribe from Thrace. It is said that after being set free he returned there and set about civilizing the people. Stories about him suggest that he pretended to return from the dead. However, the Getae also had a god called Zalmoxis, and it is unclear how much of what is known about 'Zalmoxis' refers to the god and how much to the man. The association of both Abaris and Aristeas with the cult of Apollo may not be coincidental:

> There is some reason to believe that Apollo may have come to the Greeks from an area in contact with the shamans, and in that blend of history and legend which forms so much of the early story of Greece we can trace various figures akin to shamans, Abaris, Musaeus, Aristeas and Hermotimus, Orpheus and Epimenides and Pythagoras. (Ferguson 1970, p. 80)

The only name on this list that has not been mentioned at all so far is that of Hermotimus. The stories about him contain familiar shamanic themes such as being able to leave his body and working miracles. A temple was erected to him in Clazomenae, and in later legend he became recognized as one of the earlier incarnations of Pythagoras. Although some have questioned his historicity, Aristotle treated him as both historical and philosophical. In *Metaphysics* (984b) he gives Hermotimus credit for an early attempt at framing the theory that mind is present in the whole of nature and is the basis of order in the world. If he lived, it was probably in the eighth or seventh century, but there is little to go on.

We have considerably more to go on in the case of Apollonius of Tyana, who is said to have 'raised the dead, healed the sick, and ascended bodily into heaven' (Philostratus 1970, p. 9). Apollonius lived in the first century AD. Written in the early third century AD, the biography of him written by Philostratus did much to enhance his reputation, and he seems to have become regarded as one of paganism's great assets in its tussle with Christianity. How much of what Philostratus wrote is reliable is another matter, and he seems to have indulged in some literary licence. Apollonius is said to have absorbed the teachings of Pythagoras and travelled far and wide, including to Egypt and India, to learn more. The biography relates his many journeys and claims that he had the ability to disappear from one place and magically turn up in another. He possessed prodigious healing powers, and many stories are told of how he exercised them. He had the ability to see into the future, but attributed this (IV.44) not to 'the gift of prophecy' but 'to knowledge which god reveals to wise men' (Philostratus 1970, p. 106). In the Middle Ages, he became credited with the authorship of an alchemical work known as the 'Emerald Tablet' (Marshall 2001, p. 253). Christian theologians also took note of him, and in *Preparation for the Gospel* (IV.13) Eusebius (2002a, p. 164) quotes from a work attributed to him, 'Concerning Sacrifices'. Even if only half of what Philostratus says about him is true, he was clearly a charismatic and exceptional character. Thanks to Philostratus, the posthumous fame of Apollonius spread far and wide and many temples and shrines were dedicated to him. A work attributed to Sossianus Hierocles, a governor of Bithynia under Diocletian, compared him favourably with his contemporary, Jesus of Nazareth.

There were also echoes of shamanism within early Christianity itself. Peregrinus Proteus (second century AD) was, as his nickname of 'Proteus' might suggest, someone with flexible principles, flirting with both Cynicism and Christianity, and perhaps other beliefs as well. He moved around a great deal, often because he became involved in difficulties of various kinds and found it prudent to move on. Not surprisingly, opinions about him seem to have differed, but some at least were prepared to acknowledge him as a prophet, and he himself seems to have claimed to be the Second Coming of Christ. His death was spectacular: he climbed atop a funeral pyre at the Olympic Games in AD 165. Less colourful, but more influential, was his contemporary Montanus (second century AD). At one time a pagan priest, he became a Christian. At some point around AD 157, he began to prophesy, and this led to the development of his own sect, which lasted until the sixth century. Amongst the followers he attracted were a handful of women who also claimed to possess the prophetic gift. One of them claimed to have had a visitation from Christ himself saying she saw him 'in the form of a woman' who was 'arrayed in shining garments', and he 'set wisdom upon me' (Hultgren and Haggmark, p. 129).

Another who converted to Christianity from paganism was Cyprian of Antioch (third/fourth century AD?). Although some (including the Vatican) have dismissed the stories about him as worthless fictions, it is possible that they contain something of value. Before his conversion he is said to have been an initiate in the mysteries of both Mithras and Demeter, and then gone through another initiation ritual on Mount Olympus that lasted for six weeks. Ferguson observes:

> We cannot discern exactly into what he was being initiated. Comparison with other evidence, however, suggests that the initiation may have been not just initiation as a worshipper, but at least a partial training as a seer. (Ferguson 1970, p. 181)

Part of the training, whatever its purpose, consisted of a severe asceticism. Only fruit was eaten, and only after sunset. Such asceticism became part of mainstream Christianity through monasticism, and in particular those who chose the life of the hermit. *The Life of Antony* written by Athanasius of Alexandria (2003) contains many of the elements found in *The Life of Apollonius* by Philostratus. Like Apollonius, Antony of Egypt (third/fourth century AD) is able to heal the sick and see into the future. He was much in demand and 'He helped the judges, especially advising all of them to make just decisions' (Athanasius of Alexandria 2003, p. 239). This seems to be a recurrent theme in late antiquity. The ascetic who withdraws from the world, or who at least lives on the fringes of it, is sought out by the world for help and advice of all kinds.

One of the best known of these ascetics was Simeon the Stylite (fourth century AD). After many years spent devoting himself to asceticism (and in particular fasting), he set himself up on top of a pillar at Telanissus (now known as Deir Samaan) in Syria and spent the rest of his life there. The pillar underwent some alterations during the thirty-six years he spent on it and is believed to have eventually reached a height of around sixty feet, topped by a platform twelve feet square. It is known that Simeon would often be called upon to arbitrate in all kinds of matters of a civic and legal nature, much as people like Deioces had been centuries earlier. The kind of holy man personified by Simeon was perceived as a suitable person to perform these functions because he stood on the very edge of society, both metaphorically and literally. He was sufficiently independent to be accept-able to everyone. By remaining a kind of outsider, the holy man was allied to no particular group or faction and was in no one's debt, so he could be relied upon to be objective. As Peter Brown points out:

> The rise of the holy man as the bearer of objectivity in society is, of course, the final playing out of the long history of oracles and divination in the ancient world ... The lonely cells of the recluses of Egypt have been revealed, by the archaeologist, to have had well-furnished consulting rooms. (Brown 1982, p. 135)

Indeed, in the holy men (and to a lesser extent the holy women) of late antiquity, many of whom have become regarded as saints, there is a kind of summing up of much of what was regarded as wisdom in the ancient world. While Christianity may have condemned magical practices and divination, the holy men enjoyed and deployed many of the benefits of these, performing miracles and seeing into the future. Many of them were sought out for the same reasons as the wise had been sought out through-out antiquity: for their advice, for their help, for their healing. The nickname of one of them, Gregory the Wonderworker (third century AD), is perhaps a testimony to the fact that what was sought was often found. Not all of these holy men were Christians. Much the same phenomenon can be found in paganism: 'Most major [philosophical] schools found no difficulty in accommodating the concept of the holy or divine man' (Ander-son 1994, pp. 5-6).

With Gregory, Antony, Simeon and countless other saints whose names will have to be passed over, we are coming again towards the end of the historical period covered by this book, and it is time to go back again to pick up a different thread. By way of transition, this section will end with one of the more enigmatic of the early Greek philosophers, Empedocles of Acragas (fifth century BC). As with Peregrinus Proteus, there is a spectacular story told about his death. In fact, there is more than one of them. One has it that he was taken up bodily into heaven in a blaze of light, another has it that he leapt into the crater of Mount Etna, and a third, relatively low key one, is that he drowned. E.R. Dodds describes him as

a very old type of personality, the shaman who combines the still undifferentiated functions of magician and naturalist, poet and philosopher,
preacher, healer and public counsellor. (Dodds 1951, p. 146)

Not surprisingly, an individual with so many different and varied talents
is difficult to pin down. The matter is complicated by the fact that the
surviving evidence concerning his life is sparse and sometimes contradictory, and that what remains of his work is extremely fragmentary, with
many disagreements over how the fragments should be reassembled. This
is not helped by an evidently longstanding disagreement concerning where
his basic philosophical affiliations lie. Diogenes Laertius (VIII.54-6) de-
spairingly lists the different stories about those who influenced him. One
has him as an admirer of Parmenides, another as a pupil of Anaxagoras,
another as a pupil of Pythagoras or one of his successors. Peter Kingsley
(1995, pp. 226-7) sees a close resemblance to the Persian magi. It is not
impossible that all of these claims are true and that Empedocles himself
was a true eclectic.

It is generally thought that the surviving fragments attributed to him
are from two separate poems, one called 'On Nature' and the other
'Purifications'. The notion of purification has echoes of both the Pythagoreans and the mysteries, but it was also a central feature of the Greek
religious outlook in general (Zaidman and Pantel 1992, pp. 9-11). Purification and its complement, pollution, were both important aspects of the
cult of Apollo. The specific source of pollution identified by Empedocles in
his poem is the eating of meat:

> Alas that the pitiless day did not first destroy me
> before I contrived with my lips the terrible deed of eating flesh.
> (Barnes 1987, p. 200)

The idea seems to have been that animals are in some sense kindred
spirits, and it may be noted that when Aristotle spoke of the view held by
Hermotimus, that there is an intelligence pervading the whole of nature,
he also ascribed this view to Anaxagoras, said by some to be one of the
teachers of Empedocles. However, Empedocles and Anaxagoras seem to
have been close contemporaries inhabiting different parts of the Greek
world and it does not seem to be particularly likely that one was the
teacher of the other. But the same idea could have come via Pythagoreanism. Furthermore, the idea that there were intelligent forces pervading
the natural world also appears in traditional religious beliefs concerning
nymphs.

More interesting for present purposes is the other poem, 'On Nature',
where Empedocles seems more clearly to be his own man. Here he sets out
the view that everything in the world is composed of the four elements,
earth, fire, air and water. That in itself was not original, but he animates

these elements with two fundamental forces, usually translated as 'love' and 'strife'. 'Love' is a unifying force that brings things together, 'strife' is a divisive force that pulls things apart. Because of the fragmentary evidence surviving from this time it is difficult to assess the degree to which the views of Empedocles were genuinely innovative. However, while Dodds is certainly correct in seeing in Empedocles a very old type of character, he also represents a new kind of character, the philosopher. When poetic means of expression are used it is often difficult to establish what is intended to be understood literally and what metaphorically. However, whatever the precise nuances of his poems, it is clear that Empedocles is seeking to get beneath the skin of everyday existence and reveal its fundamental structure, the basic order that underlies it. Where mythology addresses such issues through narratives and personifications, philosophy does so through principles and theories. Empedocles occupies something of an intermediate position: 'love' is sometimes Aphrodite and 'strife' is sometimes Ares, while Hephaestus is sometimes 'fire', and so on. However, while the poems of Empedocles may not be recognizable as *modern* philosophy, they can certainly be located against the developing background of *ancient* philosophy. It is to that background that I now turn.

10. The Early Philosophers

As is well known, the term 'philosophy' means the 'love of wisdom', and although not all philosophers may have been wise, a lot of them could reasonably feature in this discussion. Fortunately, there is no need to provide an A to Z of ancient philosophers here as I have already done that elsewhere (Curnow 2006b). That makes it possible to focus here on only a few of them. Furthermore, as I have argued elsewhere (Curnow 2006a), the founders of philosophical schools may be taken as the embodiments of the values of their schools. While others might emulate them, none surpassed them. Consequently, when it comes to the philosophical schools I shall concentrate on a handful of people who exemplify their principles. However, many of the early philosophers were very much individuals in their own right who neither founded nor belonged to any school. Although that does not of itself necessarily make them any more important, it does mean that they cannot be conveniently dealt with collectively. As a result, although I shall not consider all of them, I shall consider what might seem like a disproportionately large number of them. There is also another reason why the earliest philosophers might merit greater attention. As those who first attract the attention of history as philosophers, they are in effect the trailblazers of a new profession that concerns itself with wisdom. As such they occupy an important position in the narrative of this book.

I shall begin, as everyone does, with Thales of Miletus, whose name appears on every known list of the Seven Sages. Traditionally, the first attested date in the history of Western philosophy is 585 BC when Thales predicted an eclipse of the sun. This fact alone is sufficient to indicate that his interests were certainly not limited to what today would be regarded as philosophy. The extent to which he is entitled to be regarded as the first Western philosopher has been a matter of some debate, turning, at least in part, on what is meant by 'Western' and what is meant by 'philosopher'. Thales lived in Asia, may have been of Phoenician descent, may have studied in Egypt and may have had access to materials from Mesopotamia. The fluidity of the culture of the ancient world means that ideas and knowledge were often mobile and widely shared rather than static and parochial. That Thales was a polymath is apparent from all the evidence (O'Grady 2002), and he could evidently boast accomplishments across a number of fields of learning. However, the claim that he was the first Western philosopher is based on the belief that however much he owed to his predecessors, he took things in a significant new direction.

> From what we know of his contemporaries and the esteem in which he was held by later philosopher-scientists we can conclude that Thales's mind was not attuned to the mythopoeic traditions. What Thales did was to examine the natural phenomena, consider possible processes of change, and propound hypotheses ... Thales believed that the events of nature had natural causes ... (O'Grady 2002, pp. 81, 82)

It is easier to say what this new approach was than it is to determine the precise role Thales played in its development. For example, there has long been a debate over whether 'The Memphite Theology' [2.2b] should be regarded as a philosophical work or not (Frankfort et al. 1949, pp. 64-70). And as Martin Bernal has argued (Bernal 1991), arguments concerning when and where philosophy originated have often been articulated with ulterior motives. However, whether or not Thales was the first Western philosopher, he nevertheless represents an early example of a kind of thinker 'not attuned to the mythopoeic traditions', who sought to understand the fundamental order of the world according to impersonal principles. As such, philosophy emerges as a new kind of wisdom.

I shall not dwell long on the views attributed to Thales himself. The sources are few and cryptic. What seems evident is that he assigned some kind of primacy to water in explaining the nature of the world such that it was in some sense or other the origin of everything. Perhaps something of what he meant can be extracted from the views of Anaximenes, a close contemporary and also from Miletus. Anaximenes believed that everything derived from a single element that he called 'air'. This could exist in different densities and so take on many different forms. As breath, it was also the source of life. It is possible that Thales saw water in much the same way, as something that could exist as ice, water or steam, and that was a source of life. A third philosopher from Miletus, Anaximander, is sometimes thought to have been a pupil of Thales. He had yet another view of things, although there are differences of opinion as to precisely what that view actually was. He seems to have postulated an original formless mass that took on form to become the various objects found in the world. Interestingly, he believed that the first human beings evolved or emerged from fish-like creatures. It is tempting to detect in this a faint echo of the *apkallu*.

The precise opinions of these three are less important than the kind of outlook they represent both individually and collectively. Although their speculations may have had an empirical basis, they were all metaphysicians, passing from what could be immediately witnessed to what lay beyond, beneath or behind it. They can be regarded as early representatives of what is recognisably a philosophical outlook on the world and approach to the problem of order. Exactly why Thales was the only one of the three to ever make it onto any list of the Seven Sages is unclear. All that is clear is that Thales is always present whilst the others are always absent. However, if the year of 582 BC really was when the first list was assembled, then the fact that it followed very closely on the heels of the year in which Thales predicted an eclipse may be significant. It is entirely possible to understand that such a practical demonstration of such a profound understanding of the principles underlying the order of the world would make a profound impression.

11. Pythagoras and Pythagoreanism

Another name that appears on some, but not all, lists of the Seven Sages is that of Pythagoras. He is a problematic figure, one about whom many legends grew up. While it is generally agreed that he came after Thales, Anaximander and Anaximenes, he is often given the credit for coining the term 'philosopher' and so in some ways stands at the very beginning of philosophy. This position was endorsed in a work of Greek wisdom literature that hails Pythagoras as 'the first philosopher', identifying him as 'one of the ascetic learned men' (Gutas 1975, p. 63). According to Diogenes Laertius (I.12), the reason Pythagoras chose to call himself a lover of wisdom, rather than a sage, was that wisdom is divine rather than human. However, this interpretation (and the use Diogenes makes of his sources) has been challenged, and some have argued that what Pythagoras was really trying to do was distinguish philosophy from other kinds of *sophia* (Gottschalk 1990, pp. 23-9): it is not that philosophers cannot become wise, but the wisdom they seek is a different kind of wisdom from that which others seek. Given the many different dimensions of *sophia*, the idea that the early philosophers might seek to clarify what *their own* particular *sophia* was is far from implausible.

A few things about his life seem to be reasonably well established. He was born on Samos in around 570 BC. About forty years later he moved to Croton in southern Italy where he founded a community. He subsequently had to move from Croton to nearby Metapontum, and that seems to be where he died. According to tradition, he wrote nothing, and the Pythagoreans generally had a reputation for secrecy. They also had a reputation for strong friendships and living in close-knit communities. These communities followed a number of rules, including various dietary ones. On the available evidence, Pythagoras seems to have been the first philosopher to found something recognizable as a school, although perhaps in modern terminology what he founded in his own lifetime might be more accurately described as a sect. For hundreds of years after his death people identified themselves as Pythagoreans. One of those was Apollonius of Tyana who, according to Philostratus (I.7) told his father, 'I will live Pythagoras' way' (Philostratus 1970, p. 33). Historians of philosophy also identified many people, such as Empedocles, as Pythagoreans, although why is not always clear. However, it may be noted that there is no clear evidence of any school of Thaleans or Anaximandrians, suggesting that, for whatever reason, Pythagoras was seen in a very different light from the philosophers of Miletus. Pythagoras may have been the first to set up a recognizable philosophical institution of which teaching was an essential function. However, while the early Pythagoreans practised communal living as the norm, later Pythagoreans seem to be identified purely on the basis of espousing the Pythagorean view of the world.

There are many problems in establishing how much of what came to be known as Pythagoreanism actually stemmed from Pythagoras himself, and this is particularly true in the area of mathematics. The famous theorem of geometry that bears his name probably had nothing to do with him, and some have argued that Pythagoras took very little interest in mathematics of any description. However, given that his followers took a very close interest in it, a total lack of interest in it on his behalf would seem a little surprising. The clear impression is that the Pythagoreans, or at least the early ones, were a relatively conservative group, which would make it extremely surprising if one of their key concepts had no connection whatsoever with their founder. In what follows I shall discuss Pythagoreanism and leave it open as to whether or not all of these doctrines were taught by Pythagoras himself. If they were not, they are still doctrines that his followers believed that he taught.

One of the doctrines for which the Pythagoreans were particularly noted was that of the transmigration of the soul, and various legends were elaborated concerning the 'pre-incarnations' of Pythagoras ranging from Euphorbus, who fought in the Trojan War, to Pyrrhus, a humble fisherman from Delos. Some see in this doctrine strong evidence of Indian influence (Kahn 2001, p. 19). Curiously, although Pythagoras was widely credited with having studied in many different places, the surviving ancient biographies do not include India amongst them. According to Porphyry (11), after studying with Anaximander,

Pythagoras visited the Egyptians, the Arabians, the Chaldeans and the Hebrews, from whom he acquired expertise in the interpretation of dreams, and acquired the use of frankincense in the worship of divinities. (Fideler 1998, p. 125)

Others also mention Phoenicia, Crete and Persia. However, as the earliest surviving biography of Pythagoras dates to the third century AD, it is difficult to know how much of what is said can be relied upon. Nevertheless, it is interesting to observe that what Porphyry says is compatible with the views of Eupolemus and Aristobulus concerning the interconnectedness of Greek and Hebrew thought [4.5], although he does not assign any particular primacy to 'the Hebrews'. The significance of frankincense is opaque, but the association of a wise person with the ability to interpret dreams is not. Curiously, the only complete classical text on dream interpretation to survive, that of Artemidorus (II.69), is extremely scathing about the Pythagoreans:

Everything that the Pythagoreans, the physiognomists, the prophets who divine from dice, from cheese, from sieves, from forms or figures, from palms, from dishes, and the necromancers say must be regarded as false and misleading ... For the arts of these men are totally specious and they themselves do not have even the slightest knowledge of divination. Rather, they cheat, deceive and strip those that they come upon. (Artemidorus 1975, p. 134)

Like Empedocles, Pythagoras is best approached as a complex character who cannot conveniently be pigeonholed into any one particular category. However, Pythagoreanism itself came to be closely associated with the notion of number, and this seems to have stood at the heart of its understanding of the universe. Whatever the contribution to them of Pythagoras himself, the teachings associated with him had a mathematical core. The great imaginative leap of Pythagoreanism was to bring both music and the cosmos within a single mathematical model, projecting the notion of harmony found in the former onto the latter, with the result that the order of the latter became interpreted musically. However, the notion of the 'music of the spheres' was not a metaphor, because, according to Nicomachus of Gerasa (first/second century AD), 'all swiftly whirling bodies necessarily produce sounds when something gives way to them' (Nicomachus the Pythagorean 1994, p. 45). Indeed, taking the view that the seven notes of the scale were named after the seven planets (counting the sun and moon as planets), Nicomachus suggests that the music of the spheres is the fundamental musical reality, but it is number that underlines reality as a whole, with the number seven having special importance.

Although Pythagoras never actually displaced Thales on any list of the Seven Sages, it is not surprising that he found his way onto some of them. Indeed, according to Iamblichus (12), it was Thales himself who predicted that Pythagoras might become 'the most godlike of mortals, surpassing all others in wisdom' (Iamblichus 1989, p. 5). For many who followed him, Pythagoras was not only the first philosopher, but also the philosopher *par excellence*.

12. Heraclitus and Parmenides

Heraclitus (sixth/fifth century BC) came from Ephesus and even in antiquity acquired the nicknames of 'the obscure' and 'the riddler'. The passage of time, and the loss of most of his writings have not made him any easier to understand. The extent to which he was *intentionally* obscure is unclear: there is evidence to indicate that he took a certain amount of pleasure in being cryptic. On the other hand, some of his sayings seem to be paradoxical rather than cryptic, for example, 'We step and do not step into the same rivers' (Barnes 1987, p. 117), and perhaps are meant to mirror the paradoxical nature of reality, in which things are both constant and constantly changing.

The notion of change is central to the philosophy of Heraclitus. However, like Thales and Anaximenes he also thought that a single fundamental element underlay the world, and he called it 'fire'. Perhaps it would be better to describe 'fire' as a force rather than an element as it seems to designate the energy that lies behind the constant changes that are taking place in the world, most graphically demonstrated, perhaps, by the way in which fire totally alters the things that it burns. And behind fire there was a divine intelligence that he called *logos*. This elusive term originally seems to have simply meant something that was said, but then came to also mean something that was thought. It then further expanded to apply to reason. Reason in turn might be understood as law of nature and as order. Heraclitus seems to have been the first to make a technical term out of *logos*. As has already been seen it later became part of the vocabulary of Christianity [2.3], by which time it had become more closely associated with the notion of *sophia* than seems to have been the case in the time of Heraclitus.

Standing as a useful counterbalance to Heraclitus is Parmenides (fifth century BC). From Elea in southern Italy, his philosophy developed in a very different direction. He was also interested in the phenomenon of change, and seems to have understood it as a process whereby something *that is* ceases to be, and is then replaced by something else *that was not* coming into being. However, he felt that there was such a gulf between what is and what is not that such a thing could not possibly happen. What is is, and what is not is not, for all time. Consequently, change is impossible. Where Heraclitus built his system around change, Parmenides built his system around denying it. Where Thales, Pythagoras and Heraclitus had all, in their different way, sought to explain the world of experience, even if they appealed to things outside experience, Parmenides sought to dismiss that experience as at bottom illusory. (Although there is no evidence of any influence from India on Parmenides, his philosophy finds many echoes there.) Building on this basic analysis of the impossibility of change, Parmenides goes on to argue for a world that is also eternal and indivisible. As such everything is fundamentally one thing.

13. Democritus and Anaxagoras

As I have explained [4.10], it is not remotely my intention to say something about each and every philosopher. The intention is rather to give some indication of the kind of thinking associated with some of the most important names from this early period when philosophy and philosophers were emerging into history. I shall conclude the discussion of this early period with two final figures of note, Democritus and Anaxagoras.

Democritus (fifth/fourth century BC) came from Abdera. As with a number of his predecessors, he is said to have travelled widely and so been exposed to a variety of influences. Although not normally credited with inventing it (that honour tends to go to Leucippus), Democritus was a very early exponent of the theory of atomism, and as such postulated a different kind of explanation for the order of the world. He put forward an elegant and simple argument for the existence of atoms. Understanding an atom to be something that is indivisible, he argued that there must be indivisible things in the world since if things were infinitely divisible everything would ultimately resolve into nothing.

Although the ascription is no longer given any credence, the name of Democritus has long been attached to an important document bearing on an aspect of the ancient economy of wisdom that has not hitherto been mentioned: alchemy. The document (the title of which translates as 'The Physical and the Mystical') may have been the work of Bolus of Mendes (third century BC?) One of the fragments of it that remains tells of the visit of Democritus to Memphis in Egypt to raise the ghost of Ostanes, his teacher, in order to receive further instruction. The identity of Ostanes is problematic, but he seems to have come from Persia. Whatever factual basis there is for any of this, Democritus was long associated with alchemy, and alchemy in turn was clearly associated through this story with both Egypt and Persia.

The name of Anaxagoras (fifth century BC) has already been mentioned [1.3, 4.9]. He was said to have been the first philosopher to move to Athens (he was originally from Clazomenae in Asia Minor). Unfortunately his presence there was not entirely welcome and he was charged with impiety. His offence was claiming that the sun and the moon were physical objects and nothing else. He may have been helped to escape by Pericles, who had been one of his pupils. In any event he made his way to Lampsacus where he founded his own school and lived out a rather more settled life than had been possible in Athens. He espoused a kind of atomic theory, with the world made up of many different kinds of infinitely small particles. In their natural state, these particles would be randomly distributed. The fact that the world manifested a clear order of things was due to an intelligence of some kind that pervaded the world. As Plato expresses it in *Phaedo* (97d), 'it is Mind that produces order and is the cause of everything' (Plato 1969, p. 155).

It is not the aim here to dissect these different views or go into great expository detail concerning them. The main aim has been to show how these first people to be called philosophers, lovers of wisdom, addressed themselves, amongst other things, to the problem of establishing the basis of the order that pervades the world. They sought to do this in a variety of ways, and the differences between them are many. Because of the fragmentary evidence surviving from this period it is difficult to be sure as to who knew whom or what influences were at work when and where. Some have argued that Parmenides and Democritus were influenced by Pythagoreanism, but since they came up with very different theories from that associated with Pythagoras, it would appear to make very little difference whether they were or not.

It has become customary to see the life of Socrates as a watershed in the history of Western philosophy, such that those who preceded him are collectively known as the pre-Socratics. It is time now to turn to Socrates himself.

14. Socrates and the Sophists

I quoted earlier [2.1] from the words attributed to Socrates (469-399 BC) by Plato in *Apology*. The context for those words appears a little earlier in the same work [21a]. Socrates is relating a story about his friend Chaerephon who went to consult the oracle of Apollo at Delphi: 'he asked whether there was anyone wiser than myself. The priestess replied that there was none' (Plato 1969, p. 49). Such an endorsement was not unique: Myson, one of the Seven Sages [1.3], is also said to have received it, and there may have been others. An appeal to Apollo to settle matters relating to wisdom was obviously logical, given the god's particular connections with it [2.2d].

However, it is perhaps harder to see in what the wisdom of Socrates lay, and why both the oracle and subsequent generations held him in such high esteem. It may also be pointed out that whatever the opinion of Apollo, there were plenty of Athenians who disagreed with it. These included Aristophanes who savagely satirized Socrates in his 423 BC play 'Clouds'. When asked by a prospective student what he will learn, Aristophanes makes the character of Socrates reply (ll. 262-4):

> You'll become an assured, glib
> Confidence man, with a shifty tongue;
> You'll sift words fine as flour ...

> (Aristophanes 1970, p. 119)

It is clear from the play that Aristophanes regards Socrates as far from wise and instead sees him as one of, and perhaps even the worst of, the sophists. In order to understand the position of Aristophanes, it is necessary to take a look at the sophists. Fortunately, this is territory that needs to be explored anyway. Like 'sage' [*sophos*], 'sophist' [*sophistes*] is obviously related to *sophia*. More than that, both terms 'are used of Pythagoras, Parmenides, and Anaxagoras, as well as of the wise men, of physiologists as well as poets' (Lloyd 1989, p. 92n). According to Diogenes Laertius (I.12), even Homer and Hesiod had been referred to as sophists by some. Because of the range of meanings that *sophia* could carry, a range of people could claim to possess it, or be ascribed it. It is mainly during the century after Socrates that the notions of what it is to be a 'philosopher' and what it is to be a 'sophist' take on firmer shape (Curnow 2008). Because the people who came to be known as the sophists did not form any kind of organized group, it is not easy to come up with any single criterion that sets them all apart. This was also true of the Seven Sages [1.3], and at least one of the sophists, Hippias of Elis, may actually have been regarded as a sage by some (Pausanias 1971b, p. 274). However, perhaps a cluster of criteria would cover a large number of them: generally speaking it may be said that they were professional educators who often specialized in rhetoric and, insofar as they had a philosophical position, tended towards relativism. The idea that an educator was a person of wisdom was not unusual in the ancient world. In due course, the sophists and the philosophers between them provided the classical world's higher education system.

In 'Clouds' (ll. 336-44), Aristophanes lumps sophists together with 'proselytizing prophets, quack doctors, and long-haired poseurs' as well as 'fake weather-forecasters', suggesting that he regarded them all as a bunch of charlatans. The objections of Plato are both more complex and less clear. At bottom he seems to think that a number of them are frauds, because they 'claimed to be able to teach virtue without comprehending the innate essence of virtue' (O'Grady 2008, p. 57). He also seems to think that they are dangerous, and on that point he may be in agreement with Aristophanes as well.

One of the best known of the sophists was Protagoras (*c.* 485-*c.* 415 BC) who came from Abdera, which was also the home of Democritus. He subsequently moved to Athens where he made a lot of money from teaching. Like Socrates, he attracted the attention of the comic dramatists. He appears as a character in a 421 BC play by Eupolis with the telling title of 'The Spongers'. Although the play has survived only in fragments, it is evident that it does not portray Protagoras in a flattering light. The fact that many sophists made a lot of money in Athens even though they were not Athenians may have been resented by many, and Plato clearly took objection to the fact that they charged for their services at all.

In terms of what Protagoras taught, very little evidence has survived,

Socrates.

but such as there is points towards a radical outlook on life. His most famous saying, 'Of all things the measure is man, of things that are that they are, and of things that are not that they are not' (Sprague 2001, p. 18), has been interpreted in a variety of ways. Another saying attributed to him makes it clear that he was an agnostic, while yet another, 'on every issue there are two sides opposed to each other' (Sprague 2001, p. 21), suggests he was also a relativist. At the very least, it seems fair to say that he was a humanist. His approach to the gods would naturally offend conservatives while his approach to knowledge offended the philosophers.

Hippias of Elis, whose name has already been mentioned, was a younger contemporary of Protagoras. He appears to have been a man of considerable learning, cosmopolitan in outlook, and a particularly gifted mathematician. Gorgias of Leontini, another contemporary but from Sicily (where he may have studied with Empedocles), became rich through teaching rhetoric in Athens. He produced a philosophical work arguing that nothing exists and that even if it did, we could know nothing about it.

I mention these three names, Protagoras, Hippias and Gorgias, to give some sense of the kind of thinking associated with the early sophists. On the bases of these brief thumbnail sketches, it seems that in some ways they very much took an interest in areas traditionally associated with wisdom. It is true that, in the course of time, the title of sophist became attached much more specifically to those who primarily taught rhetoric, but that was after both 'philosophers' and 'sophists' had worked out a division of labour between themselves and formed themselves into competing, but also complementary, professions. But on the face of it, when Gorgias argued that nothing exists, he was being neither more nor less philosophical than Parmenides had been when he argued that nothing changes. What is perhaps notable in the work of Protagoras and Gorgias in particular is evidence of an interest in the problem of knowledge itself, and a generally sceptical approach towards it. As such, the sophists were perhaps a little ahead of their philosophical contemporaries in developing what was to become an important area of philosophy.

Although I believe the sophists merit inclusion in this discussion in their own right, the immediate reason for considering them was Aristophanes' satire on Socrates, and to Socrates I shall now return. It is well known that he wrote nothing, but that Plato wrote a lot about him, although how accurately has long been a matter of debate. It is also known that Socrates was tried and executed for 'refusing to recognize the gods recognized by the state, and of introducing other new divinities'. He was also charged with 'corrupting the youth' (Diogenes Laertius 1972, p. 171). During his defence speech, on which Plato's *Apology* is based to a greater or lesser degree, Socrates acknowledges that he has a reputation for wisdom but denies that he has any, except in the sense that he has arrived at a knowledge of his own limitations. And he did not stop at his own limitations. He interrogated a number of people skilled in a number of areas and found the same thing over and over again (22e):

> On the strength of their technical proficiency they claimed a perfect understanding of every other subject, however important; and I felt that this error more than outweighed their positive wisdom. (Plato 1969, p. 52)

What Socrates seems to be saying is that there is a kind of wisdom that many people have, but it scarcely deserves the name of wisdom at all, and there is a kind of wisdom that no people have, which is true wisdom. In between there is the kind of wisdom that consists of knowing one's limitations, and that is the kind that Socrates himself has. This kind of wisdom, although human, also had a kind of link with the divine. To know one's limitations was one interpretation of the famous maxim that was inscribed at the temple of Apollo at Delphi: 'Know Thyself'. It was not the only one, and the Seven Sages are generally given collective credit for them. The fact that they were inscribed on the temple connected them with Apollo as well.

It is interesting that the groups of people whose claims to wisdom Socrates expressly disparages in *Apology* are politicians, craftsmen and poets. It also seems to be the case that it is not simply his contemporaries he is disparaging: he is critical of the supposed wisdom of *all* politicians, craftsmen and poets. If this is so, then Socrates is taking a radical approach to wisdom, dismissing as worthless the kind of wisdom associated with many of the Seven Sages, amongst others. He is also, at least indirectly, disparaging kinds of wisdom associated with Athena [2.2]. Although the *Apology* as it stands is a literary piece, it is generally thought that Plato stayed reasonably close to the ideas, if not the actual words, of Socrates when writing it, making it reasonable to suppose that the views on wisdom expressed in it are those of Socrates himself. Furthermore, it seems extremely unlikely that the story about the oracle at Delphi is a fabrication: if it were, too many people reading *Apology* would have known it to be so. Is the oracle then endorsing a new understanding of who the wise people are? Is it endorsing a new, and superior, kind of wisdom? Is it identifying Socrates as the founder of a new kind of philosophy? This was certainly how he has been perceived by many, right down to the present day. In his *Tusculan Disputations* (V.4), Cicero hailed him as 'the first to call philosophy down from the heavens' and make it deal with 'questions about life and morality and things good and evil' (Cicero 1945, p. 435).

The claim of Cicero does not entirely stand up. There were those before Socrates who had concerned themselves with 'questions about life and morality' and there would be those after Socrates who would return philosophy to the heavens. On the other hand, if Socrates seriously claimed that his wisdom lay in being aware of what he did not know, then only the Sceptics really followed in his footsteps. It is easier to say *that* Socrates was important than it is to say exactly *why* he was important. One of the complications is that little enough is really known about Socrates. He appears mainly through the reverential eyes of his followers or the damning eyes of the dramatists. Of those followers, by far the most important is Plato.

15. Plato, Aristotle and the Schools

Plato (*c.* 424-348 BC), like Socrates, was an Athenian. Despite his fame, our knowledge of his life is very patchy. Three things at least seem reasonably certain. First, that he became a follower of Socrates, second, that he was at one time involved with political matters in Syracuse, and third, that he left behind him an institution known as the Academy. Because Plato wrote his philosophical works in the form of dialogues in which he did not appear but in which Socrates did, it has long been a matter of dispute as to precisely what Plato's philosophy was and precisely how much it owed to Socrates. It is also not clear exactly what kind of institution the Academy was when Plato died, but all those who subsequently headed it explicitly identified themselves as 'successors'.

> The third philosopher is Plato the Divine, whose precedence is acknowledged by all who came after him …. He said: The perfect sage is not he who rejoices in any of the world's pleasures or grieves on account of any of its misfortunes. (Gutas 1975, pp. 117, 133)

Although we know precious little about either, it is evident that Plato's Academy was something very different from a Pythagorean community. For example, the Academy had no known dietary laws. On the other hand, it is generally acknowledged that Plato was very much influenced by Pythagoreanism, as evidenced by the importance he attached to mathematics. The extent to which he left behind him a coherent philosophical doctrine has been challenged (Dillon 2003, p. 16), but it is indisputable that he left behind him a set of writings. The Academy and the writings clearly evolved into an institution with a body of doctrine, even if things did not start out that way. It may also be noted that although he was by no means indifferent to 'questions about life and morality and things good and evil', he took an interest in more metaphysical matters as well. Although his own precise contribution to the development may be unclear, Plato seems to stand at the beginning of what might be termed the professionalization of philosophy. As such, his attacks on the sophists may be part of an inter-professional turf war. It may be helpful, by way of context, to say a few words about how that war ended and what the profession of philosopher came to look like.

Although there was never a universally agreed arrangement, the institutions that became known as the philosophical schools generally shared a similar perception of what philosophy looked like. It became common to divide it into three different areas that were known as 'logic', 'physics' and 'ethics'. The area of 'logic' concerned itself with two main issues, knowledge and argument. With regards to knowledge, the questions that were asked concerned what we can know and how we can know it. With regards to argument, it was necessary to sift the good from the bad such that the benefits of the truth-preserving powers of good argument could be enjoyed and the errors into which bad argument led could be avoided. The area of 'physics' addressed itself to understanding the nature of the world, and as such embraced sciences that go beyond modern physics, while also going beyond science to metaphysics. Finally, 'ethics' was concerned with the application of 'logic' and 'physics' to everyday life, with the question of how to live. While it would be incorrect to suggest that no one other than philosophers took any interest in any of these issues, collectively they came to represent philosophy. Others certainly did take an interest in some of the concerns of philosophy. Indeed, it might be argued that it was the fact that, from his point of view, the sophists tended to study aspects of 'logic' in isolation that led Plato to be critical of them. They were too fond of argument and not fond enough of knowledge, let alone of 'ethics'. On the other hand, if philosophy was 'logic', 'physics' and 'ethics', different philosophers and philosophies might give different emphases to these three elements. The wisdom of the philosopher spanned all three, but not necessarily equally. This in part explains the turf wars that took place between the different philosophical schools. They not only disagreed on the nature of the world, for example, but they also disagreed on the importance of a proper understanding of the nature of the world in philosophy as a whole.

As a profession that self-consciously identified itself with the pursuit of wisdom, philosophy obviously had a special connection with wisdom and philosophers sometimes engaged in explicit reflections on its nature. Heraclitus may have been the first philosopher to do so, but these three different translations of a quotation preserved by Diogenes Laertius (IX.1) seem to justify his reputation for being obscure:

> This one thing is wisdom, to understand thought, as that which guides all the world everywhere. (Diogenes Laertius 1931, p. 409)

> The wise is one, grasping the knowledge how all things are steered through all. (Barnes 1987, p. 105)

> The wise is one thing, to be acquainted with true judgment, how all things are steered through all. (Kirk and Raven 1971, p. 204)

Other translations could also be cited, but they would do nothing to make the picture any clearer. Apart from the fact that Heraclitus is clearly a believer in the unitary nature of wisdom (whatever that means), it is difficult to be sure what he is getting at. Rather more light is shone on the matter by Aristotle (384-322 BC) in *Metaphysics* (981b-982b). He begins by offering a general observation, saying that:

> in the earliest times anyone who discovered any craft that went beyond the perceptions common to all was admired not only because he discovered something useful, but also for being a wise person, superior to others. (Cohen, Curd and Reeve 1995, p. 588)

This is an interesting point which ties in with much of what has already been seen and said, that wisdom had many different facets in antiquity. Aristotle goes on to observe that not all craftsmen are seen as equally wise because the 'master craftsman [is] wiser than the manual craftsman' (Cohen, Curd and Reeve 1995, p. 588). That is to say, there seems to be a hierarchy of wisdom. In the view of Aristotle, this leads to the conclusion that 'wisdom is knowledge of certain sorts of principles and causes' (Cohen, Curd and Reeve 1995, p. 588). He then goes on to consider the characteristics of a wise person. Such a person 'has knowledge about all things as far as possible' and 'is capable of knowing difficult things'. The wiser person in any area of study will be the one who 'is more exact, and a better teacher of the causes'. Furthermore, not all areas of study are equal. An area of study that is pursued purely for its own sake rather than for any practical purpose 'has a better claim to be wisdom'. From all this he concludes that 'wisdom must study the *first* [my emphasis] principles and causes' (Cohen, Curd and Reeve 1995, pp. 588-9). Aristotle is at pains to stress that wisdom is not productive: it is knowing for the sake of knowing. There are many reasons why Aristotle wants to, and manages to, arrive at this conclusion, and he revisits some of them in his *Nicomachean Ethics* (1177a-78a) where he argues that the reflective life (which is also the philosophical life) is the one that is most worth living. The philosopher is the type of person who leads the best life and who is the true possessor of wisdom.

He then goes on to consider some earlier thinkers, such as Thales, Anaximenes and Parmenides, in the light of his observations. In doing so, however, Aristotle might have been rewriting history:

> Clearly the fourth-century depictions of earlier thinkers as solitary contemplatives is quite misleading. In particular, they indicate that the wisdom of the early thinkers was confined to intellectual speculation. In fact, there is considerable evidence that most of these men were able performers of practical and political wisdom. (Nightingale 2004, p. 31)

What Aristotle seems to be doing is setting out his own conception of wisdom, and then fitting the wise people of the past into it. The idea that the pre-Socratic philosophers were purely contemplatives will not bear scrutiny, although the idea that they engaged in metaphysical speculation is amply attested. There is certainly a core of truth to the picture painted by Aristotle, but it does not seem to be the whole truth. Aristotle founded his own school, the Lyceum, which achieved a reputation for advances in scientific knowledge. Aristotle was 'the model of the learned men' and, through his work in logic, 'prepared a foundation for all the other sciences' (Gutas 1975, p. 159). In that respect, in the pursuit of knowledge being a major concern, in 'physics' being its primary focus, the Lyceum was perhaps unusual.

However, the idea that philosophy had (at the very least) a strong and pronounced contemplative dimension was already present in the philosophy of Plato. His theory of knowledge revolved around mysterious 'Forms' that could only be directly perceived by an enlightened few. Because the Forms were pure in nature, those who wished to perceive them had to go through a process of purification in order to be able to perceive them, and the god who presided over matters of purification was Apollo. The notion of purification therefore brought with it strong religious overtones. More than that, through acquaintance with the Forms, the individual is transformed by them. As Plato says in *Republic* (501c):

> Then the philosopher, by consorting with what is ordered and divine and despite all the slanders around that say otherwise, himself becomes as divine and ordered as a human being can. (Plato 1992, p. 174)

If the philosopher is not actually a god (for that would require immortality), becoming godlike is nevertheless a realistic and attainable ambition. This is a curious twist on the observation by Socrates that wisdom is divine. The same connection is retained, but now instead of it making wisdom impossible for humans, it becomes an argument for the godlike nature of those who attain it. The idea that the wise are somehow godlike is not a novelty: in Egypt, Imhotep and Amenhotep actually *became* gods [3.4].

An important element of Plato's philosophy was that emotion is to be curbed and reason is to rule, and he saw wisdom as closely connected to reason and knowledge. In *Republic*, Plato makes it clear that he wishes reason to rule in society as well as in the individual. He is aware that the wise must not limit themselves to metaphysical contemplation, but must also engage with the social. It is because the wise have seen the Form of justice that they are able to implement it. It is because the contemplative life is an enjoyable one that they must be *obliged* to take up their social responsibilities, for they will not wish to. Indeed, Festugière (1950) argues that only by demonstrating the social benefits of the contemplative life could that kind of life be made acceptable in the kind of society in which Plato and Aristotle lived. In a culture where ostracism was one of the most severe punishments conceivable, the person who sought to disengage from society could not help but appear to be a figure of suspicion, which was one of the reasons why the Epicureans were widely unpopular. Figures such as Antony of Egypt and Simeon the Stylite were from a very different world [4.9].

In the end, neither Plato nor Aristotle managed to corner the market in wisdom for philosophy. What they, and those who came after them, did manage to do was to carve out a distinctive territory for philosophy. Although it overlapped with others, it became sufficiently clearly demarcated and identifiable for the term 'philosophy' to gain a specific meaning and for the term 'philosopher' to denote a particular profession (although that did not prevent many philosophers from being amateurs in philosophy while pursuing their professions elsewhere). While the schools founded by Plato and Aristotle were important and had long and distinguished histories, they were not the only ones. The most famous ones to stand alongside them were the Stoa of Zeno and the Garden of Epicurus.

16. Zeno and Epicurus

Zeno (334-262 BC) was a native of Citium in Cyprus and, like Thales, may have been of Phoenician descent. Tradition has it that he arrived in Athens as the result of a shipwreck. There he met some philosophers, became interested in philosophy, and founded his own school, which became known as the Stoa after the place where he taught. So well respected was he that a statue was erected in Athens in his honour while he was still alive, and another in Citium. The philosophy he founded, Stoicism, evolved considerably over the years, and most of the surviving texts come the first, second and third centuries AD. The little we know about the teachings of Zeno and his earliest followers is fragmentary and second-hand. It is therefore possible that the picture portrayed of Zeno by later writers is not entirely accurate. However, if the figure of Zeno became somewhat ideal-ized over time, this is only to be suspected. The founder of a philosophical school was at the same time the embodiment of its ideals, the model to which all others aspired. If Zeno was not the perfect Stoic, no one could be.

Two preliminary points may be made, both of which draw on the testimony of Diogenes Laertius. First (VII.87), Zeno is said to have been the first philosopher to have set up 'life in accordance with nature' as a goal and ideal. There is some controversy about this, and it seems likely that Zeno borrowed the idea from the Cynics (while interpreting it differ-ently). Furthermore, the idea of life in accordance with nature is very similar to the Egyptian understanding of life in accordance with *maat* [2.2]. The second point (VII.39) is that Zeno was given the credit for being the first to divide philosophy up into 'logic', 'physics' and 'ethics'.

A sense of what the ideal Stoic wise man might look like is also provided by Diogenes Laertius (VII.116-125). In it he draws on a number of lost writings, including some by Zeno himself:

> For the wise man will not be afraid in any way, but will be cautious ... They say the wise man is also free of passions ... And the wise man is free of vanity ... Nor indeed will wise men feel pain ... And they are godly; for they have in themselves a kind of god ... And only wise men are priests, for they have conducted an investigation into sacrifices, foundations, purifications, and the other matters which are proper for the gods ... They say that the wise man will participate in politics unless something prevents him ... And he will marry, as Zeno says in his *Republic*, and have children ... Again, the wise man will not hold opinions, that is, he will not assent to anything that is false ... Again, the wise man is astonished at none of the things which appear to be wonders ... The wise man does everything well ... . (Inwood and Gerson 1997, pp. 198-201)

The idea that the wise are godlike has already been noted with regard to Plato, as has the connection between wisdom and freedom from passion. Lacking, however, is some of the otherwordliness of Plato's idealized

Zeno.

philosopher. The philosophy taught by Zeno was heavily materialistic, and even souls were nothing more than very fine matter. Whereas the pursuit of knowledge through acquaintance with the Forms took Plato's philosopher some way out of this world, both the feet and the head of the Stoic sage were firmly fixed in it. Knowledge was highly valued. Like Aristotle, the Stoics believed that the wise person 'has knowledge about all things as far as possible'. The ideal Stoic sage would know, or at least understand, everything. However, the reasons the Stoics had for pursuing such omniscience would not have pleased Aristotle. Far from being interested in knowing for the sake of knowing, the Stoics wanted to know in order to anticipate. This is why 'the wise man is astonished at none of the things which appear to be wonders'. Understanding how the world works, the order of things, leads to knowledge about what to expect, and so the sage is never surprised or disappointed. On the Stoic understanding of things, like the Heraclitean one, the world is ordered by the power of *logos*, and *logos* is rational. The rational human mind also possesses *logos*, which is

97

why, at least in principle, it is potentially able to understand the order of things (although to actually understand absolutely everything might require being a god rather than just being godly). Perhaps for that reason, the Stoics sometimes identified *logos* with the divine. One of the most famous surviving early Stoic writings is the third-century BC 'Hymn to Zeus' by Cleanthes which begins:

> Most majestic of immortals, many-titled, ever-omnipotent Zeus, prime mover of nature, who with your law steer all things, hail to you. (Long and Sedley 1987, p. 326)

This identification of *logos* with Zeus could be just a colourful figure of speech, but it does not appear to be. It also echoes the Egyptian *maat*/Maat where the fundamental underpinning of the order of the world is understood in both personal and impersonal terms at the same time [2.2b].

The Stoics had a general principle of a miss being as good as a mile, because 'he who is a hundred stades from Canopus and he who is one stade away are equally not in Canopus' (Inwood and Gerson 1997, p. 200). This meant that the Stoic sage was an elusive figure, perhaps to be found in only a few, perhaps to be found only in Zeno, perhaps to be found nowhere.

The idea that the wise person is 'free of passions' appears to be an original Greek one: there is no obvious evidence of it originating elsewhere. The idea that the sage was a cold individual was one that seems to have exercised the Stoics to some degree. The person without feelings might normally be regarded as less than human instead of more than human. Exactly what was involved was subject to different interpretations. At the very least it always involved freedom from the negative effects of the passions, while at the extreme it meant freedom from any kind of feelings whatsoever. In a letter (LXIII) to his friend Lucilius about the death of another friend, Seneca (*c.* 4 BC-AD 65) wrote:

> I would not have you grieve unduly over it. I can scarcely venture to demand that you should not grieve at all – and yet I am convinced that it is better that way ... Suppose someone lost his one and only shirt in a robbery, would you not think him an utter idiot if he chose to bewail his loss rather than look about him for some means of keeping out the cold and find something to put over his shoulders? (Seneca 1969, pp. 113, 116)

As Seneca was himself a Stoic, he can scarcely be accused of unfair caricature here. Quite why there was such a strong antipathy towards the emotional side of life is unclear, but I think it is possible to work towards a plausible hypothesis. The development of Greek philosophy from Thales onwards may be characterized as a process of demythologization. Scientific theories were developed to explain phenomena that had previously been explained by myth. This process led to Anaxagoras and his argument that the sun and moon were nothing but physical objects. This in turn led to accusations of impiety and the departure from Athens of Anaxagoras. Increasingly, the philosophical position towards the gods became one of agnosticism at best. And even when they believed in them, the gods they believed in bore increasingly little resemblance to the gods of the state cults or the gods of Homer. Increasingly, at least in personal terms, they become abstractions, like the primary being, the unmoved mover, of Aristotle's *Metaphysics* (1073a). Such beings are incapable of human emotions, because they are not human. Moreover, the idea was clearly developing in the thought of Plato (in *Republic* and *Symposium* in particular) that the gods were extremely similar to the Forms. Far from being anthropomorphic entities with human failings, they were the embodiments of perfection. And as perfect beings they could want nothing (in either sense of 'want'). If this new conception of the gods underlay the new philosophical conception of wisdom (and it may be recalled that one of the offences with which Socrates was charged involved 'new divinities'), then it is not surprising that wisdom was seen to sit uncomfortably alongside attributes that the gods did not, could not, possess. And once the new model of divinity became linked with the notion that wisdom made human beings godlike, it became virtually impossible for wisdom to remain in close association with the emotional side of human nature. If this argument has some merit, then it was the development of philosophy itself that lay behind the devaluation of the emotional. By stripping emotions from the gods, philosophy made them unacceptable for humans who aspired to become godlike.

However, philosophy was never a one-size-fits-all affair, and I think the argument that has just been articulated can help to explain some of the differences between Stoicism and Epicureanism. But first, some words about Epicurus (*c.* 340-270 BC). Although his family was Athenian, he was probably born on Samos, settling in Athens in around 306 BC. There he bought some land, and his school was often called The Garden. Of all the schools, that of Epicurus was perhaps the most conservative in that its teaching changed little over the centuries. He was certainly regarded as wise by his followers, while in his poem 'On the Nature of Things' (V.1-10), Lucretius went further:

> a god he was, a god ... who first discovered that principle of life which is now identified with wisdom, and who by his genius saved life from such mighty waves and such deep darkness and moored it in such calm water and so brilliant a light. (Lucretius 2001, pp. 136-7)

On the other hand, in *On Moral Ends* (II.7), Cicero observes with some disdain that Epicurus 'dared to proclaim himself wise' (Cicero 2001, p. 28), contrasting him unfavourably with the Seven Sages 'who received their title not by their own vote but by that of all peoples'. Not for the first time, Cicero overstates the case. Nevertheless, it is true that in many ways Epicurus was a divisive figure, and that while most of the other schools could tolerate each other, special opprobrium tended to be reserved for the Epicureans. This many have been at least in part due to their preference for communal living which involved collectively cutting themselves off from society to a degree. The fact that their philosophy laid a strong emphasis on the importance of pleasure meant that accusations of licentiousness tended to follow them around. Curiously, they were often accused of being atheists, even though it is clear that they were not. In a letter he wrote to someone called Menoeceus, preserved by Diogenes Laertius (X.122-35), Epicurus briefly outlines his views about the gods. They are 'indestructible and blessed' and they 'always welcome men who are like themselves' (Inwood and Gerson 1997, pp. 28, 29). They are remote, but at the same time congenial and in some ways almost human. They were certainly not abstractions. Because of this, in line with the argument advanced above, Epicureanism was able to take a more positive approach to emotions.

If the Epicureans were careless in their characterization of the gods, as seems to be one of Cicero's complaints in *The Nature of the Gods* (Cicero 1972), it is because Epicurus believed that the gods took no interest in human affairs, therefore there was little point or possible benefit in giving them much thought. The gods do not send dreams, they do not send storms, they do not act in our world at all. Consequently, there is nothing to be had from them, no reason to sacrifice to them, no point in building temples to them. This may be the basis of the accusations of atheism.

The philosophy of Epicurus was concerned with reaching 'calm water' and 'brilliant light', a state of tranquillity illuminated by knowledge. According to Diogenes Laertius (X.117-21):

> Harm from other men comes either as a result of hate or envy or contempt, which the wise man overcomes by reasoning ... And even if the wise man is tortured on the rack, he is happy ... He will resist fate, and will betray none of his friends ... He will take more delight in contemplation than other men ... He will hold firm opinions and will not be at a loss. And he will be of the same character while asleep. And he will sometimes die for a friend. (Inwood and Gerson 1997, pp. 42-3)

The comment about the rack goes to the heart of the Epicurean philosophy. Pain and suffering are two different things, and the wise man knows this and puts it into practice. Pain is physical whereas suffering is mental. When properly understood, suffering can be eliminated. Only knowledge that conduces to the elimination of suffering has any value. Once it is known that the gods have nothing to do with us, there is no value in further speculation on what they are like. Epicurus was the exemplar of all this. Plagued by poor health for years, he bore it all with fortitude and good cheer. As with Stoicism, the test of Epicureanism was the kind of lives its followers led. The wisdom of the philosopher was manifested above all in the philosophical life, and for Epicurus this was best and most easily led in a community of like-minded individuals.

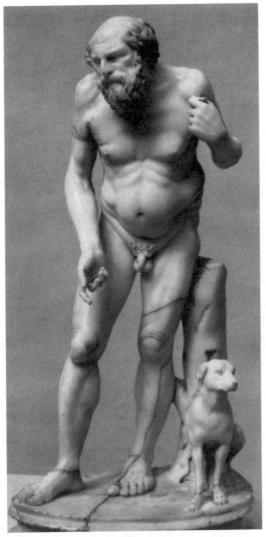

Diogenes.

17. Diogenes and Pyrrho

Two very different kinds of philosophical life were led by Diogenes of Sinope (fourth century BC) and Pyrrho of Elis (*c*. 365-*c*. 275 BC). Opinions differ as to whether it is Diogenes or Antisthenes of Athens who should be given credit for being the first official Cynic, but for present purposes nothing of importance turns on it. In any event, whether or not he was the first, Diogenes became the most celebrated. The Cynics came to recruit a far earlier figure to their cause; it was claimed that Anacharsis, one of the

101

Seven Sages [1.3], had been one. As he was the only one of the Seven who was not a Greek, it may be that the Cynics found him an appealing character because he was an outsider like themselves.

Curiously, for a philosophical school that was not really a school, and that began, and often stayed, on the fringes of society, the image of the Cynic became virtually synonymous with that of the philosopher. The cloak, sandals, staff and pouch of the Cynic became a kind of philosophical uniform. Because Antisthenes had been a friend of Socrates, some saw the origins of Cynicism in Socrates himself, a view that still has its adherents: 'Diogenes represents the Socratic *sophos* [sage] with its chief features pushed to extremes' (Dudley 1967, p. 27). The Socratic image of the gadfly might have been appropriate for the Cynics, but instead they were called dogs. This may have originated in an insult, but if it was it was one they embraced.

Separating fact from fiction is difficult where Diogenes is concerned. It was said that his father was in charge of the local mint in his home town of Sinope, and that one of them was accused of some currency offence. What does seem clear is that Diogenes adopted 'deface the currency' as a kind of philosophical motto. Because the value of currency is based on convention, defacing the currency is undermining conventional values, which is what the Cynics did. Some think that the principle of 'life in accordance with nature' entered Stoicism via the Cynics, but the Cynics understood 'nature' to be the antithesis of the conventional (an opposition and dichotomy that was frequently articulated by the sophists). The early Cynics helped to make people aware of what was merely conventional by flouting conventions of various kinds, including sexual ones. Needless to say, scandal often followed the Cynics around, although given their sometimes outrageous behaviour (Diogenes often masturbated in public, for example) one might think that they were received and treated relatively tolerantly. Certainly they often appear to have been popular figures, and when Diogenes died in his adopted city of Corinth, a memorial was erected to his memory.

The Cynics had little in the way of doctrine, and Cynicism was above all a way of life. However, they did become associated with a literary genre, the diatribe. This development was particularly associated with Bion of Borysthenes (d. 245 BC), who also seems to have been one of the first Cynics to adopt an itinerant lifestyle. (Diogenes, by way of contrast, famously lived in a barrel in Corinth for years.) Although a diatribe could technically be any kind of lecture, in the hands of the Cynics it became increasing moral in content and sharp in tone. It was not used to articulate a philosophical position, but rather to censure the failings of those who were not Cynics.

It was mentioned above [4.7] that some have drawn connections between what we know about Jesus and what we know about Cynicism. It may be appropriate to return to that topic briefly here. A number of similarities have been identified:

Cynics were known for begging, voluntary poverty, renunciation of needs, severance of family ties, fearless and carefree attitudes, and troublesome public behavior. Standard themes in Cynic discourse included a critique of riches, pretension and hypocrisy ... The Cynic style of speech was distinctly aphoristic ... Cynics were schooled in such topics as handling reproach, nonretaliation, and authenticity in following their vocation ... (Mack 1993, p. 115)

There is no need to draw out the point, or, indeed, draw any further conclusions. That there were similarities seems apparent. What they mean is a matter for conjecture. The Cynic perhaps represented the wisdom of the outsider, the onlooker, the one with detachment, the one with no personal interest, the representative of the 'natural' as opposed to the conventional or artificial. Their eccentricities were generally tolerated because they were so transparently people of principle. However, because they had little in the way of actual doctrine, some struggled to see the Cynics as philosophers at all.

The same was true of the Sceptics. But where the Cynics took a critical position with regard to society, the Sceptics took a critical position with regard to knowledge. Little is known of its founder, Pyrrho, and some of what is 'known' is contradictory. According to Diogenes Laertius (IX.62):

He was consistent with this view [i.e. the suspension of judgment] in his manner of living, neither avoiding anything nor watching out for anything, taking everything as it came, whether it be wagons or precipices or dogs, and all such things, relying on his senses for nothing. He was kept alive by his acquaintances who followed him around, according to the school of Antigonus of Carystus. Aenesidemus, however, says that he only theorized about the suspension of judgment, whereas he did not actually act improvidently. (Inwood and Gerson 1997, p. 285)

The truth may lie somewhere in between. It is difficult to believe that Pyrrho reached the age of 90 according to the way Antigonus thought he lived, but on the other hand to suggest that he did not at all practice what he preached seems extremely unlikely.

Although some suspect that he may have been influenced by Indian philosophy, the wisdom of Pyrrho in some ways resembles that of Socrates, for in the words of Photius (*Bibliotheca* 212), 'he is wise in knowing above all that nothing has been grasped securely by himself' (Inwood and Gerson 1997, p. 300). As Diogenes Laertius again puts it:

For he said that nothing was either honourable or shameful, just or unjust; similarly for all cases he said that nothing exists in truth but that men do everything on the basis of convention and custom; for each thing is no more this than that. (Inwood and Gerson 1997, p. 285)

There are clearly some similarities between this and both Cynicism and the Sophists. There are also similarities between Scepticism and both

103

Stoicism and Epicureanism since what Pyrrho believes he has found as a result of the suspension of judgment is tranquillity. Diogenes Laertius (IX.68) relates an anecdote in which Pyrrho supposedly said that 'the wise man ought to repose in ... a state of freedom from disturbance' (Inwood and Gerson 1997, p. 287). The wise man has a true insight into the human condition and by acting in accordance with that insight is able to achieve tranquillity. The insight in the case of Scepticism is that attachment to beliefs about how things are is the source of unhappiness, but there is never sufficient reason to cling to those beliefs. Once this is understood, attachment ceases, the source of unhappiness disappears and tranquillity results.

It can be seen that Zeno, Epicurus, Diogenes and Pyrrho represent and embody very different approaches to life. As the evidence of Cicero concerning Epicurus readily testifies, what some regarded as wisdom others might regard as stupidity. Nevertheless, all achieved a reputation for wisdom amongst a group of followers (although a very loose group in the cases of Cynicism and Scepticism), and all pointed to a path whereby others could also come to that wisdom, or at least a path along which they could approach it.

There were a number of other minor philosophical schools, such as that of Megara founded by Euclides, that of Cyrene founded by Aristippus and that of Elis founded by Phaedo. All of the founders were at least acquaintances and in some cases personal friends of Socrates. In the next section I take a look at two philosophers who lived centuries after the deaths of Socrates and all his friends and foes alike.

18. Plotinus and Iamblichus

Plotinus (third century AD) and Iamblichus (AD *c.* 245-325) are both regarded as Neoplatonists. However, the term 'Neoplatonist' is a new one that neither of them would have understood. As far as they were concerned, they were both Platonists. The label that became attached to them much later reflects a perception that Plotinus took Platonism in a significantly new direction. Although many have seen a mystical dimension in Plato, there were numerous ways in which his philosophy could be, and was, interpreted. With Plotinus, the mystical element explicitly and unmistakably came to the fore.

Plotinus was originally from Egypt. He studied philosophy there and later went on an expedition to Persia where he may have become acquainted with ideas from further east. He moved to Rome and spent most of the rest of his life there, attracting a number of pupils and followers. Although not much is known about his life it is apparent that he underwent some kind of profound mystical experience on a number of occasions and that these experiences coloured his whole subsequent philosophy. Indeed, the whole point of his subsequent philosophy became the development of a coherent metaphysical structure that made those experiences meaningful and understandable. In some ways his philosophy resembled that of the Gnostics as he sought to explain how the human soul had arrived in its present condition. Like the Gnostics, his reason for tracing the soul's descent was in order to provide guidance for the soul's ascent back to its source. However, he openly and vehemently dissociated himself from the Gnostics because he felt that they made the soul's ascent appear too easy. He also found Gnosticism irrational and superstitious compared with his own philosophical approach.

The contribution of Iamblichus to Neoplatonism was to take it in a more religious and occult direction. Where Plotinus rooted himself in the rational, Iamblichus tended towards the ritual. For Plotinus, the soul's struggle was a lonely one, for Iamblichus is was one that was carried out with the assistance of the divine. Iamblichus was a keen, if not always accurate, historian of philosophy and one of the surviving accounts of the life of Pythagoras was written by him. Pythagoras, rather than Plato, seems to have been the ideal philosopher in the eyes of Iamblichus, who was sympathetic to the idea that Pythagoras was the son of Apollo himself (Iamblichus 1989). His account of the early life of Pythagoras makes him the heir not only to the earlier philosophers like Thales, but also to the ancient Egyptians, Phoenicians, Mesopotamians and Persians. In Pythagoras, all the learning of the ancient world comes together as far as Iamblichus is concerned.

It is known that not all those who came after Plotinus were happy with the direction taken by Iamblichus, and he was opposed by Porphyry, the pupil, biographer and editor of Plotinus, and teacher of Iamblichus. Polemical exchanges between them were pursued in a curious Egyptian context. Porphyry wrote a *Letter to Anebo*, a real or imagined Egyptian priest, in which he set out a number of objections to the philosophy of Iamblichus. Iamblichus in turn replied with *The Reply of the Master Abammon to the Letter of Porphyry to Anebo and the Solutions to the Difficulties Raised Therein*. Quite why he chose to present himself as 'the Master Abammon' is unclear, but it is to be presumed that he is in agreement with what 'the Master Abammon' says. Towards the end of the work (X.4) he provides this as a kind of summing up:

> Only divine mantic prediction, therefore, conjoined with the gods, truly imparts to us a share in divine life – partaking as it does in the foreknowledge and the divine acts of thinking – and renders us, in truth, divine. And this genuinely furnishes us with what is good for us ... (Dillon and Gerson 2004, p. 238)

I have mentioned Plotinus and Iamblichus in order to give a sense of the direction taken by philosophy towards the end of the ancient world. As will be apparent from even these brief observations concerning Neoplatonism, philosophy and religion came considerably closer to each other in the works and lives of its adherents than they had in any of the other schools. It is not surprising that Augustine of Hippo (AD 354-430) found his philosophical inspiration in Neoplatonism and was able with little difficulty to reconcile his philosophy with his religion when he became a Christian.

19. Some Wise Men of Rome

A lot has been said here about philosophers, and a great deal more could be said. The philosophers of the ancient world are entitled to substantial coverage because it was they above all who came to be professionally associated with the pursuit of wisdom in the world of Greece and Rome. However, it has been amply demonstrated that they were by no means the only ones associated with wisdom in popular opinion. To conclude this chapter, I want to consider a handful of characters from ancient Rome who may merit a mention.

The first is Lucius Quinctius Cincinnatus (*c.* 519-*c.* 438 BC). In many ways he seems to have embodied the Roman virtues and was sufficiently well-remembered to ultimately give his name to an American city. In *The City of God* (V.18) Augustine makes complimentary remarks about his voluntary poverty. Although not a law maker, Cincinnatus once fulfilled the role of Roman dictator, a special position of great power and limited duration that was created in times of crisis. Financially ruined because of the need to meet his son's debts, his austere lifestyle may not have been entirely of his own choosing. However, it took him only a little over two weeks to rescue Rome from its plight, whereupon he willingly laid down his office and returned to his farm. Although the position of dictator tended to require primarily military skills, it also required a broader integrity, given how much power the chosen person was entrusted with. Unfortunately, it is suspected that much of the later reputation of Cincinnatus was based more on legend than on fact.

More reliable is the reputation of (Marcus Porcius) Cato the Censor (234-149 BC). Often seen as an embodiment of specifically Roman values, he was suspicious of Greek ones. He even seems to have disliked doctors because most of them were Greek. In 184 BC he was elected censor after campaigning for the position with a promise to restore traditional Roman values. He opposed luxury wherever he found it and practised what he preached in terms of austerity. An orator and author, he produced much, but little has survived. In 155 BC he was one of those most eager to remove a visiting delegation of philosophers from Rome for fear of their bad influence. Although he seems to have exuded little warmth, is said to have been cruel to his slaves and was the chief advocate of the utter destruction of Carthage, the Romans were proud of him as one of the best of their own.

(Marcus Porcius) Cato the Younger (95-46 BC) was his great-grandson.

Unlike his great-grandfather, the younger Cato had a liking for philosophy and studied with a number of Stoic teachers. Convinced that Julius Caesar would win the civil war and that the republic was doomed, he committed suicide. Although in many ways a very different man from his ancestor, many regarded him as another from that family to personify Roman values. Cicero wrote a (now lost) work about him, *In Praise of Cato*, which helped to project the image of Cato as a Stoic sage.

20. Conclusion

This chapter has ranged far and wide across the ancient world. The figures who have passed across its pages are united above all in their variety: kings, prophets, teachers, philosophers, lawgivers, architects, shamans, and many more. Yet each in his or her own fashion seems to have attracted a reputation for wisdom in one way or another. Whether every reputation was deserved is impossible to tell. Many of the figures, despite their historicity, are little more than names. But there were many more whose names are totally lost but who nevertheless followed professions or were engaged in practices that would have given them the status of wise people in their own times. The next chapter takes a look at some of those professions and practices

Wisdom in Practice

1. Introduction

The previous chapter considered a wide range of individuals from antiquity who, for one reason or another, had a reputation for wisdom. The sheer variety of people and talent on offer provides ample support for my first hypothesis, that wisdom in the ancient world was multi-faceted. The wisdom of one was not necessarily the wisdom of another, and what was regarded as wisdom was not a constant across either time or territory. More than that, there could be disagreements as to what constituted wisdom and what did not:

> Rivalry in claims to be wise starts almost as soon as we have evidence to go on in Greece, and what counted as wisdom was an extraordinarily open-ended and negotiable question. (Lloyd 1989, p. 103)

What this reveals, if nothing else, is that there was kudos attached to being wise. People competed for the honour of being so regarded. On occasions, as seen in the case of the philosophers and the sophists [4.14], this could develop into something resembling a turf war between professions. There were also many practices associated with wisdom, in particular divinatory ones. While divination as such was a constant in the ancient world in one way or another, methods might change. New ones might emerge, old ones might become discredited. In many cases we know little or nothing about those who practised them, but we often know considerably more about the practice itself. The aim of this chapter is therefore twofold. First, to pull together in a different way some of the materials that have already been examined, making more explicit what might be termed the professional as opposed to the personal dimension of wisdom. Second, to shine some light into areas associated with wisdom where there is little knowledge of any concrete individuals who might be regarded as representatives of them.

2. Ruling, Judging and Lawgiving

I shall deal with ruling, judging and lawgiving together as they may all be regarded as in one way or another political in nature. The view that in Mesopotamia 'the king was the wise man *par excellence*' (Sweet 1990a, p. 65) has already been noted [4.4]. However, the extent to which this can be taken at face value is questionable. It seems clearly desirable that those who rule should be wise, and perverse to wish that they should not be. On the other hand, the actual claims of rulers to be wise cannot be taken at face value any more than the claims of twentieth-century personality cults can or should be. While we have Hammurabi's and Ashurbanipal's estimations of their own wisdom, we do not have the judgments of those they ruled to compare them with.

However, there was a sense, both in Mesopotamia and Egypt, that rulers had to be wise almost by definition because of the special perceived relationship between the king (rulers in both lands were almost always male) and the gods. What might be termed the official ideology in both Egypt and Mesopotamia made the king the closest human approximation to a god, and sometimes the distinction between king and god might become so blurred that it is difficult to tell where one ended and the other began. The idea that humans might become gods was widespread in the ancient world, and during the period of the Roman Empire one emperor after another was posthumously elevated to divine rank. On the other hand, the history of tomb robbing in Egypt suggests that the official story was often not believed. What was *meant* to happen to those who desecrated the tombs according to the inscriptions that they bore and what actually *did* happen to them are two different things, suggesting that the official line was either not believed or, if believed at one level, not sufficiently feared at another.

I have suggested [4.4] that rulers had three primary functions, to rule well, to judge well and to wage war well, all of which were in one way or another concerned with the establishment or preservation of order. All of these requirements are at least to some extent open to objective assessment. While there might be, and doubtless were, disagreements as to what it meant to rule, judge or fight well, it was rather easier to tell when a king ruled, judged or fought badly. Although it was presumably possible to both fight well and lose, victory and defeat seem to have been widely regarded as speaking for themselves. A king who lost in battle was revealed as a king who no longer enjoyed divine support. Human affairs unfolded according to divine wishes and plans. This theme runs through the Old Testament time and again: defeats and victories both reflect the will of God.

Although the biblical story of Solomon cannot necessarily be taken as accurate in all particulars, it is interesting to note the way in which it is expressed:

> And all Israel heard of the judgment which the king had rendered; and they stood in awe of the king, because they perceived that the wisdom of God was in him, to render justice. (1 Kings 3:28)

The implication is that the wisdom of Solomon as a judge was recognized by the people at large, that the people had a sense of what judging well looked like and they saw it in Solomon. There is nothing in this of the esoteric knowledge that Ashurbanipal claimed for himself. Although perhaps no one else would have come up with the same solution to the disputed maternity claim that Solomon did, all could see the wisdom of it. Doubtless this was not always the case, and the ability of winners and losers in legal proceedings to respond to verdicts very differently is unlikely to be a modern invention.

With regard to ruling well, perhaps the most important requirement was the avoidance of chaos, of disorder. To some extent, any order was better than the absence of order altogether. A number of surviving Egyptian works develop this theme. One of the earliest is 'The Prophecies of Neferti', which has already been briefly mentioned [4.2]. As the hero of the work is Amenemhet I, it is assumed that the work was written during his reign (1985-1955 BC). It takes the form of a set of prophecies delivered centuries before, and so is written mainly in the future tense. The extent to which it reflects genuine historical circumstances is disputed. A period of great disorder is described when even nature seems to have been turned upside down:

> Shoreland will turn into water,
> Watercourse back into shoreland.

(Lichtheim 1975, p. 141)

The order of the social world, too, is reversed:

> The beggar will gain riches,
> The great [will rob] to live,
> The poor will eat bread,
> The slaves will be exalted.

(Lichtheim 1975, p. 143)

Fortunately, all will be well, because 'a king will come from the South' and:

> Then Order [*maat*] will return to its seat,
> While Chaos is driven away.

(Lichtheim 1975, pp. 143-4)

The same theme is taken up in 'The Complaints of Khakheperre-sonb', dated to the reign of Senusret II (1880-1874 BC):

> The land breaks up, is destroyed,
> Becomes [a wasteland].
> Order [*maat*] is cast out,
> Chaos is in the council hall.

(Lichtheim 1975, pp. 147)

A longer work, surviving in part, is the 'Admonitions of Ipuwer'. The surviving copy has been dated to the thirteenth century BC, although the work itself may be older. It has been characterized by Lichtheim as 'the last, fullest, most exaggerated and hence least successful, composition on the theme "order versus chaos" ' (Lichtheim 1975, p. 150). Woes of all kinds are described, but there are two main themes. The first is a lack of social order, such that people live in conditions of uncertainty and constant fear: the perils of travel are particularly emphasized. The second theme is not so much one of disorder, but of an old order that has become inverted or reversed:

> Lo, poor men have become men of wealth,
> He who could not afford sandals owns riches.
>
> See, noble ladies are on boards,
> Princes in the workhouse.
>
> See, those who owned robes are in rags,
> He who did not weave for himself owns fine linen.
>
> (Lichtheim 1975 pp. 151, 156)

The last two lines quoted seem to suggest that not only has the social order been inverted, but that even the fundamental principle of cause and effect no longer applies and no one gets what they deserve. Given that no solution is explicitly proposed, the text is a gloomy one, and perhaps the best that can be said about this kind of composition is that in portraying the miseries of disorder it is by implication a hymn in praise of Maat. And it also implies that *maat* cannot be taken for granted, the existence of order, at least on the social level, is never to be presumed but is always an achievement. It is also the primary responsibility of the ruler to establish it where it is absent and preserve it where it is present. As Raaflaub (2005, p. 53) puts it, 'the Egyptian ideology of kingship emphasized the pharaoh's protective function and his responsibility for justice and order'. The bringing together of 'justice and order' further makes the point that ruling and judging were both, in the end, the responsibilities of the king, even if he did not always carry them out personally.

It would be wrong to suggest or believe that this was a particularly or purely Egyptian outlook. It has already been noted [4.8] that Raaflaub has pointed to similarities between *maat* and Solon's notion of good government, *eunomia*. However he also suggests that this is only one element of a wider sense of common interest to be identified across the ancient world. According to him these elements include:

> A general concern for justice and good order sanctioned by the supreme god, the king as supreme leader in charge of maintaining and dispensing justice, the enactment of written law as a means to enhance justice, and a concept of social justice that protects the weaker members of society from abuse of power by the stronger ... (Raaflaub 2005, p. 54)

Raaflaub's comparisons are between Egypt, Mesopotamia, Israel and archaic Greece. Clearly the situation changed when Greece developed alternative systems of government to kingship. However, it may be argued that that did not significantly change people's expectations, only the mechanisms through which those expectations were to be fulfilled. The emphasis on the importance of a specifically *written* law raises some interesting questions. On the face of it the only difference between an oral law and a written law is the medium of its preservation and transmission, and the significance of this is not immediately apparent. Lewis (2007) points out that Lycurgus dictated that the laws of Sparta should *not* be written down.

> But Sparta was in many ways unique. Such a law 'code' is surely more of an *ethos* than a true code of laws. To become an objective part of civic life, the laws must be written and placed into public view. (Lewis 2007, p. 42, emphasis in original)

It is perhaps the reference to laws being 'an objective part of civic life' that carries the real weight here. The story is told of Solon that he went into exile after enacting his laws, and he is not the only lawgiver about whom such a story is told. There is a clear difference between the availability of a wise person to adjudicate, in the manner of Solomon, between claimants and the laws set down by a wise person for a society to follow. Although to some extent such laws may be regarded as the sedimentation of the wise person's wisdom, the point of laying down fixed laws is that they do not require the lawgiver's presence in order to be effective. It is the fixing of them that marks the transition from the subjective judge to the objective law, and writing them down is simply one way of fixing them. In practice, legal codes were often carved into the walls of public buildings, making them both objective, in the sense of equally visible to all, and fixed, in the sense of being preserved in a highly durable medium. While the memorization of their laws by the Spartans may have served to make them more like an '*ethos*', because they would have become almost second nature to those who memorized them, it is not clear that they thereby jeopardized their status as laws. Although without knowing more about them in detail it is not possible to be sure.

What such a code looked like may also be mentioned. It is clear that in some Greek states the law codes dealt with a variety of procedural or constitutional issues. Where they dealt with more substantive matters, there are clear similarities to the laws of Hammurabi. His code, it may be recalled [4.4], was a series of judgments, and as such bore a closer resemblance to English common law than to, for example, French law. By being set down as a code, however, they became fixed in time and removed from their original context. In a society that changed little, and that saw no virtue in change, this was perhaps not seen as a major disadvantage.

However, from the drastic nature of the legal reforms that were sometimes enacted across the ancient world, it would appear that the inability of legal codes to evolve meant that, as with inaccuracies in the calendar, the failure to make a series of minor changes resulted in the eventual need for major ones. Those who not only failed to put down their thoughts and ideas in writing, but objected to doing so on principle, seem to have perhaps appreciated this fact better than others. While the development of a more sophisticated body of law might be seen as progress of a kind, the separation of the objective from the subjective, of the judgment from the judge, was not always, or at least not necessarily, positive. The same principle may apply to wisdom literature: in the end, the book is a poor substitute for the writer.

3. The Scribe

Even today, in places where the general level of literacy is low, there is often a good living to be made from being able to read and write. In the ancient world, a clear division can be seen between those cultures where, to a significant extent, literacy *was* education, and those where it did little more than provide the foundations for it. It has been widely observed that the alphabetic system of writing, as found in Greece and Rome, is far easier to master than either hieroglyphics or cuneiform. As a result, those who only taught literacy in Greece and Rome were regarded as occupying the lowest end of the educational spectrum. Whereas in Egypt and Mesopotamia, to be trained as a scribe meant becoming qualified to fill any number of roles, in Greece and Rome literacy was what provided access to the kind of higher education furnished by the sophists and philosophers. In what follows, therefore, the emphasis is on Egypt and Mesopotamia. In passing it may be recalled that there was a far stronger association of writing with the divine in Egypt and Mesopotamia, a reasonable reflection of the social status of those people who possessed the skill.

To begin with Mesopotamia, it is clear that scribes there were an elite in their own right. However, because of their scarce skills they also tended to find themselves in the vicinity and employ of other elites who had a need of their services, and the two principal focal points about which the ancient world elites gathered were the temple and the palace. But there is ample evidence that Mesopotamian scribes also had an institution of their own known as the *edubba* in Sumerian and the *bit tuppi* in Akkadian, both terms meaning 'the tablet house' after one of the tools of their trade, the clay tablet on which they wrote. In these institutions boys (scribes were almost always male and usually came from the social elite) learnt their art. Because the system of writing employed was complex, a long period of training was required in order to master it. As Saggs notes (Saggs 1965, p. 77), the fact that a child was engaged in wholly non-productive activity for a number of years meant that only the children of the privileged were

Portrait of an Egyptian scribe.

likely to be able to take advantage of this kind of training even if access was not formally forbidden to the lower social orders. It is extremely fortunate (for us) that one of the methods used in learning to write was copying existing texts, which is the main reason that a number of works have survived. After the conquests of Sargon the Great (2334-2279 BC) and the formation of the first Akkadian empire, Mesopotamian culture became effectively bilingual and in time even multilingual. Although Sumer never regained its earlier political significance, its language continued to be used, including for a long period as a classical literary one long after it had ceased to be spoken. With these developments scribes had to become translators as well. Although archaeologists think they have unearthed the remains of an *edubba* in Ur, amongst other places, there is some evidence that the institution itself may have ceased to exist at some stage during the second millennium BC, with the task of

114

educating scribes moving within the precinct of the temple, but the picture is not entirely clear.

It would appear that there may have been more than one institution or more than one level within the same institution concerned with scribal education. From Babylon at least there is evidence of an institution known as the 'house of wisdom' [*bit mumme*]. While the graduate from the tablet house was a writer [*tupsarrum*], the graduate of the house of wisdom was a sage [*emqum*]. It was the sages who would be expected to fill the highest posts (McKane 1965, pp. 39-40). In any event, if the education of the scribe became or was sometimes something that happened within the walls of the temple, the subsequent employment of the scribe was certainly not confined within them. As a member of a small educated elite, the trained scribe had a number of career openings available. As Saggs (1965, pp. 75-81) points out, although writing may have originated within the temple as a kind of accountancy tool, then as now there were a number of openings for those with accountancy skills, and scribes were always in demand in the world of commerce, amongst other places.

Although it is obvious why scribes were regarded as educated, it may be worthwhile reflecting briefly on why there was a tendency to perceive them as *wise*. One obvious answer presents itself and is neatly summed up by Bertman thus: 'literacy was the link that connected the present with the wisdom of the past and its instructional and inspirational power' (Bertman 2003, p. 148). From this perspective, the scribe may be seen as the successor to the *apkallu*. Where the *apkallu* transmitted learning from the gods to humanity, the scribe transmits it to succeeding generations of humanity. Furthermore the means whereby the scribe achieves this is through the medium of writing, itself a gift from the gods. And just as the order of the world was the work of the gods, so one of the occupations of the scribes seems to have been the representation of this order through the medium of the written word. Although their precise purpose has been a matter of some debate, one way of understanding the word lists produced by the Sumerians is as an exercise in a science of order.

> The Sumerians believed in a system of ordering the world which brought with it confirmation of the working of the gods. The lists had the task of making this order manifest in connection with the main groups of objects and living creatures, including the gods. (Soden 1994, p. 146)

It may also be pointed out that given the importance attached to the act of naming in the Babylonian creation myth, the production of word lists could almost be seen as an act of re-creation in itself. More will be said about word lists when wisdom literature is discussed [6.2].

Although the ability to write was the core skill of the scribe, the scribe also represented and offered a rather more amorphous (or polymorphous) expertise. He was an educated person who might be expected to be able to deploy the benefits of that education in a variety of ways. The Akkadian word that best sums up this kind of person is *'ummanu'*. It can be variously translated as 'expert', '(skilled) craftsman' and 'scholar' (Sweet 1990a, p. 48), and it may be recalled that Dalley (2000, p. 328) suggests that Uan, the name of the first of the *apkallu*, was intended as a pun on it. Bottéro (1992, pp. 247-8) refers to a tradition that just as there was a series of *apkallu* who acted as advisors to a number of kings *before* the flood, so there was also a series of *ummanu* who performed a similar function for a number of kings *after* the flood. A list survives that matches a number of *ummanu* to their corresponding Babylonian and Assyrian kings who lived between the eleventh and seventh centuries BC. Bottéro suggests that the *apkallu* might represent the *ummanu* transposed from the realm of history into the realm of myth, with the appropriate degree of mythological exaggeration thrown in. This would be in line with my third hypothesis [1.2]. However, although the historical *ummanu* might have been the inspiration behind the advisory role attributed to the legendary *apkallu*, it is possible that this dimension was simply grafted onto an existing myth. Whichever way it is interpreted, and whether or not there was ever any kind of officially recognized position of royal counsellor, it seems obvious that rulers would sometimes have sought out those whom they believed to be able to offer them wise counsel. And those they sought out would most obviously be looked for amongst the *ummanu*, the experts of various kinds, the educated elite, those who could write. However, if the ability to write might provide the basis of a claim to wisdom, it was not in itself a requirement of wisdom. It has already been noted that few Mesopotamian kings even claimed to be literate (Sweet 1990a, p. 65).

The status of the Egyptian scribe has already been given some consideration [4.2] in the context of documents celebrating the wisdom of the greatest of them, and the claim made in the 'Satire on the Trades', attributed to Khety, that the scribal profession was the best to be had. In fact, 'Satire on the Trades' is a modern nickname for the work, which introduces itself thus:

> Beginning of the Instruction made by the man of Sile, whose name is Dua-khety [Khety, son of Duauf], for his son, called Pepi, as he journeyed south to the residence, to place him in the school for scribes, amongst the sons of magistrates, with the elite of the residence. (Lichtheim 1975, p. 185)

Knowledge of the educational system of ancient Egypt, to the extent that there was a system, is meagre. As in Mesopotamia, there was an early connection between education and the temple, between the scribe and the priest. The two professions seem to have become increasingly differentiated from each other during the period of the New Kingdom, beginning in the middle of the second millennium BC. While some scribes remained within the priestly sphere, many more seem to have become bureaucrats, servicing the administrative needs of the Empire. Whereas in earlier times the profession of scribe seems to have been open to those from different social backgrounds on a largely meritocratic basis, during the New Kingdom entry became increasingly restricted to the social elite and, as in the case of Khety and Pepi, there was often an hereditary dimension.

Some children may have literally learnt their trade at their father's knee. However, such a relationship did not have to be a blood one, and there is evidence that scribes would sometimes adopt promising youths, including ones from inferior social backgrounds. The case of Ramose is a case in point. His father was a messenger, but Ramose was adopted by the scribe Huy, and Ramose in turn adopted Kenhirkshepsef. Ramose seems to have been related in some way to Amenhotep, son of Hapu, but Kenhirkshepsef came from a poorer family. Under such circumstances, 'adoption' was very much like entering an apprenticeship. But there is also clear evidence of the existence of a number of important scribal schools in and around Thebes (modern Luxor/Karnak) on both sides of the Nile. It is possible that their establishment owed something to Mesopotamian influence (Bowen 1972, p. 31). Such schools would have constituted the training ground for the future imperial elite who would occupy the highest offices. The first stage of the scribal education seems to have begun at around the age of five and lasted for around four years (Booth 2006, p. 10). This was followed by something more akin to an apprenticeship. It is evident that even the lowliest scribe enjoyed considerable esteem and respect. According to 'the 'Satire on the Trades':

> Barely grown, still a child,
> He is greeted, sent on errands,
> Hardly returned, he wears a gown.
> I never saw a sculptor as envoy,
> Nor is a goldsmith ever sent.
>
> (Lichtheim 1975, p. 186)

The author quotes from another work: 'A scribe at whatever post in town, He will not suffer in it' (Lichtheim 1975, p. 185), which sounds as if it could have been something close to a proverb. Later, in his own words, the author asserts that 'no scribe is short of food' or 'of riches from the palace' (Lichtheim 1975, p. 191).

But if this was the least one could expect as a scribe, at the other end of the spectrum limits were set only by ambition and opportunity. The highest appointed position in the land, that of vizier, was open to scribes. On occasion, this became a jumping off point for the very highest position of all: Amenemhet I was not the only vizier who became pharaoh.

As in the case of Mesopotamia, the reason the scribe was perceived as wise rather than simply educated, to the extent that the distinction can be drawn in this context, is unclear. Whereas the claim of individuals such as Imhotep is clear, that of the profession as a whole is a little shakier.

117

Doubtless some scribes were perceived as wiser than others. Doubtless too, it serves a profession to establish a reputation for wisdom for itself. On the other hand, it would be surprising if the idea that writing was a gift of the gods did not have some impact on how the practitioners of that skill were broadly perceived. And then as now, it is unlikely that a profession would ever knowingly undersell itself.

4. Diviners and Divination

The role of divination in the ancient world was enormous and the ways and places in which it could be practised were many. It will not be possible to do much more than skim the surface here. Before proceeding, it may be worth making one fundamental point. Although it might be used for such a purpose, divination was by no means restricted to attempts to see into the future. It might also be employed to ascertain information about the present, such as the whereabouts of stolen property or matters of paternity. It was also used to obtain advice, about careers, prospective marriage partners, and so on. Many Greek colonies attributed their locations to the advice of the oracle of Apollo at Delhi in particular. Politically, divination might help to select, or at least endorse, a new king, while militarily it was used to decide when to fight. The extent to which it was taken as decisive is unclear, and there are episodes that suggest people were not beyond manipulating the process to get the right result. But one way or another it was deeply woven into the fabric of everyday life in many ways and at all social levels.

In Mesopotamia, divination was as central to the way the world worked as kingship, and it is apparent that the two often came into contact with each other. While diviners were not limited in their activities to the palace, they were certainly not barred from it. Just as there were different kinds of divination, so there were also different kinds of diviner. One such specialist was the *ashipu* who brought the divinatory arts to the practice of medicine. Generally speaking, it was the task of the *ashipu* to provide a diagnosis, and possibly treat it through magical means, although there was also the *asu* whose medical responsibilities were (by modern standards) more conventional and who might prescribe (again by modern standards) more conventional treatments.

Although the precise division of labour within the Mesopotamian divinatory world is not entirely clear, the pre-eminent position within it seems to have belonged to the *baru* who formed a definite elite. '*Baru*' is an Akkadian word, but texts containing its Sumerian equivalent have been dated to as far back as 2650 BC, and there is evidence of haruspicy (divination by the inspection of entrails) from around the same time. Another popular form of divination was libanomancy, which involved the study of the smoke produced by incense. Both of these forms of divination were closely connected to sacrificial practices. Two other forms of divina-

118

tion that were practised were lecanomancy and aleuromancy, which involved the study of patterns created by dropping oil and flour respectively onto water. There were also the interpretation of dreams and astrology. From the evidence available it would appear that astrology and dream interpretation became more popular over the centuries and, perhaps as a result, some other methods of divination went into a relative decline. Although all of these forms of divination might have their specialists, the *baru* seems to have been the specialist in divination *per se*, and a person of considerable importance and stature. The name of at least one is known, Asqudum who lived in Mari during the eighteenth century BC, and whose archives were discovered in the palace there, evidence of how close a *baru* could be to the centre of power. However, in many ways the *baru* was more like a priest (although there is no evidence of them being formally attached to temples), and the practice of divination always had a religious dimension even when it was not directly connected with acts of sacrifice. In Mesopotamia, divination was primarily concerned with ascertaining the will of the gods, who directed and decided the destiny of the world and all who lived in it. In one way or another, the gods were always part of the picture. And because destiny was in the lap of the gods, nothing was inevitable because they could always change their minds. Consequently, divination was located within a broader complex of practices that also included magic [5.9].

While the *baru* might provide services to the palace, the divinatory arts were more widely sought out, and there was certainly a private market for them as well as a public one. In 'Ludlul bel nemeqi' (line 52) the author complains that he 'cannot stop going to the diviner [*baru*] and dream interpreter [*sailu*]' (Pritchard 1969, p. 596), and although he is certainly not from the lowest ranks of society, equally certainly he is not a king either. The *sailu* was a particular kind of dream interpreter, often female, and perhaps of lower social status. Although the evidence is sparse, the *sailu* may have been a more intuitive kind of interpreter whereas the art of the *baru* became increasingly systematized and more scientific. From around the time of Hammurabi onwards, information about omens of all kinds was collected and organized into an increasingly complex and comprehensive system. One way of looking at dreams is as a special class of omens. Similarly, the different configurations of and markings on the liver, the favoured organ for those who studied entrails, could also be thought of as omens of a particular kind. Two points may be made about these collections of omens. First, each omen took a standard format, consisting of a protasis (what was observed) and the apodosis (what it presaged), presented in a conditional relationship: if the protasis, then the apodosis. However, there is always an implied 'unless' to be understood. The protasis did not cause the apodosis, but pointed towards it. The apodosis was not inevitable; rather it was what should be expected unless the gods could be prevailed upon to change their minds. It may be noted that this 'if ... then' formula was also used in the substantive part of Hammurabi's code, and just as the code contained the king's judgments, so omens related to the gods' judgments on the world. It was no coincidence that Shamash was the god of both justice and omens. A work on dreams of uncertain date declares:

> Shamash, you are the judge – judge my case!
> You are the one who makes the decisions – decide my case!
> Change the dream I had into a good one!
>
> (Oppenheim 1956, p. 300)

The second point to note is that whereas originally collections of omens seem to have related only to what had actually been observed, the study of omens gradually went beyond the observed to anticipate the potentially observable. A number of basic variables could be worked through systematically, in particular right/left, number, colour and direction (north/south/east/west). The result was that collections of omens traced a network of connections that embraced more and more of the world as they expanded. Collections of omens of all kinds therefore all contributed to the attempt to describe the order of the world. Because the order of the world was seen as the creation of the gods, the idea of a scientific law would have had nowhere to root itself. Consequently, although collections of omens might sometimes 'describe' something that had never been seen and perhaps never would be, and so go beyond the empirical strictly speaking, nevertheless the approach taken was always concrete and never abstract. The primary task of the diviner was to understand the order of the world as revealed through omens, and as collections of omens became increasingly comprehensive, so divination increasingly came to resemble a science more than an art. But art or science, it was never perfect and it was always open to abuse. It is known that the Assyrian king Sennacherib (704-681 BC) regarded his *baru* with a degree of scepticism, and diviners seem to have gone to inordinate lengths at times in order to ensure that they came up with something favourable. Sennacherib's pragmatic solution was to divide them into two groups and compare their results. A similar story was told by Herodotus [I.46-50] about Croesus (sixth century BC), who sent the same enquiry to several different oracles as a test. However, Croesus had a very significant advantage over Sennacherib, having taken care to arrange things so that he knew in advance what the correct answer should be.

Prophecy was also practised in Mesopotamia. A document from the time of Esarhaddon (ruled 680-669 BC) preserves a number of prophecies along with the names of those who uttered them such as Ishtarlatashiat, Baia, Belitabisha and Ladagalili, all of whom were from Arbela, and 'the woman Rimute-allate of the town Darahuya which is in the mountains' (Pritchard 1969, p. 605). Arbela was a major centre of the cult of Ishtar, and it may

120

be that all the prophets from there were attached to it. The prophecies do not seem to serve as answers to any particular questions, so they may have been purely spontaneous. However, there is also clear evidence of direct questions being put to the gods:

> I ask you Shamash, great lord, whether this drug which is now placed before your great divinity, and which Ashurbanipal, crown prince of the Succession House (is to) drink – (whether by drinking this drug he will) be saved, (and escape). Be present in this ram, place (in it) a firm positive answer ... (Leick 2001, p. 238)

The implication of the final sentence is that the answer is to be sought through an examination of a sacrificial ram's entrails, a standard Mesopotamian practice. In ancient Egypt, a common form of divination involved cult statues. When they were being carried in procession on special days, questions might be put to them and the response of the god would be indicated by the way in which the statue moved. Presumably the questions that were put either presented alternatives between which a choice could be made, or were answerable with a simple 'yes' or 'no'. This kind of binary oracle seems to have been available at a number of cult centres in Egypt. At Soknopaiou Nesos two pieces of papyrus were found, dating to the second century BC. They both bore the same question (concerning the advisability of ploughing a particular piece of land), but on one there was a positive response and the other a negative one. Clearly the god (Sobek in this case) would somehow have been expected to indicate his preference between the two in some way or other.

Another method found in Egypt and many other places was the dream oracle, an institution that became particularly closely identified with the cult of Asclepius. Dream oracles were sought through the process of incubation, which typically involved a process of preparation and purification, followed by a night spent sleeping in a special part of a temple complex. The oracle of Bes at Abydos was one of the better known Egyptian ones, although Bes seems to have used other means of communication as well.

That the dream was widely regarded as a significant personal event is apparent, although precisely how significant, and precisely what the significance actually was, were matters for dispute. Herodotus (IX.16) tells the story of Xerxes having a dream and sending for Artabanus to explain it. Artabanus seeks to reassure Xerxes that the dream is nothing to worry about, because:

> dreams do not come from God. I ... will tell you what these visions are that float before our eyes in sleep: nearly always these drifting phantoms are the shadows of what we have been thinking about during the day. (Herodotus 1965, p. 423)

121

This naturalistic explanation was later taken up by Aristotle and the Epicureans, while the Stoics insisted that dreams were indeed sent by the gods. In Egypt, the dream was certainly seen as significant, and the story told in Genesis of Joseph reaching the highest position in the land because of his ability to interpret dreams is entirely plausible whether historically accurate or not. The Egyptian scribe Kenhirkhepshef (thirteenth/twelfth century BC) evidently took an interest in dreams and a papyrus belonging to him has survived on which he wrote about how they should be interpreted. It is thought that at least some of the materials in this dream book (the reverse of the Chester Beatty III papyrus) are considerably earlier than Kenhirkhepshef himself, perhaps by a margin of five hundred years (Kaster 1965, p. 153). The work lists a number of dreams and then provides an interpretation, first in terms of whether the significance is good or bad, and then more specifically what it connotes. There is no single pattern: the associations between dreams and meanings are of many kinds. Sometimes the symbolism is obvious, sometimes not. Dreaming of drinking one's own urine is good because it means acquiring wealth from one's children. Dreaming of drinking warm beer is bad and portends suffering. Dreaming of copulating with a cow is good and points to a pleasant day at home. Dreaming of copulating with a woman is bad and is associated with mourning. Kaster (1965, p. 154) suggests that many of the associations made in the book would find themselves fully at home in a modern psychoanalytic work. As in Mesopotamia, it would appear that while Egyptians regarded dreams as signs, what they portended was not inevitable, for the dream book ends with a spell for exorcising bad dreams.

While the logic of Kenhirkhepshef's dream book needs unravelling and deciphering by the reader, *The Interpretation of Dreams* by Artemidorus (1975) seeks to provide a systematic and scientific guide to the subject. Written during the second century AD, it is a veritable encyclopaedia of ancient learning on the subject. Book I of the work sets out some basic principles. First, there is a distinction between *oneiros* and *enhypnion*. The former are meaningful and relate to future concerns, while the latter have no meaning and relate to current concerns. The latter are simply a continuation of the thoughts of the day, as Artabanus explained to Xerxes. Some dreams (theorematic ones) point directly to future events while others (allegorical ones) point more indirectly. People only dream about things they have previously thought about. The interpreter of dreams needs to know about the dreamer as well as about the dream. The dreamer's age, occupation, health, financial and social status may all be relevant to interpreting a dream. In the end, however, only so much can be learnt from manuals such as this one; natural talent is also required for success. This observation reflects a distinction that was frequently made in the ancient world, between natural and artificial divination, or as it might be more often articulated today, between the intuitive and the inductive. Some are able to practise divination with little or no formal

A Roman augur.

training. They may possess certain natural aptitudes, or they may be prone to entering into certain psychological states that are associated with divination. This kind of diviner is perhaps more akin to the prophet, although the border between the two is blurred in the case of those who enter into certain psychological states intentionally, with or without chemical assistance. The other kind is more scholarly. It would appear that the practice of augury at Rome, for example, required little more than observing the skies and then checking what was seen against the manual. However, even in these cases, Artemidorus seems to suggest, those with some natural flair may fare better than those who do not. Unless an omen is completely unambiguous and subject to only one possible meaning, there will be a need for interpretation, and some interpret better than others. As Artemidorus puts it (III.66):

In judging a dream, therefore, one must imitate the diviners. For they know how each individual sign fits into the whole and base their judgments as much on the sum total of the signs as on each individual sign. (Artemidorus 1975, p. 176)

Not all diviners or interpreters were equal. For reasons that are entirely unclear, the people of Telmessus in Caria had a particularly high reputation as diviners, such that Clement of Alexandria in his *Stromata* (I.16) even claimed that they invented dream interpretation. The Galeotae, a soothsaying clan, supposedly originated from there, although in historical times they were associated with the city of Hybla Geleatis in Sicily. Pausanias (V.23) notes that the inhabitants of this place were famous for being 'interpreters of dreams and omens' (Pausanias 1971b, p. 269).

And if not all diviners were equal, then neither were all forms of divination. It has already been noted [4.11] that Artemidorus had a dim view of a number of practices that went under this name. He was quite clear about those who were worth consulting and those who were not (II.69).

The only things left that are true are the utterances of sacrificers, bird augurs, astrologers, observers of strange phenomena, dream interpreters, and soothsayers who examine livers. (Artemidorus 1975, p 134)

The examination of the entrails of sacrificed animals, extispicy or haruspicy, had a long history in the ancient world. Although particularly associated in classical times with the Etruscans, it first appears in Mesopotamia. The liver was the organ to which most attention was paid, and Babylonian clay models of livers, obviously designed for reference or training in the art of extispicy, have survived dating back to at least 2,000 BC. Finds of similar items at such places as Megiddo and Ugarit indicates the spread of the practice. The reason for the special attention paid to the liver is a matter of some dispute. Halliday (1913, pp. 198-202) considers a few of them: it was easy to examine, many regarded it as the seat of life, some thought demons resided there. Robert Temple suggests that the origins of extispicy may be more prosaic and lie in an interesting physical fact about the organ: 'I discovered that if you pull the liver out of a freshly slaughtered lamb it will act as a perfect mirror' (Temple 1992, p. 66). The fact that the liver was able to function literally as a mirror of reality may have led to the belief that it was also able to 'reflect' reality in more metaphorical or supernatural ways.

If there was a naturalistic explanation for divination by examination of the liver, then it could have spontaneously developed in more than one place. The Romans were convinced that the Etruscans had invented it, and the Etruscans were convinced that it was the gift of Tages. (Tages was an enigmatic figure who was believed to have emerged from the ground, instructed the Etruscans in a variety of matters, including religion and divination, and then disappeared back into the ground again.) A bronze model of a liver discovered at Piacenza has shed a great deal of light on how the Etruscans practised it.

> Indeed, it becomes clear that the priests were not relying on intuition as they examined the entrails of the sacrificial animal, but on specific formulas which were almost mathematical in conception. For the liver was divided into four quarters and each of these quarters into four, each section having its meaning in terms of a well thought out cosmography. In short the haruspex was not examining a piece of flesh as he held the liver in the palm of one hand and felt its conformation with the fingers of the other; he was examining a microcosm of the universe. (Wellard 1973, pp. 145-6)

What is interesting, if I understand both Temple and Wellard correctly, is that the Babylonian clay model of a liver had 55 sections whereas the Etruscan one had 16. This in itself *might* suggest that the Etruscans developed the practice independently of the Babylonians, or, at the very least, developed it in a significantly different way. According to Cicero in *On Divination* (I.42), the people of Telmessus were celebrated practitioners of extispicy as well as dream interpretation. The practice continued to be used at least until the fourth century AD. Writing about Diocletian (AD 245-316) in his essay 'On the Deaths of the Persecutors' (X), Lactantius (d. AD 326) says that the emperor 'was offering a sacrifice of cattle and was seeking from their entrails what things were to happen' (Lactantius 1965, p. 148).

The examination of entrails, although it achieved and generally retained a high reputation throughout antiquity, was not a particularly accessible form of divination. For one thing, it was expensive, and for another, there was only a limited supply of suitably qualified priests, haruspices (although in *On Divination* (I.132) Cicero suggests that there were 'village haruspices' who were presumably relatively cheap but with a level of competence to match). The hundreds of oracles spread across the ancient world testify to their popularity and persistence. While visiting a major one might incur considerable expense, there were often cheaper and handier options available (Curnow 2004). It is evident that the popularity of individual oracles, including the most celebrated ones, was far from constant, and there are stories of bribery which suggest that officials were not incorruptible. There were also what might be termed 'recycled' oracles, oracular pronouncements that were collected and then passed on. Mention has already been made [4.8] of Onomacritus who seems to have done this, and been caught out forging some new ones. After his banishment from Athens, he travelled to Persia and managed to be admitted to the court of Xerxes. As Herodotus relates it (VII.6), he was careful to make sure that Xerxes heard what he wanted to hear:

Etruscan bronze model of a liver.

Babylonian clay model of a liver.

A haruspex examines the entrails of a bull.

Any prophecy which implied a setback to the Persian cause he would carefully omit, choosing for quotation only those which promised the brightest triumphs, describing to Xerxes how it was foreordained that the Hellespont should be bridged by a Persian, and how the army would march from Asia into Greece. (Herodotus 1965, p. 415)

It is scarcely surprising that Aristophanes could not resist making the oracle collector, the chresmologue, the butt of his humour in one of his plays, 'Birds'. On the other hand, the Sibylline books, thought to contain the authentic pronouncements of the Sibyl, were among the most treasured possessions of the Romans. The whole institution of divination was founded on the belief that it was possible to attain to a kind of knowledge normally denied to humans but that could be made accessible through contact with the divine, or, if not the divine itself, those close to the divine.

This last category included the dead, and necromancy was a recognized form of divination. Because the gods had knowledge of the future, their advice was far superior to human advice. While some diviners were regarded as better than others, in the end the diviner was no more than a medium for divine wisdom.

A form of divination that took on an increasingly important place in the ancient world after emerging in Mesopotamia, and that even today has its adherents, is astrology. Astrology and astronomy (to the extent to which the two are separable in Mesopotamian culture) seem to have originated in the first half of the second millennium BC. The study of the skies might be undertaken for a variety of practical reasons connected with the calendar, the seasons and the weather. The heavens were also a potential source of omens that could be collected and organized like any others. It is not clear at what point an interest developed in systematically collecting routine data pertaining to the night sky as opposed to noting unusual celestial events, but it seems to have been a relatively late development and much of the work was done after the Persian conquest. However, the dividing line between what might be regarded as omens and what might be regarded as data is not always clear.

> An abundant correspondence from the Neo-Assyrian empire [746-609 BC] attests the importance at the royal court of the diviners and the astronomers who apprised the king of the portents, and the exorcists who were expert in averting ill-boding forecasts via their rituals. The astronomers regularly conveyed to the king such routine reports as the monthly sighting of the new moon and the date of the opposition of sun and moon as well as reports on various predictable and predicted celestial and meteorological phenomena, such as conjunctions, occultations, and rain and thunder. More than a thousand years earlier, in Mari, the correspondents reported on such extraordinary events as torrential rains and thunder. (Reiner 1995, pp. 63-4)

While the sighting of the new moon might be regarded as a routine event from one perspective, it might be regarded as an omen from another. The consequence was that the collection of information relating to celestial omens also became the collection of astronomical data.

It may have been only in the time of Nabonidus (ruled 555-539 BC), the last king of an independent Babylonia, that astrology supplanted extispicy as the preferred Mesopotamian form of divination, and perhaps not even then. The king is said to have asked for the significance of a lunar eclipse to be clarified through the examination of a liver (Reiner 1995, p. 74), suggesting that a strong faith was retained in tried and trusted methods. It may also be noted that up to the time of Nabonidus, astrology was essentially a matter of state or, to the extent to which it was a personal matter, the only person who mattered was the king. Astrology was the study of celestial omens for the primary purpose of guiding political and military decision-making. Cyrus the Great added Babylonia to his Persian

Empire in 539 BC, and the earliest surviving personal horoscopes date from after this time. Consequently, some have seen the development of personal astrology as the result of Persian influence (Baigent 1994, pp. 174-6). It was this new kind of astrology that was taken up by the Greeks, although they also became familiar with the astronomical data generated by the older kind. Astrology in all its forms remained strongly associated in the popular mind with Mesopotamia. Saggs notes that:

> in the Hellenistic world ... the term 'Chaldaean', properly relating to the last native Babylonian dynasty, became a synonym for soothsayer or astrologer. (Saggs 1978, p. 127)

In the end, it did not particularly matter what form of divination was practised. The very different procedures that were employed were only of secondary importance. None would have had any value if there were not some reason to believe in their efficacy. The basis of this belief in Mesopotamia was the notion of order:

> the entire world order was thought to be pervaded by signs, and these signs consisted of every perceptible and imaginable phenomenon occurring in the world, not only above, but also below ... . (Rochberg 2004, p. 166)

Furthermore, 'the entire world order' was itself the work of the gods. Consequently, the understanding of the order of the world was thoroughly bound up with, if not indistinguishable from, the understanding of the divine. Omens were revelatory of both, whether spontaneous (as celestial phenomena were) or actively encouraged (as those discovered through the examination of entrails were). Just as there was one world order, so there was also one 'science' of omens, even though it might have many different branches.

> The conception of a divinely created order underlies the various forms of Mesopotamian divination, which functioned as a system of divine communication with human beings by means of perceptible patterns of phenomena. The idea of an ordered universe is ... expressed clearly in, for example the divine epithet that refers to certain gods as the 'ones who draw the cosmic designs'. (Rochberg 2004, p. 45)

Mesopotamian divination provides one of the contexts in which the connection between wisdom and order is very close to the surface. The gods created the order of the world, and the world was one great book in which the wisdom of the gods could be read. Diviners were those with the special talent, or special training, to read this book. While divination came to be rejected by Judaism [4.5], it was generally speaking a constant across the ancient world. While sceptics of all kinds might dismiss it, it retained a firm grip on the popular mind. Cato the Censor's remark, recorded by

Cicero in *On Divination* (II.52), that he found it difficult to understand how two soothsayers could keep a straight face when they met each other, might have reflected the attitude of the more educated elite, and perhaps there were some less educated who distrusted it too. Yet the evidence is there to indicate that people returned to it time after time. And while some philosophers and philosophical schools poured scorn on it, others came up with ever more ingenious justifications of it.

5. Counsellors and Advisors

Although there is relatively little to say about counsellors and advisers, it may be worth making a few explicit points about them since they have only been obliquely dealt with up to this point. It is perhaps in the context of counsel and advice that meritocracy is most evident in the ancient world. While many skills may be learnt by many people, good sense is harder to come by. To some extent, the role of the counsellor or advisor is a parasitic one, in that it relies on someone else requiring advice or counsel in order to exist, and in practice the sycophant is perhaps as likely to catch the royal or governmental ear as the sage is. Furthermore, just as there are many different issues on which advice might be sought, so there are many different kinds of advisor who might be in a position to give it.

An example of this is given by Gammie (1990). He mentions three figures who received the title of 'friend of the king' during the Ptolemaic period in Egypt. Demetrius of Phalerum (b. c. 350 BC) was a statesman and pupil of Theophrastus who turned up in Egypt when it was no longer possible or politic for him to remain in Athens. There he gained entry to the court of Ptolemy I and went on to advise him on legal matters and, perhaps, on the foundation of the Mouseion in Alexandria. Sosibius (third century BC) served under both Ptolemy III and Ptolemy IV in a variety of capacities, including envoy and advisor on military matters. Agathocles was a close contemporary who shared the work of reorganizing the Egyptian army. The extent to which being a 'friend of the king' was an official post, or more of an honorary title to indicate the special value attached to the advice and support of a particular individual, is not clear. However, the collective term 'friends of the king' seems to have denoted some kind of group (or sub-group) of advisors that persisted over time in some form or other. Williams suggests that the paucity of evidence for similar figures in earlier Egyptian history may have had something to do with 'the dogma of the ruler's divinity' (Williams 1990b, p. 97). He does, however, note at least one exception in the case of Nebneretu who served under Osorkon II (874-850 BC): an inscription on his statue claims that he was one 'who guides the land by his counsel' and 'whose sagacity has promoted his person' (Williams 1990b, p. 99).

As a default position, I think it must be presumed that while the ability to provide sound advice was certainly not the only requirement of a vizier (administrative skills, to give just one example, were certainly also at a premium), it would always have been reckoned a highly desirable one. As already indicated [5.3], some viziers in Egypt took the step to the throne itself. This phenomenon was not unique to Egypt. Indeed, it seems that Nabonidus claimed descent not from a king but from a counsellor, and seems to have been close to the throne before manoeuvring his way onto it. The example of Joseph suggests what might happen to someone of exceptional talent in an area of expertise that was particularly in demand at some time or other for some reason or other, but there is no obvious reason to think that the story of Joseph represents the norm. It would seem more likely that advice and counsel was a function of those of exceptional talent who progressed through the normal channels. Indeed, there would appear to have been levels of achievement and attainment within the scribal community and profession that itself decided and determined who stayed at the centre and rose to the top and who was despatched to the peripheries. On the other hand, the training of a scribe involved becoming familiar with the genre of 'instruction' literature whose purpose was to inculcate both good values and good sense [6.3]. If the average scribe was not expected to possess exceptional wisdom, there was nevertheless a presumption that it would be manifested to some degree.

Both the Cynics of Greece and Rome and the prophets of Israel might be regarded as 'freelance' advisors and counsellors, offering unbidden, and often unwanted, advice to all and sundry, but especially to rulers. The character known as Diogenes the Sophist (first century AD), who is generally thought to have been a Cynic, took it upon himself to launch a public verbal tirade against Titus (son of the emperor Vespasian) and his mistress in AD 75, and was flogged for it. Heras, another Cynic, did the same at a different time and was beheaded. In this regard, the Cynics seem to have taken up the mantle of Socrates who considered himself a social gad fly. Where the counsel of the ancient prophets of Israel always revolved around God's will and God's commandments, the message of the Cynics was both more amorphous and more demanding. Their object was to make people think for themselves. Technically it might be argued that the Cynics had no social role to play since they lived on the very fringes of society if not outside it. However, if their values might put them beyond the pale, physically they remained close to the heart of things. Indeed, it was clearly impossible to shock people without encountering them, and visibility rather than remoteness was in the Cynics' interest.

Something has already been said about the role of the 'holy man' in late antiquity [4.9]. It may be appropriate to go on to say something more about that figure now as clearly some kind of generic association with counsel and advice seems to have been part of the popular perception of this individual, even if there were other associations too.

We have found the holy man central to the way in which different milieus coped with increased freedom and its consequent dangers: for the farmers of Syria, he brought leadership; for the townsmen, the objectivity of a stranger; for innumerable individuals, an oasis of certainty in the conflicting aims and traditions of the world. Such a need for certainty and for leadership is not usually experienced by more stable societies, where the objectivity associated with the supernatural is more securely lodged in impersonal and enduring institutions – in great temple sites, whose prophets are often thought of as totally transparent to the divine and whose grave priests (as in Egypt) emerged only in low relief against the facade of ancient wisdom. We know that the later Roman Empire was the very opposite of such a society. On every level of life, institutions that had seemed capable of receiving the awesome charge of permanence and divinity in classical times either declined or exploded. Men were left with nothing to fall back on than other men. (Brown 1982, p. 148)

It is not only rulers and leaders who need counsel and advice, so do ordinary people. When they are left, or feel, rudderless, whole societies may seek advice. In this context, Brown notes that the holy man seems to have taken over some of the functions of the oracle, at least in some places. He also notes that these holy *men* tended to supplant an older type of occultism that was primarily associated with *women* (1982, pp. 150-1).

Psychologically, as with the oracles, all that counsellors and advisors were often asked to provide was at bottom no more than reassurance. Should I marry this person? There is no right answer. If it goes wrong, there is always the possible response that not marrying that person would have turned out even worse.

6. Architects and Planners

The importance of architecture in the ancient world may perhaps best be judged by the extent of the resources the ancients ploughed into their buildings and, judging by what is left, both the quality and the quantity of them. The stories associated with Imhotep are so many and various that it is difficult to sift fact from fiction, and his later identification with Asclepius points towards a formidable reputation for healing. However, if it is also true that he was the designer of the step pyramid at Saqqara, then he was also a giant in the world of architecture. Because they sought to immortalize themselves in the buildings (and the inscriptions) they left behind, the pharaohs of Egypt were keen builders, and only the most important buildings were constructed of stone. Architects therefore frequently found themselves close to the centre of power. In Mesopotamia, there is evidence that wisdom was attributed to those who were involved in the construction of buildings (Sweet 1990a, pp. 58-9). Those identified as such appear to be the craftsmen and architects. The term *ummanu* applied to a craftsman [5.3] is also that sometimes used more generically for a sage. It has been noted [4.5] that Bezalel and Aholiab, the builders of

Israel's Tabernacle were credited with wisdom. To them might be added the name of Hiram from Tyre who produced the extensive bronze features of Solomon's temple in Jerusalem, and who was 'full of wisdom, understanding, and skill, for making any work in bronze' (1 Kings 7:14).

While for much of the ancient world we have to surmise what people thought about architecture from the physical remains, there is one notable exception. *The Ten Books of Architecture* by Marcus Vitruvius Pollio (first century BC) is a complete surviving systematic treatise on the subject, a subject he interprets very broadly (Vitruvius 1960). Here are not only instructions on how to design a building, but also where to locate it, how to build it, how to decorate it, and so on. It is with a clear sense of pride that Vitruvius begins his treatment of his subject with the following words (I.1.1,3):

> The architect should be equipped with knowledge of many branches of study and varied kinds of learning, for it is by his judgement that all work done by the other arts is put to test ... Neither natural ability without instruction nor instruction without natural ability can make the perfect artist. Let him be educated, skilful with the pencil, instructed in geometry, know much history, have followed the philosophers with attention, understand music, have some knowledge of medicine, know the questions of the jurists, and be acquainted with astronomy and the theory of the heavens. (Vitruvius 1960, pp. 5-6)

Why is such a wide range of expertise and such extensive knowledge required? Vitruvius goes on to explain. A good education is required so that the architect can write well about the subject. The ability to draw well, incorporating a knowledge of geometry, needs little explanation or justification. (Vitruvius notes that a knowledge of arithmetic is also useful when it comes to quantity surveying.) The requirement for a knowledge of history is more a requirement of a knowledge of the history of architecture than a knowledge of history as such. A knowledge of the history of architecture gives insight into how architectural traditions have evolved and why. This makes it possible to not only work with them but also to explain them (I.1.7).

> As for philosophy, it makes an architect high-minded and not self-assuming, but rather makes him courteous, just and honest without avariciousness. This is very important, for no work can be rightly done without honesty and incorruptibility. (Vitruvius 1960, p. 8)

In other words, the point and the value of philosophy is that it produces people of good character. An understanding of music, with its theoretical principles substantially shaped by Pythagoreanism, brings with it a knowledge of mathematics. Furthermore (I.1.8), a knowledge of music enables the architect to 'tune ballistae, catapultae, and scorpiones to the proper key' (Vitruvius 1960, p. 8). 'Ballistae, catapultes and scorpiones' are all mechanical weapons that throw things. They do so by putting 'strings of twisted sinew' under tension. The correct tension seems to be established in the same way that the correct tension in the strings of a lyre is established, by listening to the sounds produced. This is a useful reminder of the fact that the defences of a city were a key element in its design, and that architects were expected to have a knowledge of weaponry.

A knowledge of medicine is needed in order that buildings are constructed only in healthy locations. A knowledge of law covers both land law and building regulations, and again needs little by way of justification or explanation. A knowledge of astronomy and the heavens is required for a very mundane purpose: so that the architect can design and construct sundials.

Having outlined the requirements of the architect, Vitruvius then (I.2) goes on to explain the basic principles of architecture. These are order, arrangement, eurhythmy, symmetry, propriety and economy. In fact, these all feed into and are difficult to distinguish from each other. Order, arrangement, eurhythmy and symmetry and propriety might all be characterized as different aspects of, or different ways of thinking about, architectural harmony. They are all concerned, in one way or another, with ensuring that a building is properly proportioned and unified in conception. Economy is not directly about harmony but about the very practical problems posed by actually constructing a building. But even here there is an indirect sense of harmony. An architect should not design a building that cannot be constructed from materials that are not easily available, and what is easily available depends on where the building is to be constructed. This might be seen as a requirement that a building such be materially in harmony with its environment as well as aesthetically.

It might be suggested that the architect is not only concerned with order in the narrow sense, 'an adjustment according to quantity', as Vitruvius (I.2.2) puts it (Vitruvius 1960, p. 13), but also with order in a wider sense. In that sense, order is not simply part of harmony, but harmony itself is order, and the wisdom of the architect relates to this particular kind of order. But there is more to it than that. It is less apparent in Greece and Rome, but in Mesopotamia and Israel (at least) there was a strong sense that the order embodied in architecture was in some sense a reflection of a higher order. Some of the works that have been written on this topic are undoubtedly fanciful and perhaps owe more to imagination than information. However, they are not the sole occupants of the field.

There are two themes to be considered here. The first is where human architecture is a kind of replica of divine architecture, or guided by divine command. and the second is where human architecture is understood as some kind of macrocosm of the universe. A classic case of the former can be found in the vision of Ezekiel (40ff.) where he is shown a temple. The vision goes into great detail, and the only credible reason for going into so much detail, including precise measurements, would appear to be that this

134

is a 'model' for a temple that is to be built. The vision of Ezekiel has its precedent in Exodus (24ff.) where Moses is given equally precise instructions on how to construct the tabernacle. Although less detailed, the vision of the new Jerusalem related by John in Revelation (21) is also clearly intended to convey something that is, or will be, real, rather than a pure fantasy.

> We see in both the Old and New Testament passages an important pattern, according to which the prophet is given a shaman-like vision on a mountain both prior to building the temple (where he views the heavenly model in order to transfer its architecture to the earth), and (as in the case of Ezekiel and John), where he views either the temple or the heavenly temple-city prior to their *restoration* to the earth at the end of time. (Lundquist 1993, p. 11)

Something similar can be seen in Mesopotamia with regard to the Esagila, the principal temple of Marduk in Babylon. The original temple was said to have been built on Marduk's orders by the gods themselves, taking as their model Esharra, the home of the gods. It thus occupied an ambiguous status, or, to put it another way, it served as a meeting point between two realms (Ascalone 2005, p. 335).

With the Egyptians, Greeks and Romans the picture may be a little different, but perhaps the differences are not as significant as might at first appear. It seems clear that they regarded their temples as the *homes* of the gods to whom they were dedicated. As such, even if they were not *modelled* on divine prototypes, they nevertheless had to be regarded as homes that were *fit for* gods. Indeed, it is not clear that divine prototypes existed. Apart from stories about Mount Olympus (which may have been relatively late) there does not seem to have been a very clear idea about where many gods lived when they were not in their temples.

The idea that the temple was a microcosm is better evidenced in the East than in the West. However, the idea that the *city* was a microcosm can be found at the very heart of the West:

> Romulus founded the city of Rome by ploughing a circular furrow around the Palatine Hill. This circle was called the world (*mundus*) and was divided into four quarters like the cosmos. In historical times this legendary action was repeated at the foundation of every new Roman city, when a priest, or augur, would draw a circle on the ground and quarter it with lines running to the four points of the compass. (Humphrey and Vitebsky 1997, p. 13)

In Mesopotamia, as perhaps might be expected given its understanding of the nature of kingship, the physical distance between and separation of the temple and the palace diminished and disappeared over time so that:

> in the Assyrian and neo-Babylonian Empires, the temple was structurally integrated with the palace. On the one hand, such a step served to enhance

the majesty of the king. On the other hand, it symbolized, through architecture, the subordination of sacred activities to secular control. (Bertman 2003, p. 192)

It clearly suited the purposes of kings to blur the distinction between the gods and themselves and, in any event, a temple might be regarded as simply a palace for a god, which might in turn suggest that a palace was a temple for a king. Some of the constructions of the pharaohs showed a similar development. While the great temple built by Ramesses II at Abu Simbel was also technically dedicated to Amun, Re and Ptah, above all it was dedicated to Ramesses himself, as is evidenced by the colossal images of the pharaoh, not of the gods, that greet those who approach it. On the basis that far more temples appear to have been built in Egypt than could ever remotely have been needed, it seems reasonable to conclude that there was an element of excessive egotism if not megalomania in the construction projects of many pharaohs. Architecture was an important vehicle for royal self-promotion, which was doubtless one of the reasons for the importance of the architect.

It has already been noted that for Vitruvius architecture extended well beyond what might be regarded as the remit of the architect today. It may therefore be appropriate to say something here about the people who would today be regarded as planners. The names of most have long since been forgotten, but the name of one stands out, that of Hippodamus of Miletus (fifth century BC). Hippodamus was credited with inventing the grid system for laying out a city. He developed plans for Piraeus, the port of Athens, Thurium in Italy, and a number of others. Some came to regard him as a Pythagorean, although it is not apparent that he actually was. Nevertheless, his approach to town planning seems to have incorporated principles of number and harmony that made an association with Pythagoreanism both natural and credible. From what Aristotle says about him in *Politics* (1267b-68b), it is apparent that an interest in town planning but was but part of a wider interest:

He also aspired to understand nature as a whole, and was the first person, not actually engaged in politics, to attempt to say something about the best constitution. (Aristotle 1998, p. 45)

In other words, perhaps, the physical order of the city was only one particular element of the social order, and it seems clear that the ultimate aim of Hippodamus was to design a city where its physical design supported, encouraged and manifested its political arrangements. And the physical design, if the purported associations with Pythagoreanism reflect an important truth, might have in some way replicated the 'natural' order of things as manifested in mathematics. But that is admittedly speculative.

In the end, given the importance of architects and architecture, it is perhaps surprising that the names of so few have survived. But as Sir Thomas Browne put it in his 'Hydriotaphia', 'Herostratus lives that burnt the temple of Diana, he is almost lost that built it' (Browne 1965, p. 135). A number of architects managed to leave memorials to themselves, but far more have vanished without trace.

7. Scientists and Science

The topic of science has already been touched on obliquely in a number of ways. It is possible to regard Thales [1.2, 4.10] as working in the field of science as much as, or as well as, the field of philosophy, and the level of astronomical knowledge that was achieved in Mesopotamia seems to have taken it beyond the mere collection of data [6.4]. The kind of architect that Vitruvius [5.6] had in mind had to have a widespread practical knowledge of scientific matters. The ancient Egyptians had a system of mathematics. How much of the theoretical underpinnings were understood by the various practitioners of early technologies is not known, or how much of the technologies themselves were the product of nothing more sophisticated than trial and error.

Because professions were often hereditary in the ancient world, the creation of new professions was often anything but straightforward. However, parallel to the 'professions' were looser 'roles'. In ancient Greece, at least, the proliferation of Seven Sages suggests that the 'wise man' was recognized as a kind of role, and one that was moreover never apparently perceived as hereditary. There is evidence (Lloyd 1989, pp. 83-90) of 'wisdom contests' in ancient Greece and elsewhere. In Greece these seem to have paralleled poetry contests and drama contests, as well as the better known games. Given the close connection between poetry and wisdom in ancient Greek thought, and given that some early philosophers chose poetry rather than prose as their preferred literary vehicle, it seems at least possible that the 'wisdom contests' may have developed out of poetry ones, since poetry could be the form at the same time that philosophy was the content. Interestingly, one of the pieces of evidence for poetry contests comes from Hesiod. In *Works and Days* (ll. 650-8) he proclaims:

> ... As for me, I crossed
> To Chalcis, to wise Amphidamas' games:
> The great-souled hero's children had arranged
> For many contests, advertised abroad.
> And there, I say, I conquered with a song
>
> (Hesiod 1973, p. 80)

The significance of the attribution of wisdom to Amphidamas in this context is suggestive, but probably not strong enough to support anything more than speculation.

On the wider point, Lloyd suggests that the notion of the 'wise man' was 'one that was flexible enough to *permit* innovation', and so 'afforded some of the early cosmologists a category within which to work' (Lloyd 1989, p. 87). The extent to which 'a category within which to work' was actually *needed* is debatable. It is not clear that the early philosophers were anything but intelligent people with time on their hands thanks to the fact that Greek society made extensive use of slavery. On the other hand, respect for tradition in the ancient world meant that 'knowledge' and 'innovation' were frequently in tension with each other. When professional knowledge is being passed on, the point is to acquire it, not to challenge it. This is evident in the conservatism of the Egyptian approach to the education of the scribe. Seen in this perspective, it may be relevant that Thales is said to have travelled widely, including to Egypt. The importation of knowledge from cultures recognized as ancient ones might have been regarded as an acceptable form of 'innovation'.

Whatever the origins, it is apparent that in certain areas of thought and activity, new ways of thinking developed, such that certain areas of thought and activity became more recognizable (to us) as scientific in nature. This did not happen all at once, it did not happen in all areas, and new ways did not always drive out old ways. However:

> implicitly or explicitly, the investigators into nature laid claim to a new kind of wisdom, a wisdom that purported to yield superior enlightenment, even superior practical effectiveness ... They were wise men of a different kind, unlike the old seers in important respects, though again much closer to them in others than aspects of the self-image they projected would lead one to expect. They successfully demystified many a mythical, mystical, symbolic, or traditional assumption. For all that, the science they presented was, in some cases, no more than the myth of the elite that produced it. (Lloyd 1989, p. 49)

The story told about Thales and his prediction of a solar eclipse [4.10] indicates a degree of sophistication with regard to the use astronomical data, while the speculations of atomists such as Democritus [4.13] point to sophistication in a different direction. Rather than attempt to look at many different areas of science, I shall proceed in the next section to consider one example, medicine.

8. Healers and Healing

Although this section is in some ways a case study in the development of science as a form of wisdom in the ancient world, the world of healers and healing was a very diverse one and although what we would now regard as science made serious inroads into it, it never established sole control. And before considering the development of Greek scientific medicine, it is necessary to go back to an earlier age and other cultures in order to appreciate the full complexity and diversity of this important area of practice.

Mention has already been made [5.4] of the *ashipu* and *asu* who practised medicine in Mesopotamia, but from different perspectives. A somewhat similar situation seems to have prevailed in Egypt, which has been described as having a:

> three-pronged approach to healing ... It consists of a combination of magical spells, rituals and practical prescriptions, all of which would have been considered equally essential to the recovery of the patient. (Shaw and Nicholson 1995, p. 177).

A figure recognizable as a physician, the *sinw* or *sunu*, existed in Egypt before the middle of the third millennium BC. The earliest mentions of such a figure date to the Third Dynasty (2686-2613 BC), which is also the time of Imhotep. That may not be coincidental, given the strong connection the Egyptians made between Imhotep and medicine. Ancient Egypt also had its surgeons, who were the priests of Sekhmet, a lion-headed goddess associated with healing. Like many deities, she was an ambivalent figure. While she was sought as a healer, she was also feared as a bringer of disease. The celebrated second century AD Greek physician Galen tells of medical archives housed in temples at Memphis, a logical place for them if healing is associated with the divine. Indeed, the temple seems to have become increasingly the repository of learning of all kinds in Egypt. The significance of the pulse was understood, but although it was believed that the blood circulated around the body, it was also believed that other bodily fluids did the same. The Berlin Papyrus (from the middle of the second millennium BC) describes a pregnancy test. The medicinal effects of many substances were known, including honey and garlic. A number of medical tracts have survived, and it is known that many more have been lost. Probably the oldest medical work ever found was that unearthed at the site of the Sumerian city of Nippur, which contained a number of remedies. The library of Ashurbanipal at Nineveh was home to over eight hundred clay tablets containing the accumulated medical wisdom of Mesopotamia.

From this brief background, it is apparent that Greek medicine did not appear out of nowhere, but that the ancient world had a great deal of medical knowledge from many different sources to draw on, although not all was equally reliable and not all was equally scientific. The emergence of scientific medicine in Greece is intrinsically linked with the name of Hippocrates [2.2d]. There is little doubt as to his actual historicity. He came from Cos and was born in around 460 BC. He was evidently a successful physician who taught medicine to others. However, far more works became ascribed to him than are believed to have been by him. Consequently the body of writings known collectively as the Hippocratic Corpus is doubtless the work of many hands, and it is unclear what is to be attributed to the hand of Hippocrates himself and what is not. Consequently, the precise contribution of Hippocrates to the history of medicine remains a matter of dispute. The matter is complicated by the fact that there are internal tensions within the Hippocratic Corpus such that it would be misleading to suggest that it collectively articulates a single point of view. On the other hand, it would be fair to suggest that collectively the writings do seek to move medicine in a particular direction, although not without resistance. The anonymous author of a text sometimes known as 'The Science of Medicine' and sometimes as 'The Art of Medicine' describes the general position thus:

> First of all, I would define medicine as the complete removal of all distress of the sick, the alleviation of the more violent diseases, and the refusal to undertake to cure cases in which the disease has already won the mastery, knowing that everything is not possible to medicine. It is my intention to prove that medicine does accomplish these things and is every capable of doing them. (Lloyd 1978, p. 140)

The same argument is repeated over and over again throughout the text: when a physician cures someone, luck has nothing to do with it. Although different anonymous authors take different lines in a variety of ways, there is a consistent underlying message: medicine works because it is underpinned by fundamental principles. It may not always be obvious what these are, and there may be disagreement as to how many there are, and 'medicine' has to include every dimension of therapeutic intervention. This meant such factors as diet, for example, in addition to pharmacology. Another Hippocratic text, 'The Sacred Disease' discusses epilepsy, and contrasts the soundness and scientific nature of the medical approach to it with the bogus claims and dubious practices of those who approach it from a magical or religious point of view, with their supposed cures 'consisting merely of ritual purification and incantation' (Lloyd 1978, p. 237).

As Greek medicine developed it interacted with philosophy in a variety of ways. In particular, there was a divergence between the more speculative and the more sceptical approaches. The Empiricist school, which emerged in the third century BC, generally frowned upon theoretical speculation and sought to restrict itself to observation and induction. The Methodist school, which developed a little later, also laid a strong emphasis on the importance of observation. What the Empiricists and Methodists brought to the science of medicine was a new stage and level of reflectivity, where the very assumptions of the science were questioned and the proper limits of the science were reconsidered. This might also be seen as part of the process whereby the profession of medicine sought to clarify its own identity and the practice of medicine sought to more accurately locate itself within the division of labour pertaining to wisdom in the ancient world.

As a footnote to this discussion, and a link to the next, a text has survived that purports to have been written by Thessalus of Tralles (first century AD) to the emperor Nero (AD 37-68). The real Thessalus was a celebrated physician and one of the founders of the Methodist school. The text attributed to him may have been written some centuries after his death (Ogden 2002, pp. 52-4). In it he described a journey to Egypt during which he visited Thebes. There one of the priests arranged for him to have a vision of Asclepius in order that he might augment his medical knowledge. The idea that certain kinds of knowledge need to be revealed to humans by the gods was a theme running across the ancient world and has already been noted many times. Epistemology and mythology were closely linked in a variety of ways. Human knowledge is often presented as a fragment of divine wisdom.

9. Magic and Magicians

Magic differs from divination in that divination is concerned with seeking to obtain information or advice, whereas magic is concerned with influencing the course of events. The two often went together in the ancient world. In Mesopotamia it seems to have been clearly understood that omens revealed what might happen, not what must happen, and magic was the means whereby what was foretold by a bad omen might be averted. The need to use magic, as opposed to more mundane means, derived from the fact that the unfolding of events was understood as dictated by the will of the gods. Magic was a means whereby the gods were approached with a view to them changing their minds. The principal responsibility for such matters fell to the *mashmashu*, a priest with special responsibilities for magic. He it was who knew the correct incantations and rituals to counteract whatever bad omens had occurred. The extent to which such procedures were thought to *compel* the gods to change their minds is unclear. There is little concrete evidence concerning the religious views of the ordinary people in Mesopotamia, but it seems clear that magic was closely associated with wisdom: 'Generally "wisdom" refers to skill in cult and magic lore, and the wise man is the initiate' (Lambert 1996, p. 1).

As well as the gods, magic could also be used with regard to demons, and here the boundary between magic and exorcism is often difficult to establish with accuracy, as is the boundary between exorcism and healing. There was a highly developed demonology in Mesopotamia. Some demons were of divine origin, some were ghosts, and some were creatures of the underworld. They could take on all shapes and sizes, could move very quickly, and were extremely cunning. On the other hand, they also seem to have been quite gullible and even stupid, going by the ease with which they could apparently be outfoxed by a competent *mashmashu*.

In Egypt, magic was also a longstanding and widespread practice. As in Mesopotamia, it went hand in hand with religion, and the person especially connected with it was known as a lector-priest. It was his primary responsibility to recite spells, but he might also be able to interpret dreams or charm scorpions. Although an official of the temple, it seems likely that the lector-priest also carried out some of his duties outside the temple, so providing a link between temple and community. Another important personage seems to have been the *Sau*, and there is evidence of both men and women occupying this role. An important function of the *Sau* seems to have involved amulets, whether making them or in some way empowering them once they had been made. Although the use of amulets was by no means restricted to ancient Egypt, they were particularly popular there. Although they might be used in a variety of contexts, they had one basic function, which was to protect. The deity most connected with magic was Heka, who seems to have been a very ancient god, although no major temples ever appear to have been built to him. Inscriptions dating to the period of Roman rule in Egypt describe him as 'Lord of Oracles, Lord of Miracles' (Oakes and Gahlin 2007, p. 441), while a preserved hymn to him 'manifestly identifies Heka as the power behind crops, the producer and nourisher of all vegetation' (Frankfurter 1998, p. 39). As with Maat and *maat*, Heka is also understood as *heka*, as an impersonal power as well as the personification of it.

Egypt evidently had a longstanding reputation as a place of wisdom, learning and magic in the ancient world, and many stories are told of journeys made there by those wishing to learn its secrets. The extent to which Egypt was genuinely the source of practices elsewhere is unclear and unfathomable, but whatever the facts, its reputation remained intact for centuries. That magic was practised elsewhere is manifest. In *Republic* (364b-c) Plato gives a caustic account of some of the practices and practitioners of his time:

> Begging priests and prophets frequent the doors of the rich and persuade them that they posses a god-given power founded on sacrifices and incantations. If the rich person or any of his ancestors has committed an injustice, they can fix it with pleasant rituals. Moreover, if he wishes to injure some enemy, then at little expense, he'll be able to harm just and unjust alike, for by means of spells and enchantments they can persuade the gods to serve them. (Plato 1992, p. 39)

While the evidence from Mesopotamia and Egypt is overwhelmingly of magic being used to ward off evil or effect cures, Plato makes it clear that there was another dimension to it, whereby it could be used to bring about harm as well as good. To some extent, this ambivalence is built into the very fabric of magic. If events unfold according to, or at least influenced by, the will of the gods, then if people can 'persuade the gods to serve them', they may be able to guide events in the direction of their choice. It has already been noted [5.8] that the Egyptian goddess Sekhmet was associated with both the bringing of disease and the healing of it, and it has also been noted [5.9] that Apollo was the Greek god associated with both pollution and purification. Because the gods of the polytheistic religions of the ancient world were understood to often be in contention with each other, and in some ways no better than humans (although more powerful), there was in principle nothing to prevent gods being invoked to support bad causes as well as good ones. It is notable that the society that seems to have first and most decisively moved against magic in the ancient world was that of Israel. It may be recalled [4.5] that King Saul 'put the mediums and the wizards out of the land' (I Samuel 28:3). It is difficult to believe that such a move was unconnected with the simultaneous move towards monotheism.

A variety of magical characters and personages roam the pages of Greek and Latin literature. While some of the works doubtless contain a substantial degree of fiction, it is unlikely that what is recorded even in those pages falls so far outside everyday experience as to be incomprehensible. The love potion, for example, that features in a number of myths and centuries later became a useful item in the toolbox of librettists, was clearly taken seriously in works purporting to be factual. According to Suetonius (*Caligula* 50), Caligula 'is believed to have been given a love potion by his wife Caesonia, but it turned him mad' (Ogden 2002, p. 105). A number of manuscripts and fragments have survived indicating a widespread belief that members of the opposite (or sometimes the same) sex could be attracted by means of magic, with the required paraphernalia included such diverse objects as mussel shells, bats' eyes, lamps and apples (Ogden 2002, pp. 233-6).

In itself, the idea that chemicals can be used to bring about changes in people is unexceptional. The effects of poisons and intoxicants have doubtless been known since well before the beginnings of recorded history. It seems likely that the attribution of the effects of some substances to 'magic' betrays little more than an ignorance of the wholly natural ways in which those substances work. In many cases there may have been a magical dimension to what was done (incantations, spells, etc.) that in fact made no difference whatsoever to the outcome. The recognition of that fact was one of the things that made the gradual separation of medicine from magic possible.

10. Conclusion

A number of practices and practitioners have been examined in this chapter that all, in one way or another, fit into a multi-faceted picture of wisdom in the ancient world. More could have been mentioned: no place has been found here, for example, for the philosophers and sophists, the educators of the Greco-Roman world for centuries. However, these particular purveyors of wisdom have been adequately dealt with elsewhere [4.10-18]. Poets and musicians might also have been mentioned, but they have also been touched on, although more lightly, elsewhere [4.8]. Priests and practitioners of theurgy might also find a home here. Priests too have appeared on occasion elsewhere, while theurgy will be considered where the *Chaldaean Oracles* are discussed [6.8]. It seems apparent from the evidence that all of the people and practices discussed here were widely associated with wisdom across the ancient world. In some cases the reasons are easier to see than in others.

I have suggested [1.2] that the idea that most helpfully binds together ancient perspectives on wisdom is that of order. If that is the case, then again it is easier to see in some cases than it is in others. However, the picture may become a little clearer if the idea of order is understood in a more dynamic and less static way. The fact that the Egyptian god most associated with magic seems to have been Heka is instructive in the regard. As power, Heka/*heka* guides the unfolding of events in the natural world. That power does not operate randomly, any more than *logos* does [4.12]. There is an order to how events unfold, just as there is an order of how things are. There does seem to have been some tension widely felt across the ancient world as to the extent to which fate was simply the whim of the gods and the extent to which it was stable and trustworthy. Ideas about wisdom perhaps reflect this tension. On the one hand, divinatory practices were concerned with ascertaining what the gods had in mind, on the other the development of science across the ancient world, in a fragmented and often primitive way, began to reveal the possibility that the world had an order of its own that perhaps the gods had nothing to do with, or were even part of.

It may be recalled that the ancient Egyptians had a 'three-pronged approach to healing' and that all the prongs 'would have been considered equally essential to the recovery of the patient' (Shaw and Nicholson 1995, p. 177). That picture is probably generally true of the practice of medicine across the ancient world for centuries. However, that does not mean that all of these prongs were regarded as of equal value everywhere all the time. Scientific medicine, it might be argued, emerged in part because it was discovered that some of the prongs were more important than others, and presumably the making of that discovery went hand in hand with the realization that certain supposed causes of disease were more influential than others. It could only have been when there was confidence that gods were not *causing* diseases that the incantation element of the *cure* could be safely dropped. If wisdom is a virtue connected with order, then as understandings of the basis of order changed it would be only natural for understandings of wisdom was to change too.

Wisdom Literature

1. Introduction

In an often quoted passage that introduces his book on Babylonian wisdom literature, W.G. Lambert writes:

> 'Wisdom' is strictly a misnomer as applied to Babylonian literature. As used for a literary genre the term belongs to Hebraic studies and is applied to Job, Proverbs, and Ecclesiastes. Here 'wisdom' is a common topic and is extolled as the greatest virtue. While it embraces intellectual ability the emphasis is more on pious living: the wise man fears the Lord ... Babylonian has a term 'wisdom' (*nemequ*), and several adjectives for 'wise' (*enqu, mudu, hassu, etpesu*), but only rarely are they used with a moral context ... . Though this term is thus foreign to ancient Mesopotamia, it has been used for a group of texts which correspond in subject-matter with the Hebrew Wisdom books, and may be retained as a convenient short description. The sphere of these texts is what has been called philosophy since Greek times ... . Some of the works deal with ethics: practical advice on living, others with intellectual problems inherent in the then current outlook on life. Other types of literature not so intimately revealing thought patterns are included because they are conventionally classed as 'Wisdom': fables, popular sayings and proverbs. (Lambert 1996, p. 1)

Although I find myself in substantial disagreement with it, the passage provides a useful starting point. I suggested at the beginning of this book [1.2] that although many discussions of wisdom in the ancient world begin with wisdom literature (and often go no further), I afford it a position of less importance. Lambert also points to a problem that besets the discussion of ancient wisdom literature. The Bible is taken as a starting point, the genre is defined by reference to it, and other works are accepted or rejected as works of wisdom literature on the basis of it. This seems doubly mistaken. First, the idea that Job, Proverbs and Ecclesiastes form a self-evident coherent genre is itself highly problematic. One book is a narrative, the second a collection of sayings, the third an essay. Secondly, there is no obvious reason why the Hebrew understanding of wisdom should be seen as authoritative. It was at best one understanding among many, and there is no reason to believe that it was either the earliest or the most important. Two paths are indicated, one follows the line of vocabulary, the other the line of theme. One path says that wisdom literature is literature that explicitly mentions or discusses 'wisdom', whatever that term might mean in the particular context, the other that wisdom literature is literature that addresses 'wisdom-related topics', whether or not the term 'wisdom' is actually used. As will be seen, I have taken a path that falls between or combines the two. While the use of the term 'wisdom' is obviously a useful indicator, it is not the only one. Furthermore, as with any genre, there will always be grey areas around the edges where opinions may differ. My aim here is to reveal both continuities and variety.

2. Mesopotamia

As long as what might be called the sub-genres of wisdom literature to be found in the Bible are not taken to be exhaustive, there is no objection to taking them as useful and familiar starting points. Perhaps the most obvious starting point is the book of Proverbs, as the proverb appears to have been a widespread currency in the ancient world.

The Sumerians were evidently fond of proverbs and assembled a number of collections of them. The earliest known Mesopotamian proverbs date back to the first half of the third millennium BC. However, the collections that have been discovered tend to contain not only proverbs but also anecdotes, witticisms, poems and so on. For example, the work known as 'The Instructions of Shuruppak to his son Ziusudra' is described by its editor and translator as a 'Sumerian proverb collection' (Alster 1974, p. 7), but on closer inspection the claim appears to be an exaggerated one. Although some lines can be construed as containing proverbial wisdom, others cannot. 'Love maintains a family, hatred destroys a family' (Alster 1974, p. 17) may pass muster as a proverb, but 'Do not steal anything, do not kill yourself!' (Alster 1974, p. 37) just sounds like good advice. Whether or not there ever actually was a king called Shuruppak, the attribution of the work to him is presumed to be a literary fiction, designed to enhance the work's authority. However, the work makes the point over and over again that it is meant to be a father's instructions to his son, and that is a fair characterization of how it reads. While there may be a liberal sprinkling of proverbs throughout the work, it is not simply a collection of them. Although the 'instruction' sub-genre and the 'proverb' sub-genre of wisdom literature may overlap, it is unhelpful to confuse the one with the other.

Because instruction literature is intended as a guide to getting on in the world, works belonging to this sub-genre tend to tell us quite a lot about the times and places in which they were written. The same is true, although perhaps to a slightly lesser extent, of proverbs.

> The dominant imagery of the Sumerian proverbs reflects agriculture and animal husbandry, a life-style which formed the basis of Sumerian culture ... Sumerian proverbs reflect many of the jobs and occupations within the society ... Other concerns include a women's [*sic*] daily routine, family

146

relationships, good and bad manners, the good man, the liar, legal proceedings, Fate, the temples and their gods, as well as historical and ethnic allusions. (Alster 1997, p. xxiii)

Another work that incorporates proverbs is the one sometimes known as 'Wisdom of Ahiqar' (Pritchard 1969, pp. 427-30) which is set in the time of the Assyrian king Esarhaddon. Ahiqar (or Ahikar) is depicted as an old man, a scribe, and former high official. Part of the text is a narrative concerning the relations between the king and the scribe, but a large part is given over to Ahiqar's sayings, fables, reflections on wisdom, and so on. It is a matter of speculation as to how far the narrative is simply an excuse for bringing the rest of the contents of the work together. Because the oldest surviving text of Ahiqar was found in Egypt it is sometimes considered as a work of Egyptian literature, although it was written in Aramaic. The character of Ahiqar was also known to the author of the book of Tobit, suggesting a considerable international reputation and circulation.

Writing about biblical wisdom literature, Katherine Dell observes:

> When we examine the material from the cultures of the ancient Near East, we find that Proverbs appears to have most in common with Egyptian wisdom and some Semitic wisdom, such as the Wisdom of Ahikar, and we find that Job and Ecclesiastes tend to have more in common with Mesopotamian genres. (Dell 2000, p. 98)

A Mesopotamian work with which Job is often compared is 'Ludlul bel nemeqi'. The poem tells of a man who for no obvious reason has suffered appallingly, but who is finally rescued from his sufferings by Marduk, the god of wisdom. A similar theme appears in the work often known as the 'Sumerian Job' (late third millennium BC?) where again the theme is of someone who seems to be suffering for no good reason, although he acknowledges that 'A sinless child was never born of its mother' (Beyerlin 1978, p. 141), suggesting that human suffering is never entirely undeserved. Trusting in the gods is the only solution. In the work known as 'The Babylonian Theodicy' suffering is again the subject, but this time there is a debate between two people as to its nature and origin. Both parties to the dialogue are described as wise, and the author identifies himself specifically as an exorcist (Pritchard 1969, p. 601). However, there is no resolution to the dialogue, in the sense of any solution to the problem, other than throwing oneself on the mercy of the gods: 'May the god who has abandoned me give me help' (Pritchard 1969, p. 604).

If we consider what grounds there might be for regarding these works as examples of 'wisdom literature' in the light of what we know about Mesopotamian culture rather than in the light of what we know about biblical wisdom literature, then it seems to me that the notion of order provides the key. Even if two of the works are seen as nothing more than laments, they are nevertheless laments that are set against a certain background of expectations. They are more than simple complaints. There is a sense that suffering can either be deserved or undeserved. In the end it is all in the lap of the gods, but there is an expectation that the gods are not normally fickle or unjust. Their ways may not always be transparent to humanity, but there is a fundamental trust in them. The order they have created is expected to be more than simply an absence of chaos; it is also expected to be an order that is just. The order of the world has a moral as well as a physical dimension, and each of these works of wisdom literature is, in its own way, a meditation upon the nature of this order.

Another type of Mesopotamian literature is sometimes included within the wisdom category, although the reasons for doing so do not seem to be compelling. This is the 'dispute' genre, where two things (generally animals or plants) hold a debate as to which of them is the more valuable. While they may not lack insight, they seem to be devised more as entertainments. The same might be said of some of the fables that are preserved. The fact that a superficially frivolous piece of literature might make a serious point scarcely seems adequate cause to include it within the wisdom genre and I think it is unhelpful to do so.

Brief mention has already been made of the Sumerian word lists [5.3], and it is appropriate to say something more about them here. From as early as the third millennium BC the Sumerians were producing lists of words, the purpose of which has been a matter of some debate. Some have seen them as in some way scientific, or at least proto-scientific:

> Sumerian science lacked the conceptual framework of formulated principles ... and simply ordered nominal expressions one after the other in a one-dimensional fashion, without any kind of elucidation. (Soden 1994, p. 146)

In a sense it could be said that the order *was* 'the conceptual framework'. Similarly, lists of kings were produced where the order of the names on the list reproduced the historical order of the kings. Here no further 'elucidation' was presumably necessary: the first on the list was the earliest in time. In due course, Mesopotamian culture became bilingual, with Sumerian retained alongside other languages. This led to the production of lists with equivalent terms in other languages put alongside the Sumerian one. Such works were perhaps better understood as dictionaries rather than as having any theoretical import. But in a script that is not alphabetical, some other system of arranging terms is necessary, otherwise what will be produced will be just a *collection* of terms. Such a system, or at least the foundations of one, can be seen in the determinative signs that cuneiform acquired at some point in its development. Although there never seem to have been a large number of them, they could be seen as articulating a very basic system of categories which included 'man', 'god', 'wood' and so on (Bienkowski and Millard 2000, p. 85). The extent to which problems posed by writing actually led to the development of conceptual categories is unclear. Once they existed, the determinative signs provided a basic structure that more sophisticated attempts to make sense of the world could build on. According to Soden:

> The purpose of the topically ordered, monolingual Neo-Sumerian lists was not to present ideas of the cosmic order, but rather to depict inventory rolls according to the main categories in the world of objects and living creatures. (Soden 1994, p. 151)

However, the very purpose of a category is to serve as the basis for a way or ordering things. The use of determinative signs meant that what was perceived as the natural order of things (as reflected or embodied in the categories employed in conceptual thought) was reproduced or recreated in the written order of things, a phenomenon that is entirely absent from cultures employing alphabetical writing. If wisdom is intrinsically linked with order, then the Sumerian lists could qualify as a kind of wisdom literature. And if by 'wisdom literature' we mean simply written works that are concerned with wisdom, then the collections of omens could be regarded as equally well qualified, perhaps. It rather depends upon how much is expected of 'wisdom literature' other than it being in some way about wisdom. Collections of omens do not discuss wisdom, but by laying out before the reader the order of the world, they have clear connections with it.

3. Egypt

It is common to identify two genres of Egyptian literature as sub-genres of wisdom literature, and these are the 'instruction' and the 'lament'. 'Instruction' here is a translation of the Egyptian word *seboyet*. Two things may be noted concerning the Egyptian word. First, Martin Bernal has argued (1991, p. 458) that *seboyet* is the origin of the Greek word *sophia*, suggesting a very real connection between the 'instruction' and wisdom literature. Secondly, however, Alan Gardiner (1947, p. 5) has pointed out that *seboyet* can stand for instruction in quite a broad sense and its usage is not limited to the genre of literature to which it is routinely attached. For example, the 'Onomasticon of Amenope' discussed earlier [4.2] identifies itself as a work 'for instruction of the ignorant', but it is very different from the kind of work normally associated with the 'instruction' genre. However, if we see in the 'Onomasticon of Amenope' a parallel to the Sumerian word lists, and if we assign the Sumerian word lists a place within the literature of wisdom, then the extension of the genre of instruction to cover the work of Amenope might be seen as entirely justified.

A number of instruction works have survived either in their entirety or in part. This survival rate is connected with the fact that they were frequently copied as part of a scribe's training. Because of the tendency to attribute these works to notable personages of an earlier time and because they were copied for century after century, it is often difficult to identify with precision the period in which they originated. However, although it may not have been written by him, it is generally agreed that the work attributed to Ptahhotep can be dated to the Old Kingdom, while the latest examples of the genre may have been produced during the second century BC. This means that they may have been written at a time when Egyptian had been exposed to Greek philosophy, and some see clear evidence of influence from that direction (Lichtheim 1983).

The identification of a work as a piece of instruction literature is generally a matter of self-identification. The early work attributed to Ptahhotep begins, 'The instruction of the superintendent of the capital, the vizier, Ptahhotep' (Kaster 1970, p. 166, slightly amended), while the much later (second century BC?) 'Instruction of Ankhsheshonqy' declares, 'This is the instruction which the divine father Ankhsheshonqy ... wrote for his son' (Lichtheim 1983, pp. 69-70). Different scholars have tended to emphasize either the continuities or discontinuities in the history of Egyptian instruction literature, and both exist. Pharaonic Egypt was a deeply conservative state, and the principle of *maat* was essentially one of a static rather than a dynamic order. If instruction literature was concerned with passing on advice of how to live and prosper in the world, and if that world changed very little, then it is to be expected that the advice would also change very little. On the other hand, there were foreign invasions, there were shifts of power, different social classes had different perspectives on the world, and even if the general Egyptian worldview changed very slowly, it would be a gross exaggeration to say that it did not change at all.

Early instruction literature was attributed to, where it was not actually written by, high officials and pharaohs. Since in the Old Kingdom the high officials were more often than not members of the royal family, the literature reflects the outlook of a small social elite that was close to, if not actually occupying, the centre of power. Three of the earliest surviving works are those attributed to Ptahhotep, Hardejedef and Kagemni, although only the first of these survives in its entirety. Nevertheless they all seem to have the same purpose, and in each one a high official wishes to pass on his learning to his child or children. In Ptahhotep there is a short narrative at the beginning explaining that in his old age Ptahhotep wished to lay down the burden of high office and be succeeded by his son. At the end of Kagemni, a son also succeeds his father as vizier, but it is made clear that what is passed on is more than simply professional advice: 'The vizier had his sons and his daughters called, when he completed his writings on the ways of mankind and on their character as encountered by him' (Kaster 1970, p. 17). Much of Kagemni is missing, and what remains has no particular bearing on preparation for high office. In Ptahhotep there is a mixture of the general and the particular, of life in general and the life of a high official. Sometimes the two seem to be brought closely together:

150

6. Wisdom Literature

'Give out your thoughts in the council of your lord. One ought to say plainly what one knows and what one knows not' (Kaster 1970, p. 169).

Sometimes the advice seems to be strangely impersonal: 'If you are a man of note, who sits in the council of his lord, fix your heart upon what is good' (Kaster 1970, p. 171). Without wishing to make too much of this, it may be that this incorporation of the impersonal reflects the fact that Ptahhotep is concerned to instruct his son 'in the thoughts of those who have gone before' (Kaster 1970, p. 166), and so is passing on advice that he himself was given when younger. In any event, as McKane (1970, p. 10) points out, the search for coherence and unity in instruction literature may be misguided, and different works might best be seen simply as different collections of proverbs, maxims and bits of practical advice. Perhaps there is nothing more, nothing deeper. On the other hand, as Lichtheim (1975, p. 97) observes, works such as Ptahhotep, being relatively early examples of the genre, are also relatively crude compared with some later examples which display greater organization and depth. It is also possible to argue that the purpose of a work of instruction literature itself provides a measure of coherence and unity. If the aim is to provide instruction so that people may live good or successful lives, that sets a limit to what may or may not be regarded as relevant. What looks like (and may indeed be) a loose collection of sayings from one perspective may appear to be a carefully selected set of pieces of good advice from another. Certainly the late (second century BC?) example of the instruction genre to be found in the Papyrus Insinger (by which name it is normally known) is carefully arranged into thematic sections, although some of the sections are more thematically coherent than others. Whether this development is one of natural internal evolution or attributable to external influence is a matter of conjecture (Lichtheim 1983).

If Ptahhotep is a good early example of an instruction work attributed to a high official, then the 'Instruction of Merikare' is a good example of an early one attributed to a ruler. Merikare was a pharaoh during the First Intermediate Period, although it is not clear whether he ruled the whole of Egypt or only part of it during this period of turmoil. The 'instruction' is presented as his father's advice to him, and Lichtheim (1975, p. 97) believes that it probably dates to Merikare's reign even if his father was not the author. The historical context suggested by the work points to a time of civil unrest and disorder, making a First Intermediate Period dating plausible. The beginning of the text is missing, but at the end its purpose is made plain:

> Do not neglect my speech,
> Which lays down all the laws of kingship,
> Which instructs you, that you may rule the land ...
> May you be called 'he who ended the time of trouble,' ...
> Lo, I have told you the best of my thoughts,
> Act by what is set before you!
>
> (Lichtheim 1975, p. 107)

151

Just as a work of instruction intended for the benefit of a high official sets out guidelines for success in that area of expertise, so a work intended for the benefit of a future pharaoh addresses the challenges of rulership. Some of the advice is clearly pragmatic in nature: 'Strengthen your borders, your frontier patrols' (Lichtheim 1975, p. 100). However there is much else besides, and there is a clear concern for reputation as well as for success. Merikare is advised to surround himself with good advisors and to read and learn from what his ancestors have written. (This suggests that Egyptian rulers, unlike their Mesopotamian counterparts, were assumed to be literate?) There is a concern not just for order but for a just order; there is a concern for *maat*.

Another surviving example of a work purportedly produced by a ruler for his son is the 'Instruction of Amenemhet'. The Amenemhet in question, the first of that name to rule Egypt, was the founder of the twelfth dynasty, and seems to have come from humble origins. The evidence suggests that he rose through the ranks to become vizier to the previous ruler, Mentuhotep IV, before deposing him in 1985 BC and becoming pharaoh himself. Whether or not he was the actual author of the work attributed to him, it seems to have been written by someone with plenty of experience of intrigue:

> Be on your guard against subordinates, lest unforeseen terrors happen. Approach them not when you are alone! Trust not a brother, know not a friend, and make not for yourself intimates; in these there is no satisfaction. (Kaster 1970, p. 176)

There is little in the way of elevated tone or wider concerns here. The message of the instruction is that trusting no one is the key to survival. Amenemhet had good reason to be distrustful and it is thought that he was assassinated. It is not clear from the text whether it is meant to have been written by Amenemhet after his assassination, or whether it is understood to have been written after an earlier unsuccessful assassination attempt. However, as with the 'Instruction of Merikare', even if the work is not by its putative author, it seems at least to be a product of the period in which it is set.

Amenemhet clearly creates some difficulties for automatically identifying works of instruction as works of wisdom literature. While the opening lines of Amenemhet clearly state that it is a work of instruction, it is difficult to regard the contents that follow as wise in any interesting sense of that term. The tone of Amenemhet is more street-fighter than sage, and in the specific context of Egyptian wisdom literature, there is no evidence of any concern with *maat*. The use of the term 'instruction' does not seem a sufficient reason to regard this as a work of wisdom literature, even if it shares something of the form of other works of wisdom literature. In the end wisdom must be about content rather than form, and that is bound to render Amenemhet problematic.

But if Amenemhet is problematic, many would want to argue that Amenemope is paradigmatic. Ptahhotep and his kind were viziers, Merikare and his kind were pharaohs. With the 'Instruction of Amenemope' we move slightly further away from the centre of power. Amenemope announces himself as an official whose responsibilities concern the administration of land and the distribution of grain. He is evidently of the scribal class, and the son of a scribe. There are disagreements as to the dating of the surviving text, although all estimates fall within the first half of the first millennium BC. There is no agreement as to when it was first composed, but it was probably sometime during the second half of the second millennium BC. Such questions might be regarded as of minor importance were it not for the fact that Amenemope is the work of Egyptian literature that most resembles a work of biblical wisdom literature. Indeed, it is sometimes called the 'Proverbs of Amenemope' and the similarities between Amenemope and Proverbs were noted in the early 1920s when Amenemope was first published. Some have seen the similarity between the two as evidence that the Egyptian work had a Jewish author (Leclant 1963, pp. 9-10), while others have addressed themselves to the question of which borrowed from which, or whether there was a common source from which both of them borrowed. Because Proverbs is itself a collection of collections, dating is problematic. What seems indisputable, however, is that there is a clear and very substantial overlap between Amenemope and Proverbs 22.17 to 24.22.

Amenemope begins:

The beginning of instruction for living and precepts for well-being;
of everything for entering into the councils of the elders, and of precepts for courtiers;
of knowing how to return answer to him who speaks, and how to report back to him who sent him;
to set one right on the ways of life, and to cause him to prosper in the world

...

(Kaster 1970, p. 179)

As with other works already considered (with the exception of Amenemhet), there is a mixture of the more general and the more specific. For example, the advice Amenemope gives that one should not accept bribes is only worth giving to one who is likely to be in a sufficiently important position to be worth bribing, but his advice that one should be truthful and sincere may be offered to anyone. Although the work is arranged in thirty sections, the divisions do not always manifest an obvious thematic unity. Lichtheim (1983, p. 45) has pointed out that many of the sayings in the work concern one or other of the two types of human being she labels the 'silent' man and the 'heated' man, but this dichotomy does not seem to have significantly guided or structured the composition of the piece. As the opening lines make clear, the advice given is about both having a good life and having a good career, but the two are never seen as in tension with each other, and the same fundamental values run through both kinds of advice. Given its multi-faceted nature, the best term to summarize these values is *maat*, which can underlie both the truthfulness of the common man and the justice of the high official. The order of *maat* is not a rigid order in the social sense, for the instruction literature itself is testimony to a certain degree of social mobility, and some who achieved high office had humble beginnings. But there is a clear sense of a moral order, in the sense that virtue is rewarded and vice punished: the silent man will prosper and the heated man will suffer. One way of looking at Amenemope is as an essay on *maat*, not in the sense that *maat* is *analyzed* in it, but in the sense that it could be seen as an extended meditation on *maat*, with many examples brought together to illustrate many different ways in which *maat* may be manifested. Whether this is how the 'Instruction of Amenemope' was intended to be read is another matter. Nevertheless, it is evident to even the most casual reader that the work is far from being a pragmatic and amoral treatise on how to succeed.

Probably a little earlier than Amenemope is the work known as the 'Instruction of Any'. Surviving only in fragmentary form, it may have been written during the eighteenth dynasty (1550-1295 BC). Like Amenemope it is presented as the work of a scribe, but Any is an official of lower rank than Amenemope and his 'instruction' is all about everyday living with no reference to any kind of professional concerns. This work incorporates the novel feature that it ends as a dialogue when Any's son appears and complains that his father's instructions are difficult to follow. The Egyptians evidently did not believe that receiving instruction was the same thing as learning.

It may be noted that other examples of scribal instruction literature have survived, but I shall turn now to two late examples of instruction literature, the 'Instructions of Ankhsheshonqy' and the Papyrus Insinger. Neither has survived complete, but in each case what remains is substantial. Ankhsheshonqy bears some resemblance to Ahiqar in that it has a narrative framework. Ankhsheshonqy is identified as a wise physician who falls out of favour with pharaoh, and he writes his 'instruction' to his son while he is a prisoner on the ancient Egyptian equivalent of death row. The 'instruction' is a mixture of observation, advice, maxim and positive and negative injunction. Some of the advice is extremely pragmatic: 'Do not lend money at interest without a pledge in hand' (Lichtheim 1983, p. 81). Some observations come in clusters, for example those concerning the different kinds of 'wealth' (understood both literally and metaphorically), and there are many observations about married and family life. Lichtheim (1983, p. 45) notes that there are many references to 'the wise man' and 'the fool', who seem to have replaced the silent man and the heated man of earlier times (Ankhsheshonqy was probably written around a thousand years after Amenemope). Lichtheim also points out (p. 39) that there is no explicit mention of *maat* in Ankhsheshonqy. Nevertheless, there is a clear sense of order permeating the work:

> Do not insult the common man.
> When insult occurs, beating occurs.
> When beating occurs, killing occurs.
> Killing does not occur without the god knowing.
> Nothing occurs except what the god commands.
>
> (Lichtheim 1983, p, 87)

The order of things in one way or another is a recurrent theme of the work and, as Lichtheim observes (p. 43), wisdom seems to lie in perceiving and grasping the complex network of relationships that the work makes manifest. The extent to which Ankhsheshonqy also manifests external influences is a matter of dispute. A direct acquaintance with Ahiqar is argued for (Lichtheim 1983, p. 65), and if Ankhsheshonqy is to be dated to the period when the Ptolemies ruled Egypt (305-30 BC), which seems extremely likely, then familiarity with a wide range of Hellenistic learning (including the major schools of philosophy) is a distinct possibility.

Papyrus Insinger, from the same period, is a more organized work than Ankhsheshonqy but like Ankhsheshonqy it has a number of observations concerning the wise man and the fool. It often strikes a somewhat fatalistic tone, returning to the refrain that 'fame and fortune' are the gift of the gods on a number of occasions, yet it is not uniformly or universally fatalistic and the sense of an order that is stable and predictable rather than fickle runs through much of the text. Although there is some modest development of ideas, there is no real argument, and although there are groups of sayings organized according to different themes, in the end it remains more a collection of sayings than anything else. It is also a collection of sayings that compared with most other 'instruction' works lacks a clear context. Where there are instructions for pharaohs, high officials and scribes, Papyrus Insinger is more, perhaps most, like instruction for anyone, for everyone.

I have already mentioned that the 'lament' is sometimes seen as an Egyptian sub-genre of wisdom literature along with the instruction, and it may be appropriate to briefly say something about that sub-genre at this point. Whereas instruction literature generally identifies itself, the identification of a lament requires a little more judgment. The standard feature of the lament is a bewailing of the disorder into which things have fallen. Sometimes there are specific historical references to identify a particular period of disorder, but Lichtheim (1975, p. 139) argues that 'the theme "national distress" was an intellectual problem that became a literary topos'. If this is correct, then there is no guarantee that the periods of disorder described by the authors were those they had actually experienced, and some may even have invented fictitious periods of disorder for purely literary purposes. That may be important from the perspective of history, but not from the perspective of wisdom. What is evident is that a body of literature grew up around the theme of disorder, whether real or imagined. Because of the connection of Maat with *order* and with wisdom literature, it is easy to see why meditations on the problem of *disorder* might also qualify as wisdom literature, as forming the 'dark side' of the genre. Such examples as 'The Complaints of Khakheperre-sonb' and the 'Admonitions of Ipuwer' have already been noted [5.2]. One further example may be given, again thought to come from the First Intermediate Period, a work known as 'The Dispute of a Man with his Soul'. Again, the theme of disorder is prevalent, as evidenced by the following extracts:

> To whom shall I speak today?
> The evil have a contented countenance;
> good is rejected in every place.
>
> To whom shall I speak today?
> He who by his evil deeds should arouse wrath
> moves all men to laughter, though his iniquity is grievous.
>
> To whom shall I speak today?
> Brothers are evil;
> a man is treated as an enemy for his uprightness.
>
> To whom shall I speak today?
> There are no righteous ones;
> the land is given over to the doers of evil.
>
> (Kaster 1970, pp. 203-4)

Whereas some laments point to the order of nature being disturbed, and others are more interested in upheavals within the social order, 'The Dispute of a Man with his Soul' is most obviously concerned with the moral order of things: the wicked prosper and the virtuous suffer. What is missing is *maat*, what is required is a return to *maat*. The 'instruction' may give advice on how to live in accordance with *maat*, the lament graphically describes what happens when *maat* is absent.

4. Israel

It is not entirely clear when the wisdom literature of Israel first became identified as such. The traditional division of Hebrew scriptures that emerged was one employing three categories: the law, the prophets and 'the writings'. 'The writings' was a loose grouping negatively defined as what was neither law nor prophets. At some stage a group of the writings came to be identified as forming their own genre, wisdom literature. Opinions differ a great deal as to when this may have happened. One theory is that it happened at around the same time as the emergence of the rabbinical sages, that is to say, around the second century BC. Although dates are confused and contested, many assign the book of Ecclesiastes to the third century BC. Along with Job and Proverbs it forms 'the Wisdom Literature *par excellence* in the Old Testament' (Wood 1967, p. 55). Perhaps it is not unreasonable to believe that this idea of a group of wisdom writings did not emerge until after the third and last of these works had appeared? Two later Apocryphal books, Ben Sira (second century BC) and the Wisdom of Solomon (first century BC), are also normally regarded as works of wisdom literature. It is notable that the five works are in all kinds of ways very different from each other, suggesting that none of them was self-consciously produced as a work in the same wisdom 'genre'. And a genre within which no one consciously works scarcely qualifies as a genre at all. The debate as to what does and does not count as 'wisdom literature' has also been one taken up by modern scholars of the Bible. There has been much talk of 'wisdom influence' (for example in Dell 2000) and some seem to see it almost everywhere. This simply reinforces the basic point that the study of wisdom is not greatly helped by an excessive concentration on 'wisdom literature' as this tends to provoke discussions of genres, styles and forms that in the end miss the point. Wisdom, like stupidity, can appear in a variety of guises.

Where the secondary literature on non-Israelite wisdom literature from antiquity is relatively thin, there is a great deal on the biblical books, far more than can be reflected here. Fortunately, not all of it is relevant (for reasons I have just indicated), but there remains more than enough that is, and it will not be possible to do credit to it all here. Instead I shall restrict myself to the relatively straightforward task of briefly discussing each of the five above-mentioned books in turn in order to give some sense of their purpose and scope. It may be noted that in the case of the Old Testament texts, Proverbs, Job and Ecclesiastes, the authors are unknown and it is generally thought that they are works of more than one hand over a period of time.

Proverbs is in some ways both the easiest and the hardest to begin with. That wise sayings should be regarded as the distilled wisdom of wise people is in many ways a reasonable enough assumption, although calling something a wise saying is not enough to make it so. However, the book seeks to authenticate its contents by an initial invocation of a recognised authority (1:1-7):

> The proverbs of Solomon, son of David, king of Israel:
> That men may know wisdom and instruction,
> understand words of insight,
> receive instruction in wise dealing,
> righteousness, prudence and equity;
> that prudence may be given to the simple,
> knowledge and discretion to the youth –

the wise man may also hear and increase in learning,
and the man of understanding acquire skill,
to understand a proverb and a figure,
the words of the wise and their riddles.

Whether or not any of the proverbs in the book belong to the three thousand said to have been uttered by Solomon, they certainly do not all claim to be and Proverbs is clearly a collection of collections, one of which (22:17-24:22) is sufficiently similar to Amenemope to suggest either direct borrowing or a common source. The use of the term 'instruction' as early as the second verse clearly points to a connection of some kind with the Egyptian sub-genre. As with Egyptian instruction literature, there is a mixture of observations, some distinctly more profound than others. While it may be a good idea to keep your supply of water to yourself (5:15-16), and fair to say that a foolish son causes anguish to his parents (17:25), it scarcely requires a Solomon to observe these things. Although there are some recurrent themes in the book, including the importance of wisdom, and much of what is said has the ring of experience, it is too fragmented a work to make it easy to see any coherent overall view of the world underpinning it. There is, perhaps, a general sense that the world manifests a kind of order where both the wise and the foolish, the just and the unjust, get what they deserve. On the other hand, while this order is sometimes portrayed as an impersonal one, at other times it is clear that is it God, not some kind of natural law, that is at work. As has already been noted [2.3], it is also in Proverbs that the personified figure of Wisdom first appears in the Bible.

Job is a very different book. While it is not the single work of a single author, it nevertheless possesses a genuine coherence as it addresses the single topic of suffering. The general outline of the book is a simple one. Job suffers, but does not believe that he deserves it. His friends assume that if he is suffering he *must* deserve it. But there is a story outside this story, one that reveals that Job's faith is being tested by this suffering which, in terms of justice, he indeed does not deserve. As a meditation on suffering, there are parallels with earlier works from Mesopotamia. Parallels are not so easily found in Egypt. There the 'lament' was essentially about social disorder rather than personal misfortune (although the two could obviously be linked). However, while it is easy to see what Job is *about*, it is not so easy to see what it *says*. Job discusses his plight with four other people, and they all put forward their own positions and their own arguments, but no clear winner emerges. Pragmatically all is resolved when 'the Lord answered Job out of the whirlwind' (38:1), but the answer is more of a statement of omnipotence which, by implication, might be taken as a divine assessment of how insignificant humanity really is. Interestingly, Wood (1967, p. 66) suggests that parts of the answer that range like 'an encyclopaedic list' over various aspects of the natural world might have had their origin in 'conventional, stereotyped lists commonly found in Egyptian literature'.

Ecclesiastes is different in form again, a meditative piece on the ultimate insignificance and meaninglessness of everything. The prevailing mood is sceptical and pessimistic:

> Then I saw that wisdom excels folly as light excels darkness. The wise man has his eyes in his head, but the fool walks in darkness; and yet I perceived that one fate comes to all of them. Then I said to myself, 'What befalls the fool will befall me also; why then have I been so very wise?' (2:13-15)

The distinction between the wise and the foolish that was a staple of Proverbs and a commonplace in Egyptian instruction literature is here proclaimed as an irrelevance. In the end we are all dead. And before then? In the manner of an Egyptian lament the author bewails the fact that the whole order of things has been turned upside down and that wickedness is found where righteousness and justice ought to be (4:17). Make the most of life and enjoy it while you can; that seems to be the message, which might seem more like commonsense than wisdom, or perhaps it is a convergence of the two.

I have considered these three books in the order in which it is generally believed that they were composed. However, each shows signs of evolution and editing such that putting them in a strict chronological order is problematic and lines of development are difficult to trace. Do the three books follow parallel tracks, representing three different kinds of approach to wisdom? Or does the understanding of wisdom in Proverbs somehow *become* that of Job and *then* that of Ecclesiastes? In the end it has to be pointed out that they are *only* three books and as such are perhaps inadequate to support the great weight that has been put upon them.

Ecclesiasticus, or Sirach, or Ben Sira (as the book is variously known) leads us into new territory. Ben Sira is by a named author, Jesus Ben (i.e. son of) Sira, translated by his grandson, according to whom:

> after devoting himself especially to the reading of the law and the prophets and the other books of our fathers, and after acquiring considerable proficiency in them, was himself also led to write something pertaining to instruction and wisdom, in order that, by becoming conversant with this also, those who love learning should make even greater progress in living in accordance with the law. (Prologue)

Formally, the book announces itself as being in the instruction tradition. In terms of content, there is a clear and strong emphasis on the law (Torah) right at the outset, and wisdom is closely associated, if not actually identified, with it. This can also be observed in the *Pirke Abot* [4.5], pointing to this being a widespread rabbinical understanding of the nature

159

of wisdom and not a personal eccentricity of Ben Sira. However, this is not the only perspective on wisdom that the book contains and a number of different themes are developed in one way or another. The first verse of the book proper (after the grandson's prologue) declares that 'All wisdom is from the Lord and is with him for ever.' It is not entirely clear how this is to be interpreted. Is human wisdom simply a misnomer? Is the attainment of wisdom impossible without divine grace? Is wisdom impossible without revelation? In the light of the identification of wisdom with the divinely revealed law, perhaps the last is the most likely. Elsewhere the idea that 'the fear of the Lord' is, or is the beginning of, wisdom is taken up on a number of occasions, a theme that was also present in Proverbs and Job. Again, it is possible to point to connections between 'the fear of the Lord' and 'living in accordance with the law'. More controversial, problematic and difficult to explain is the appearance in Ben Sira of the personification of Wisdom. Hengel (1974, pp. 154-5) suggests that an increasingly transcendental understanding of the divine may have created a pressure towards the creation of intermediaries such as angels and the personification of wisdom. On the other hand, there is evidence of a certain eclecticism in Ben Sira, and the presence of a personification of wisdom in Israel's wisdom literature was certainly not without precedent, as has already been seen. Perhaps there was a revival of an old idea for a new reason.

Ben Sira also links the profession of scribe with wisdom:

> The wisdom of the scribe depends on the opportunity of leisure;
> and he who has little business may become wise.
> How can he become wise who handles the plough,
> and who glories in the goad,
> who drives oxen and is occupied with their work,
> and whose talk is about bulls? (38:24-5)

The engraver, the smith and the potter are also contrasted unfavourably with the scribe. They have skill, perhaps even knowledge, but not wisdom. The scribe, the *soper* (plural *soperim*) is an enigmatic figure in the history of Israel before this time. As Hengel puts it:

> The great period of these *soperim* lay in the two hundred years between the only two bearers of the title known to us by name, Ezra about 398 and Ben Sira about 180 BC; this is a period of considerable obscurity. (Hengel 1974, p. 79)

The prestige of the scribe and the connection with wisdom seems to have been a constant across the ancient world, but there is little hard evidence concerning the actual social role of the scribe in Israel before this time (leading some to compensate for this fact by drawing analogies with the role of the scribe elsewhere). This uncertainty makes it difficult to get a clear view of who the authors of the wisdom literature were, and who the intended consumers of it were. With Ben Sira we finally emerge into the light. However, by the time this happens we are also in an ancient world that has by now been substantially Hellenized as a result of the conquests of Alexander the Great and his successors.

This is perhaps more apparent in the Wisdom of Solomon (8: 7):

> And if anyone loves righteousness, her labours are virtues;
> for she teaches self-control and prudence, justice and courage;
> nothing in life is more profitable for men than these.

Self-control, prudence, justice and courage are collectively recognisable as the list of 'cardinal virtues' set out by Plato in his *Phaedo* (69c). The author of the Wisdom of Solomon (who was definitely not Solomon) was evidently familiar with Greek thought in some form, although not necessarily with Greek philosophy as such.

Like Ben Sira, Wisdom of Solomon brings together a number of different ideas and themes. While there continue to be many differences of opinion as to exactly what the structure of the book is and how it was put together, there is general agreement that it falls into a number of different sections, each with its own theme, the main ones being eschatology, wisdom and history. The section on wisdom begins by extolling its merits in various ways. For example (6:24):

> A multitude of wise men is the salvation of the world,
> and a sensible king is the stability of the people.

However, it soon moves on to become a hymn to the personified Wisdom, in terms that sometimes border on the erotic. This Wisdom who is admired and desired is the same Wisdom found in Proverbs who helped to create the world: Wisdom of Solomon calls her 'the fashioner of all things' (7:22) and 'a pure emanation of the glory of the Almighty' (7:25). While there are passages that might be construed metaphorically, others seem to clearly go beyond that and intend the personification of Wisdom to be taken utterly seriously. Some have seen in this the influence of the Egyptian cult of Isis (Crabbe 1997, p. 65) and, as with Ben Sira, the authority of Proverbs stood behind such a personification. But once wisdom becomes understood in personified terms, what it means to *possess* wisdom becomes problematic. However, the list of cardinal virtues that appears in Wisdom of Solomon points to an ethical understanding of wisdom, while elsewhere (7:17-22) there is a list of areas of knowledge that also seem to be associated with it, somewhat resembling the 'encyclopaedic list' found in Job. The extent to which the Wisdom of Solomon genuinely *synthesizes* these different elements, as opposed to simply juxtaposing or listing them, is highly questionable. In terms of articulating a coherent view of wisdom, it is not clear that either Ben Sira or Wisdom of Solomon constitutes any genuine improvement on Proverbs.

Although these five books are generally regarded as 'the' biblical books of wisdom literature, many have detected a 'wisdom influence' in a number of psalms, the books of the prophets Amos, Hosea, Micah, Isaiah, Ezekiel, Daniel and Jeremiah, the Pentateuch and the historical books (Dell 200, pp. 77-95). This may be taken to reflect two things. First, the lack of clarity as to what 'wisdom literature' is, and, second, the fact that books that talk about wise people are not always regarded as wisdom literature. The book of Daniel is perhaps the most obvious case in point, and that leads to another theme, apocalyptic.

5. Apocalyptic

Because apocalyptic is a genre that transcended cultural boundaries, it may be appropriate to allocated it its own section in this discussion. On the other hand, some might question its presence here at all. Consequently, the first task of this section is to clarify what apocalpyticism is and what its connection with wisdom is.

The term 'apocalypticism' itself is a recent one and so not the name of a genre within which ancient authors consciously wrote. However, a number of ancient works announce themselves as apocalypses, or revelations, so there does seem to have been a certain sense of what an 'apocalyptic' work should look like. The revelations that form the subject matter of these works are generally concerned with the end of history, which is more often than not portrayed as an imminent rather than a distant event. Insofar as apocalyptic works claim to relate what God has revealed to the (usually pseudonymous) author, it is reasonable to argue that they should naturally belong within the broader wisdom literature genre. In the same way that an oracle might reveal a glimpse of divine wisdom, so might a revelation granted to an individual. If the argument of this book is that wisdom has a strong association with the problem and phenomenon of order, then a revelation relating to the order according to which future historical events will unfold would seem to have a connection with that theme. Furthermore, the message of apocalyptic is often also concerned with the 'new order' that is to follow the end of history. The normal promise of apocalyptic is not annihilation for all, but a new age, a new order, characterized by justice. The fate of the evil, however, is often eternal obliteration. A late work (possibly written as late as the fourth century AD), the 'Apocalypse of Elijah' (5:22-4, 36-9), is fairly typical in its predictions of what will happen at the end of history:

> It will come to pass on that day that the Lord will hear and command the heaven and the earth with great wrath. And they will send forth fire. And the fire will prevail over the earth seventy-two cubits. It will consume the

sinners and the devils like stubble. A true judgment will occur ... On that day, the Christ, the king, and all his saints will come forth from heaven. He will burn the earth. He will spend a thousand years upon it. Because the sinners prevailed over it, he will create a new heaven and a new earth. No deadly devil will exist in them. (Charlesworth 1983, pp. 752-3)

Although the 'Apocalypse of Elijah' clearly belongs within a Christian context, apocalypticism was not confined to any one religious outlook. Apocalyptic writings have emerged from not only Christianity but also from Judaism, Zoroastrianism and Gnosticism, as well as from other religious perspectives not covered by this book. For reasons that are fairly obvious, it has often been thought that apocalyptic writing is the product of troubled times or disenchanted peoples or both. It is the nature of apocalyptic writing to look forward to the future, which is regarded as a better time. This strongly suggests a dissatisfaction, for whatever reason, with the present. There is a certain similarity to the Egyptian 'lament' sub-genre, and to some extent the two are complementary. The Egyptian lament bewails the present and the absence of *maat*, the apocalyptic work is full of praise for the future when moral order will be restored. However, while the apocalyptic work may be read as an implied lament, the lament does not necessarily carry with it the faith in the future restoration of order that is a feature of apocalyptic writing.

Sometimes the lament is explicit rather than implied, but with a twist. This may be illustrated by the book of Daniel. It is generally thought that the apocalyptic parts of it were written in around 167 BC, because they reasonably accurately reflect historical developments up to that point, ending with persecutions of the Jews under Antiochus IV Epiphanes, the Seleucid king of Syria (175-164 BC), but without mentioning setbacks Antiochus received at the hands of the Jews in 164 BC. However, the setting of the book of Daniel is some four hundred years earlier. Consequently the 'lament' is written in the form of a prophecy, and an account of present sufferings is dressed up as a prediction of future ones.

Technically, an apocalyptic work is, as its name indicates, nothing more than a revelation, and revelations could be about anything. The example of the book of Enoch has already been noted [3.3] and may be recalled in this context. However, 1 Enoch is unusual in a variety of ways. It is clearly assembled from a number of different works, which helps to explain its very substantial length. At least five different constituent parts have been distinguished by scholars, while some have argued for even more. Although some parts might be regarded as stereotypically apocalyptic, some are not. To some extent, this is a retrospective judgment, as Enoch seems to have been come relatively early in the development of apocalyptic literature. As such it may have helped to shape the genre but received little shape from it. The most obvious 'odd one out' of the various parts is the section dealing with astronomical matters, known as 'The Book of the Itineraries of the Luminaries of Heaven'.

Related to the apocalyptic genre, and included within it by some, are the works known as the 'Sibylline Oracles'. The original Sibylline books, purchased by the Romans but later destroyed by fire, were presumably simply collections of oracular pronouncements of the kind well-known across the ancient world [2.2d]. There is no obvious reason to believe that they were anything more than this. The texts known as the 'Sibylline Oracles' that have survived to the present day are something quite different. Whereas an oracular pronouncement would normally have been given in response to a specific query, the 'Sibylline Oracles' are extended prophecies, clearly constructed as literary works. The surviving works come from many different places and times. It is thought that the earliest are to be dated to the second century BC and the last to perhaps as late as the seventh century AD, while places of origin vary from Egypt to Syria to unknown. Some works survive in only a fragmentary state, some are clearly composite works. Some elements clearly emerge from a Christian background, some from a Judaic one, some from a mixture of both. There are also elements that belong to no particular religious outlook, and here the political is often to the fore.

It is difficult to make any overall sense of the 'Sibylline Oracles' since they lack internal cohesion. However, it is possible to point to recurrent themes that predominate. Of these, the most persistent one is eschatology. A description of what will happen at the end of history, how the present world will end and what will follow it, is discussed many times, with different degrees of detail and different apparent audiences. There is no one consistent line taken throughout. Some books are distinctly more pessimistic than others. The return of Nero, said not to be dead but to be living amongst the Parthians, is envisaged by some books.

However, while the eschatological elements discuss what is (at least from the view point of the authors) the restoration of order, other elements address the subject of order from a different direction. Another recurrent theme running through the books is that of a number of ages, empires and generations into which history can be structured. This was not a new idea in itself, and the idea that history could be divided up in this kind of way goes back at least as far as Hesiod who tells in his 'Works and Days' (ll. 105-202) of how one race was created after another. There are clear parallels between Hesiod and Book 1 of the 'Sibylline Oracles' where a similar story is told. However, the approach taken in some other books is very different from that taken by Hesiod. Book 4 of the 'Sibylline Oracles', for example (ll. 49-101), depicts the successive dominance of the Assyrians, Medes, Persians and Macedonians. Combined with its eschatological elements, the book might be taken as an early example of the philosophy of history, for according to it, history has both a structure and a point. Because the book is regarded as a composite work, put together in the first century AD, the contribution of its editor would appear to be the bringing together of two very different works in such a way that something superior to both emerges. In its way, the book lays out the order of the whole of human history, while at the same time locating it within a wider cosmic order, with the wisdom of the Sibyl as the guarantor of its accuracy.

However, it is questionable whether the *point* of Book 4, or any of the other books of the 'Sibylline Oracles', was to be in any way philosophical. They are widely regarded as having been designed to primarily serve a polemical purpose. On the one hand they function as propaganda aimed at the powers whose destruction is predicted, on the other they encourage the persecuted to stand firm because history will vindicate them. Descriptions of the punishment of sins are not meant to be read neutrally, but as warnings about the perils attendant upon moral failings. Condemnations are liberally sprinkled throughout the texts, with idolatry and all kinds of sexual transgressions (especially homosexuality) the most frequent targets. In eschatology, it might be said, concerns about the cosmic order and the moral order come together.

It is not surprising that there is much in common between apocalypticism and Gnosticism, since both are concerned with the human predicament and the way out of it. Indeed, there are works such as the 'Apocalypse of Adam' that are both apocalyptic and Gnostic (Charlesworth 1983). However, Gnostic theology sees the way out of the human predicament as a spiritual retracing of the steps taken to create the world whereas apocalyptic eschatology looks forward to the end of the world as the solution. For Gnosticism the whole of the history of the world might be regarded as one big mistake, but apocalypticism eagerly looks out for the signs that are omens of its imminent end.

The origins of apocaplypticism are a matter of dispute. Some favour a Zoroastrian source, others the mythology of Mesopotamia, others see it as a development of wisdom literature. As has been seen, the boundaries of apocalypticism are not neat and that in itself makes it difficult to be authoritative as to origins. Moreover, the significant degree of exchange and interpenetration between cultures in the ancient world means that multiple influences probably have to be presumed more often than not. The idea that the world comes to an end in a mighty conflagration, for example, which occurs in a number of apocalyptic writings, was an element of Stoic thought. Indeed, one of the driving forces behind Jewish apocalyptic writings seems to have been precisely the fact that Judaism was becoming increasingly vulnerable to external influences during the Hellenistic period (Hengel 1974). While some welcomed this, others did not and those who did not resorted to various forms of cultural self-defence, of which apocalyptic literature was one. In the end, despite their prophecies of far off events and their surveys of the whole of human history, apocalyptic writings generally had their eye on the short term rather than the long term and the immediate community rather than the whole of humanity.

6. A Sapiential Selection

This section looks at a variety of texts that are brought together here for the sake of convenience. While they might be assigned to other sections for a variety of reasons, they also straddle a number of different boundaries such that they have no obvious home anywhere. However, they are sufficiently significant to warrant a mention.

> Phocylides, the wisest of men, sets forth
> these counsels of God by his holy judgments, gifts of blessing.
> (Charlesworth 1985, p. 574)

So begins the work known as 'The Sentences of Phocylides', also sometimes known as 'The Sentences of Pseudo-Phocylides' as Phocylides was not its author. Phocylides himself was a poet from Miletus, writing in the sixth century BC. A few authentic fragments of his work survive. Although the provenance of 'The Sentences' is uncertain, many are inclined to see it as the work of an Alexandrian Jew writing in the first century BC or first century AD. It is essentially a work on ethics constructed mainly from short sayings. Sometimes a theme is developed and extended over a number of lines, but there is relatively little in the way of structure. The first sentences appear to be a reworking of the Ten Commandments, which one would expect in an ethical text by a Jewish author. However, there is also evidence of a knowledge of Stoicism, and the number of references to the importance of moderation might indicate familiarity with Aristotelianism. Lines on the positive value of hard work (ll. 153-74) seem to echo Egyptian works of instruction more than anything else. As with the 'Sibylline Oracles', there are a number of admonitions concerning sexual misconduct. However, it might fairly be said that many of the pieces of moral advice proffered are over-determined and could come from any of a variety of sources and backgrounds. As such, the work in many ways transcends both religious and philosophical boundaries. It ends (ll. 228-30):

> Purifications are for the purity of the soul, not of the body.
> These are the mysteries of righteousness; living thus
> may you live out (your) life well to the threshold of old age.
> (Charlesworth 1985, p. 582)

Another collection of sayings attributed to an early Greek author is 'The Sentences of Menander', usually referred to as 'The Sentences of the Syriac Menander' to emphasize both the language in which the work has survived and the fact that it was not the work of the third-century BC Greek poet of that name. On the other hand, it is possible that some otherwise lost genuine fragments of Menander are preserved in this work alongside many other elements. As a collection, dating is problematic, but the text may have reached its present state in the third century AD. A later epitome of the work also survives. It does not fit easily into any category or genre. Similarities to Pseudo-Phocylides have been observed, but also to Ahiqar and Ben Sira. As a collection of sayings it is entirely possible that materials have been taken from all over the ancient world, and, moreover, materials that have themselves been passed through a variety of hands. As such, the Syriac Menander may be a useful illustration of the international nature of ancient wisdom. On wisdom itself, the 'Sentences' say (ll. 27-33):

> If your son grows out of his boyhood
> (as one who is) humble and wise,
> teach him the 'book of wisdom',
> for the book is good to learn (wisdom) from.
> (Wisdom) is bright eyes and an excellent tongue.
> Eyes that are bright will not be blinded,
> and a tongue that speaks wisely will not begin to stammer.
>   (Charlesworth 1985, p. 593)

It is interesting to note that one manuscript substitutes 'philosophy' for 'book of wisdom' here, suggesting the kind of 'wisdom' that may be meant. As with Pseudo-Phocylides, the Syriac Menander is mainly concerned with moral matters. The basic tenets of the Ten Commandments can be found here along with various elements of Greek philosophy, and in the condemnations of laziness and talking too much there are further echoes of Egypt. Indeed, the Syriac Menander has much in common with Egyptian works of instruction. Divination, however, is expressly dismissed (ll. 292-3):

> Divination gladdens the hearts of fools,
> astrology infatuates the mind of the stupid.
>   (Charlesworth 1985, p. 600)

'The Sentences of Sextus' is another collection of sayings, probably compiled in Egypt in the second century AD. The fact that it has survived in the Greek original as well as in Latin, Syriac, Armenian, Georgian and Coptic translations is adequate testimony to its popularity and readership. Henry Chadwick has described it as perhaps an example of 'the wisdom-literature of early gentile Christendom' (Chadwick 1959, p. ix). However, the extent to which the sayings are genuinely Christian is a matter of dispute. This is reflected in a longstanding debate concerning the identity of Sextus, for while some assumed him to be one of the first two popes of that name, others have claimed Sextus to have been a Pythagorean. What seems clear is that Christians *believed* it to be a Christian work, even if others saw other things in it. Moreover, the general message of the sentences had an appeal well beyond the confines of Christianity:

The single theme of the maxims, running through them in all forms and variations, is the way to achieve moral and spiritual perfection. The believing soul is to pursue the moral ideal, which is to be made like unto God. Yet that impassible divine life is far distant from this mortal existence swayed by passion and earthiness. Accordingly, the first task of exhortation is to awaken the soul to self-realisation, to arouse it to know to how high and weighty an office it is called. Man must first reckon that the animal life of pleasure and passion is below his dignity and self-respect. (Chadwick 1959, p. 97)

Perhaps the whole of the book can be summed up in one single sentence (167): 'Wisdom leads a soul to God' (Edwards and Wild 1981, p. 37). Wisdom and the wise person comprise a theme running throughout the work. For example:

> (168) Nothing is closer to wisdom than truth.
> (190) Respect the wise man as a living image of God.
> (309) Next to God, nothing is as free as a wise man.
> (417) The soul of the sage always perceives God.
> (418) The soul of the sage is always in union with God.
> (Edwards and Wild 1981, pp. 33, 37, 39, 43, 45, 49, 51, 69)

This glowing picture of the sage (who is frequently implicitly identified with the philosopher elsewhere in 'The Sentences of Sextus') is one of the most extensive and detailed to be found. The sage is almost superhuman, or semi-divine. The sage is also there as a model and an inspiration for others, and in this there are echoes of the roles played by the founders of the philosophical schools. And the sage in turn emulates God, insofar as that is possible. Self-control is a recurrent theme, and it seems apparent that the way to wisdom lies through asceticism.

I shall finish this section with a discussion of 'The Teachings of Silvanus'. Although the name 'Silvanus' appears more than once in the New Testament, it is generally thought that the author of this text had nothing to do with any of them, but was probably using the name of one of them pseudonymously. The text is dated to around the end of the second or beginning of the third century AD, and is thought to have been written in Alexandria or the surrounding area. Although it is usually described as a Christian text, it manifests a wide variety of influences. The style is that of an Egyptian instruction (85): 'Listen, my son, to my advice!' (Robinson 1977, p. 347). There are also some familiar Egyptian elements of substance as well as style (97):

> A wise man (however), does not blurt out every word, but he will be discriminating toward those who hear. Do not mention everything in the presence of those whom you do not know. (Robinson 1977, p. 352)

As with 'The Sentences of Sextus', there is a strong emphasis on the importance of self-control. However, whereas 'Sextus' is a Christian text (to the extent to which it is one) that is silent about Christ, 'Silvanus' is not (106): 'For the Tree of Life is Christ. He is Wisdom' (Robinson 1977, p. 354). 'Silvanus' therefore brings together a wide variety of elements, but itself fits into no obvious category. It borrows from instruction literature, there is a clear moral dimension, the figure of Christ as Wisdom is one of its themes.

All of these works have something to contribute to the wider discussion. Collectively, they illustrate the diverse nature of wisdom literature and the difficulty of drawing its boundaries. Their eclecticism is in itself testimony to the inter-cultural dimension of wisdom in the ancient world. The fact that an Alexandrian Jew writing at least five hundred years after the death of Phocylides might think of appropriating the poet's name for his own work is instructive in itself. However, although only a few examples have been considered here, it is known that other collections of sayings were in circulation during the Hellenistic period and that a number of them were attributed to earlier Greek poets. Moreover, stripped of any metaphysical context, many sayings would make as much sense to a Christian as to a Jew, as to a pagan, as to anyone. Much of what passed for wisdom in these collections might equally well be characterized as the common sense of ages. While social contexts might change, a bad idea in one place and time was often a bad idea in another place and time as well. To that extent, collections of saying, whatever they may lack in terms of articulating a systematic outlook on the world, to some extent reinforce the long-term stability of the human condition by returning to the same themes not only across geographical and cultural boundaries, but also across centuries, and even millennia.

7. Hermetica

'Hermetica' is the term applied to a wide range of writings, all of which were supposedly written, inspired or revealed by the god Hermes. This Hermes, usually known as Hermes Trismegistus (the thrice great), was identified with the Egyptian god Thoth. The writings themselves seem to be of mainly or wholly Egyptian origin. However, they are not generally included within Egyptian 'wisdom literature' for a variety of reasons, but two in particular. First, they do not fall within the genres to which the term 'Egyptian wisdom literature' is normally limited. Secondly, they tend to be perceived as more international than national in character, the blending of Hermes and Thoth being but the most obvious indicator of this. Furthermore, the surviving texts are all in either Greek or Latin rather than Egyptian. Disputes about the dating of the writings have been going on for centuries. The modern consensus points towards the first three centuries AD, although that does not mean that none of the texts incorporates older materials or that none of the texts are from a later period. Furthermore, while this may be a consensus, it is not one that approaches unanimity, and some have put forward arguments for pushing the dates of the earliest texts back as far as the sixth century BC (Bernal 1991).

The problem of origins and dating is compounded by the fact that there are various kinds of Hermetic writings. There are works on medicine and astrology, magic and alchemy. There is also a body of philosophical writings, often referred to somewhat misleadingly as the Corpus Hermeticum, as if the Hermetica comprised only these. Of all these different writings, it is thought that the magical texts may be the most authentically Egyptian. There seems to be considerable continuity between magical literature associated with Thoth and magical Hermetica, and it is thought that some of the texts may be Greek translations of Egyptian originals.

Many think that (Western) alchemy was the product of Greeks living in Egypt, with the name of Bolus of Mendes often cited as the author of the first known work on the subject in around 200 BC. Either there is an unknown earlier tradition, or the association of Hermes Trismegistus with alchemy was a later anachronistic development. One of the most important alchemical writings, usually known as the Emerald Table or Emerald Tablet, was supposedly discovered in a cave, 'inscribed on a plate of emerald held in the hands of the corpse of thrice-greatest Hermes, Hermes Trismegistus' (Holmyard 1957, pp. 98-9). According to one legend, the discoverer was none other than Apollonius of Tyana [4.9]. The tablet contains the famous Hermetic saying, 'That which is above is like to that which is below, and that which is below is like to that which is above' (Holmyard 1957, p. 97). Although the contents of the Emerald Tablet are cryptic in the extreme, the central subject of its terse sayings is clear: 'It purports to summarize the principles of change in Nature and therefore lies at the root of alchemical doctrine' (Holmyard 1957, p. 97).

Although the tendency is to see alchemy as originating in Egypt, but from a Greek rather than an Egyptian cultural background, the picture may not be quite that simple. As has already been seen [5.9], Egyptian magic had a principle of *heka*, also personified as the god Heka.

> *Heka*, for the ancient Egyptians, conveyed a sense of the catalyst or energy that made creation possible. So every time a ritual was performed involving *heka*, it was as if a further development was thought to have been made in the process of creation. (Oakes and Gahlin 2007, p. 440)

Creation might be regarded as the ultimate 'change in Nature', and the energy that helped to bring it about, as well as subsequent changes in the world, might well be regarded, directly or indirectly, as a principle of such change. It is therefore tempting to see some continuity between Egyptian magic and its *heka* with the development of alchemy. Furthermore, 'sympathetic' magic was known in Egypt, whereby humans might associate themselves at appropriate times with appropriate deities to help them through difficult situations. A similar notion of sympathy can also be found in Hermetic writings:

> Among the basic intellectual common denominators of the technical Hermetica – and an important element also in the philosophical texts – is the notion that all phenomena, in the divine and the material realms alike, are linked by 'sympathetic' powers or energies into one pleroma. (Fowden 1986, p. 76)

The extent to which the Hermetic writings genuinely do articulate a single identifiable outlook is a matter of debate, but the presence of the notion of 'sympathetic' powers in a number of them is certain, and the principle according to which 'That which is above is like to that which is below, and that which is below is like to that which is above' is widely apparent.

In turning to the philosophical Hermetic writings, their concerns are at once both spiritual and practical. They are spiritual, in that they address the inner life and the divine, and practical in that they are concerned with achieving a particular goal:

> for the Hermetist, no product of human intellectual investigation, not even knowledge of God, was an end in itself: for underlying all human thought is the desire for release from this world of flux and materiality, for the salvation of the soul. (Fowden 1986, pp. 112-13)

The salvation of the soul is perceived as the attainment of immortality, and the primary route to this is through self-purification. Self-purification, in turn, is liberation from the material world. Some of the basic principles are set out in one of the shorter Hermetic texts, Libellus IV. In it, Hermes is addressing his son, Tat.

> If you do not first hate your body, my son, you cannot love yourself ... It is not possible, my son, to attach yourself both to things mortal and things divine ... You see, my son, through how many bodily things in succession we have to make our way, and through how many troops of daemons and courses of starts, that we may press on to the one and only God ... It is impossible that an incorporeal thing should be manifested to a thing that is corporeal ... . (Scott 1992, pp. 62-3)

On the face of it there is much here that seems similar to Gnosticism [2.3]. How close Hermetic writings and Gnostic writings are to each other is a matter of some debate, given the different interpretations that can be applied to both. There are ways of bringing them closer together and ways of pushing them further apart. And just as there are different forms of Gnosticism, so some would argue that there are different forms of Hermeticism. The idea that the Hermetic writings form a coherent corpus is not held by all. Nevertheless, the aspiration after salvation and the understanding of salvation as liberation from the material world is at the very least a bridge that links the Gnostics and the Hermetics.

171

It is generally acknowledged that the philosophical Hermetic writings reveal an acquaintance with a wide range of learning, most or all of it traceable to sources far outside traditional Egyptian learning. Stoic, Platonist and Pythagorean elements have been identified by some, as well as influences emanating from further east. Rather than seeking to identify specific connections with other places and systems of thought, it might be simpler to recognize the cosmopolitan and eclectic nature of Egyptian culture during the periods when it was ruled by first the Greeks and then the Romans, and bearing in mind that the Persians had also added Egypt to their empire in 525 BC and were the dominant power there for nearly two centuries.

One of the best known and longer of the philosophical Hermetic writings is the tractate known as 'Poimandres' Even its title is a source of interest, as one explanation of it is that it is a translation of the Coptic *p.eime.n.re*, meaning 'The Knowledge of Re' (Cartlidge and Dungan 1980, p. 243). The text itself presents something of a puzzle. As 'an excellent example of the religious syncretism that flourished during the Greco-Roman age' (Cartlidge and Dungan 1980, p. 243), it is difficult to know how to relate to each other its disparate elements that clearly come from very different traditions. The work is presented as the recollection of an anonymous author who has had a vision of someone introducing himself as Poimandres, 'the True Mind'. The first part of the vision concerns how the world was created and how the immortal and mortal, the spiritual and the material, became intertwined. The second part tells how this process can be reversed, how souls can become liberated from bodies. The third part sees the anonymous author sent on his way to preach what has been revealed to him. He declares (29):

> I became the mystic guide of the human race. I taught them doctrines (*logos*) of how and in what manner they should be saved; I sowed among them the doctrines of wisdom (*sophia*), and they were nourished from the ambrosial waters. (Cartlidge and Dungan 1980, p. 250).

The range of writings that found their way under the shelter of the Hermetic umbrella is a useful indicator of what was regarded as wisdom during the period in which they were produced and brought together. The Hermetic tag, with its clear association with Thoth, the Egyptian god of wisdom, serves as a kind of marker that helps to delineate the economy of wisdom at this time, although exactly what 'this time' is is not entirely clear. Later generations evidently thought that the Hermetic writings brought together and preserved the knowledge, both esoteric and exoteric, of ancient Egypt. In fact it seems likely that they did both more than that and less than that. More than that, in that sources beyond the frontiers of Egypt seem to have been incorporated, and less than that, in that there is no reason to suppose that their coverage is encyclopaedic.

172

8. The *Chaldaean Oracles*

I turn now to a very specific text, the *Chaldaean Oracles*. Although the text itself has not survived, fragments have been preserved in a variety of places. Unlike the Hermetic writings, the origin of the *Chaldaean Oracles* is relatively clear. The work is attributed to two people, father and son, both called Julian. More is known about the son, Julian the Theurgist, who was born during the reign of Trajan (AD 98-117) and served in the Roman army during the reign of Marcus Aurelius (AD 161-80). The father was known as Julian the Chaldaean. The *Chaldaean Oracles* achieved an enormous significance and became what might be regarded as the founding text for the practice of theurgy, which was to play an important role in the spirituality of late antiquity, and through the work of Porphyry and Iamblichus [4.18] became taken up by and incorporated within Neoplatonism.

The extent to which the *Chaldaean Oracles* was an actual collection of oracles is unclear. It is known that that is what the two Julians claimed it to be, and that a number of the oracular pronouncements contained within it were attributed to Apollo, Psyche and Hecate. It is suspected that at least some of the contents of the work were produced by the two Julians themselves. It was Porphyry who brought the *Chaldaean Oracles* to the attention of Neoplatonists, and he regarded them as authentic sayings of divine wisdom. His discussion of them in his *On the Philosophy of the Oracles* has been preserved through long quotations from it in Eusebius' *Preparation for the Gospel* (Eusebius 2002a) and Augustine's *The City of God* (O'Meara 1959). From what can be gleaned from these sources, the work contained a number of moral commandments and prohibitions, and some have seen similarities with some Hermetic writings (Lewy 1956, p. 35). Porphyry's work on oracles seems to have had the *Chaldaean Oracles* as its major source of material. Although it was written a hundred years or so before his time, he seems to have been the first to make it well known. At the same time, he put a specifically Platonist interpretation on it. The theurgical dimension was further developed by Iamblichus, and it was Iamblichus' teachings which came to the attention of the emperor Julian (AD 331-363). They were also taken up by Plutarch of Athens (fourth/fifth century AD), who became the first Neoplatonist teacher in Athens. His disciple was Syrianus, who in turn was succeeded by Proclus, who was particularly attached to the *Chaldaean Oracles*. Most of the fragments of the work that have been preserved come from his writings. Next in importance as a source is Damascius (fifth/sixth century AD). He drew on the works of Proclus and Iamblichus, and was the last Athenian Neoplatonist. Thereafter there were no further Neoplatonist commentaries on the *Chaldaean Oracles*.

The contents of the work appear to have been very wide ranging, and more than a modicum of eclecticism is evident. The basic structure of the universe is explained. Planets seem to have been identified with both gods and virtues, with possibly Mercury (or Hermes) identified with wisdom (Lewy 1956, p. 50). Another possible connection with Hermeticism is suggested by the work's 'basic magical belief in the sympathy of all the powers of the world' (Lewy 1956, p. 157). As in Gnostic works, the *Chaldean Oracles* seems to have contained its fair quota of demons, and they were often the cause of disease. There is also an emphasis on the importance of purification, which could have come from a variety of directions. The personification of evil in the form of Hades might be Zoroastrian in origin. The very title *Chaldaean Oracles* points to an eastern influence, although the extent to which the work contains genuinely Chaldaean, or Babylonian, materials is difficult to ascertain.

Although it is possible to see similarities between the *Chaldaean Oracles* and other works and belief systems, it is more interesting to look at what is most distinctive about the work, and this is theurgy. The term itself may have made its first appearance in this work, although its derivation is obvious enough, combining as it does the notions of the divine and work. Theurgy is therefore a means of attaining communication with the divine by the performance of certain actions. This might appear to be a form of divination, and to some extent it is. However, a surviving fragment makes it clear that the creators of theurgy intended it to be regarded as the only legitimate form of divination: 'The wide-winged aerial flight of birds is never true, nor yet the slicings of the victims and of other entrails. These are all toys, lending support to mercenary fraud' (Lewy 1956, p. 255). By way of contrast, theurgy was regarded as scientific, and its integrity and authenticity guaranteed by the fact that it had been divinely revealed.

Three types of people seem to have officiated in the rituals of the theurgists; priests, 'callers' and 'recipients'. The function of the first is unknown, the second invoked the gods, and the third acted as mediums for them. Both callers and recipients had to go through forms of purification. The principal theurgical ritual was a playing out of 'the destiny of the soul of the initiate after his bodily death' (Lewy 1956, p. 210). In its focus on the liberation of the soul from the body and its subsequent immortality, there were similarities between theurgy and both Gnosticism and the mystery cults [2.3, 2.2c]. However, theurgy had a far stronger magical dimension than either of them did.

More than one kind of ritual seems to have been practised by the theurgists, and Julian the Chaldaean actually claimed to have conjured up the soul of Plato. The connections between the *Chaldaean Oracles* and Platonism appear to be quite complex. It has already been noted that both Porphyry and Iamblichus were enthusiastic about the work and sought to introduce its teachings into their interpretation of Platonism. However, there is also some evidence that at least part of its teachings were actually based on Platonism. It has been claimed that elements of the *Chaldaean*

Oracles can be traced to the influence of Numenius of Apamea (second century AD) and Albinus (second century AD), although it may be noted that most regard Numenius as as much a Pythagorean as a Platonist. Again, it may be unhelpful to seek to be too precise in terms of identifying influences:

> It cannot be considered an accident that the origination of the Chaldaean system should be temporally coincident with the most flourishing period of the Oriental mystery-religions, of the Hermetic theosophy and of western gnosticism, as well as with the revival of the metaphysical tendencies of Platonism. (Lewy 1956, p. 312)

In short, theurgy was very much a product of its time, and its emergence is more likely to be overdetermined than underdetermined. For the faithful it promised a blessed life after death in the manner of the mysteries. The means of achieving this was to become as godlike as it was possible for humans to be, and the whole theurgical outlook was underpinned by the claimed revelatory status of the *Chaldaean Oracles*. Whether or not the contents of the *Chaldaean Oracles* were all genuine, the work itself is a significant milestone in the history of wisdom in the ancient world. It is clear that the usual reason for people visiting oracles was advice of various kinds, often on very specific personal issues. While whole communities might seek collective advice, it was still advice rather than any kind of overarching view of the world that was sought. The activities of the chresmologues in collecting oracles was for retail, not philosophical, purposes. What seems to have happened with the *Chaldaean Oracles* is that oracular pronouncements were seen as collectively yielding a coherent cosmology, philosophy and mystery cult. Just as Mesopotamian collections of omens began to reveal the outlines of the structure of the world as they became increasingly organized and systematized, so collections of oracles underwent the same kind of process at the hands of the two Julians. In this way, oracular pronouncements became seen not as isolated responses to individual concerns, but as fragments of the wisdom of the gods, and, moreover, fragments that could be assembled by those with the insight and imagination to do so into a coherent worldview and philosophy. Seen this way, it is little surprise that those who took the *Chaldaean Oracles* seriously found the work so exciting and innovative.

9. Conclusion

As with every chapter, there is much more that could be said. I have particularly not mentioned here the writings of the philosophers, yet clearly they dealt with wisdom, either directly or indirectly: directly when they explicitly discussed the topic, indirectly when they guided the reader in the direction of the wise philosophical life. However, as neither philosophers nor philosophy have been underrepresented in this book, their contribution to wisdom literature receives only this brief acknowledgement here. Similarly, Gnosticism has been dealt with elsewhere [2.3] even though Gnostic writings would easily fit within the category of wisdom literature.

If the notion of wisdom is broad and multi-faceted, so must the notion of wisdom literature be. Attempts to restrict it to a narrow range of genres purely on the basis that these are to be found in the Bible are unhelpful and must be rejected. The sole advantage of that approach, perhaps, is that it helps to keep wisdom literature within easily manageable bounds, but the price of such convenience is serious distortion and misrepresentation. Once it is liberated from such restrictions, wisdom literature becomes more representative of ancient wisdom itself.

In considering the full range of wisdom literature, certain practices that have received little or no attention elsewhere in the book have emerged, such as alchemy and theurgy. Other works reveal the fascination with proverbs across the ancient world and the willingness to ascribe them to almost anyone with a reputation for wisdom. The extent to which proverbs were genuinely international, in the sense of being *exchanged* internationally, has often been debated. While the possibility certainly should not be discounted, the idea that one nation needs another nation to come up with basic good advice about everyday life is not, on the face of it, particularly plausible. On the other hand, the idea that a particularly felicitous way of expressing a particular insight might, over time, gain a certain international currency seems rather more likely. In many of the writings considered here there is also a considerable measure of eclecticism, which might be regarded as another form of internationalism.

Because we have no idea how much has been lost, it is difficult to tell with regard to the earlier periods how representative the texts that survive are. What is evident from the evidence there is is that there was a certain conservatism in much of the literature, such that the same texts were being read for centuries, and the same materials were being recycled under different names in different places. Many of the materials discussed here simply offer insights into certain areas of life. Valuable though these may be, they do not articulate a wider vision of the world in the way that philosophical or Gnostic texts do. The Hermetica, *Chaldaean Oracles* and apocalyptic writings are broader in scope and do seek to present the bigger picture. In the end, the variety of styles and contents are a reflection of the many facets of ancient wisdom itself.

7

Conclusion

Since Job's question, 'But where shall wisdom be found?' was first posed in this book [1.1], it has become apparent that the ancient world was prepared to entertain many different answers to it. Certain individuals were widely regarded as paradigms of wisdom. On that exclusive list we might include such as Imhotep [3.4], Solomon [4.5] and Thales [4.10], as well as the founders of the philosophical schools [4.16, 4.17]. Even when legend has been separated from history, it remains clear that these were exceptional people. Perhaps it was wisdom's association with such people that led so many to stake a claim to it. Hammurabi and Ashurbanipal [5.2] are just two early examples of those who publicly announced their own wisdom to the world. However, while these were amongst the most celebrated claimants, they had ample company. But it was not just individuals; whole professions declared their dedication to or possession of wisdom of one kind or another. While those who followed these professions can never have constituted more than a minority of the population in any society, they were not a rarity either.

Why were some people thought to be wise? Why did some people feel entitled to claim to be wise? From all that has been said, I think it is clear that there is no simple answer. Even with Imhotep, Solomon and Thales, we have three quite different people with very different personal accomplishments. With the professions, we have different technical accomplishments. I suggested earlier [1.2] that wisdom was the pre-eminent virtue in the ancient world, and that 'virtue' in this context was to be understood in terms of 'excellence'. So it might be said that the wise were those who excelled, and that certain types of accomplishment, such as writing in Egypt and Mesopotamia [5.3], were widely regarded as evidence of, or kinds of, excellence in themselves. This is broadly in line with the observations of Aristotle [4.15], who also points out that hierarchies exist with regard to individual excellences, such that some people are recognized as superior exponents of them to others.

When the Seven Sages were discussed [1.3], an attempt was made to extract what they might have in common, and this proved to be a far from simple task. Having now roamed over many more instances of and observations concerning wisdom in the ancient world, the problem may be revisited. A number of associations with wisdom have emerged from time to time. One of these is knowledge. The cases of Enoch [3.3] and the Stoics [4.16], among others have witnessed a connection between wisdom and encyclopaedic knowledge, a connection that Aristotle would also endorse. Solomon was also said to have had such knowledge, although the precise connection between this and his wisdom was unclear. Instead, his reputation for wisdom was apparently based principally on his judgment. However, the famous example of his judgment was itself based on a kind of knowledge, knowledge of human nature. Solomon correctly resolves the dispute between the two women who claim to be the mother of a child because he knows that the real mother would rather give her child up than have the child killed. Threatening the life of the child therefore reveals the identity of the real mother. When it is borne in mind that the kind of knowledge that Aristotle and the Stoics associated with wisdom was not knowledge of an endless stream of isolated facts but rather a fundamental insight into how the world works, the gap between the knowledge of Solomon and the judgment of Solomon begins to look less significant than it might at first appear. Both might be said to involve an understanding of, or insight into, the order of things.

The theme of chaos versus order runs through a great deal of ancient wisdom literature. Egyptian laments paint graphic pictures of chaotic times when *maat* has been lost, and one of the purposes of instruction literature is to ensure the preservation of order in future by passing on the knowledge of the past [6.3]. And when Lipit-Ishtar and Hammurabi announce that they have established justice in their lands [4.4], they seem to be thinking of much more than the fair resolution of disputes between individuals, or promulgation of particular laws. Justice is a manifestation of order at the social level and the king is its guarantor and giver. In a similar way, Ea is responsible for order at a higher level, as explained in 'Enki and the World Order: The Organization of the Earth and its Cultural Processes' [2.2a]. At the individual level, it would be possible to construe both the 'life in accordance with *maat*' of the Egyptians and the 'life in accordance with nature' of the Stoics and Cynics [4.17] to mean 'life in accordance with the order of things'. And among the many possible interpretations of the 'Know Thyself' that were associated with both the Seven Sages and Apollo [4.14], one was 'Know your place' (Wilkins 1979), or more fully perhaps, 'Know your place in the order of things'.

What this points to is a hierarchical understanding of order within which three basic strata might be identified: the cosmic, the social and the individual. Perhaps the greatest shift in understanding with regard to cosmic order was the one traditionally initiated by Thales [4.10], whereby something at least resembling science came to replace myth, and something like laws of nature replaced divine will as the basis of cosmic order. Occupying the middle stratum is social order. While cosmic order might in a sense be 'out there' to investigate, social order had to be imposed. This meant not only keeping internal tensions in check but also protecting society from external destructive forces. This is one of the reasons why waging successful war was one of the requirements of a ruler. At the lowest, individual, level order is manifested in what might be termed the well-ordered life.

The three strata of order were interdependent in a number of ways. It was difficult to live a well-ordered life in a society that was in chaos. However, some philosophies and religious movements might be regarded as coping strategies for dealing with just such a state of affairs. The disengagement of the Stoics and the other-worldly focus of the mystery cults [2.2c], for example, might fall into this category. On the literary side, apocalyptic writings might be regarded as meditations on this theme [6.5]. Establishing and maintaining social order was not something that happened by accident. The fact that divination played such an important part in public life in the ancient world is evidence of the need felt by rulers to understand the ways of cosmic order [5.4]. And on the individual level, a sense of the proper order of things provided a guide to life in those areas that rulers overlooked or took no interest in.

Earlier [1.2], I suggested that a connection with order offered a way into making sense of the many different shapes and sizes that wisdom came in in the ancient world. However, while I think it has much to offer in this direction, it is necessary to consider those areas in which its role is more problematic. It may be recalled that Akkadian seems to have had twenty different words meaning 'wisdom'. The items on the list Sweet provides (Sweet 1990a, pp. 49-50) compiled from the *Akkadisches Handwörterbuch* and *Chicago Assyrian Dictionary* are clearly not all identical with each other, and some might be regarded as more, and some as less, centrally related to wisdom. Certainly the terms appear to derive from a surprising variety of roots. The fact that there are more entries under 'wisdom' than under 'wise man' (seven) and 'wise' (ten) put together might suggest a tendency towards a broader rather than a narrower interpretation. In the case of Hebrew and Greek, we know that the important terms of *hokma* and *sophia* evolved and changed meanings over time. The Bible calls Jonadab wise [4.5] even though he appears to have been a very different character from Solomon, and a fairly unsavoury character altogether. This might suggest that a particular talent for *anything* might have once been sufficient for ascribing *hokma* to someone, just as Aristotle seems to suggest that Greeks used to recognize *sophia* in almost any craft or skill at one time. All of this might in turn suggest that over the course of time, wisdom became associated with a progressively narrower range of accomplishments.

In Mesopotamia, too, this seems to have been the case. The *apkallu* brought all of the learning that made civilization possible, and they were indubitably regarded as both wise and the transmitters of wisdom [3.2]. However, the list of things that Adapa and the others taught humanity was very wide-ranging. While later Mesopotamian generations might well hold those who had mastered the skills of literacy in high esteem, did they equally revere those who had mastered the skills involved in working the land? It appears not, yet knowledge of agriculture was certainly one of the gifts of the *apkallu*. It is tempting to see a socio-political dimension to this. Were the kinds of skills and knowledge that became most valued by society those that the social elite appropriated to themselves and professionalized and/or made hereditary? Whatever the reason, what might be termed an epistemological class system seems to have developed over time and across large swathes of the ancient world, with wisdom occupying its upper echelons.

Because wisdom had a history, any generalizations about it are bound to be problematic. It is also the case that as far as the ancient world is concerned, we know rather more about its later history and significantly less about its early history. That makes tracing the course of its evolution difficult. However, from what we do know I believe that the general trajectory of its history is largely explicable in terms of the points that have just been articulated. A highly polymorphous notion that saw wisdom in a wide variety of human achievements became more limited in scope over time, and increasingly attached to 'higher' rather than 'lower' accomplishments. What 'higher' and 'lower' signified differed from place to place and from time to time, but there were identifiable general trends. What became regarded as 'higher' included the esoteric, that which dealt with the gods, that which required the longest training, that which was most abstract, and that which was most associated with the higher strata of society. The ultimate expression of this line of development was not only to assign wisdom to the gods, but to assign wisdom *only* to the gods. This gave it a truly elevated status.

In order to move this final chapter towards its end, it may be useful and appropriate to return to the four hypotheses I set out in the first chapter [1.2] and reconsider them in the light of all that has been said since then.

The first hypothesis, that wisdom in the ancient world was a multi-faceted affair is the least contentious, and I think the point has been demonstrated over and over again. Unless we are to impose retrospectively on the ancient world a narrow definition of wisdom and then refuse to acknowledge anything that does not conform to it, we can scarcely fail to see the truth of the first hypothesis. However, it is worth pointing out that not every facet of wisdom was apparent in every culture at every time. The second hypothesis is clearly more problematic. As I indicated at the outset, I am not convinced that this hypothesis fits all the facts. However, I believe it may be possible to argue that wisdom progressively evolved in the direction of concerning itself with the phenomenon of order such that the connection with order became increasingly strong and important over time. The connection was there from the earliest days, in the association of Ea with both wisdom and order, for example, but this aspect gradually became more dominant. Seen this way, it perhaps becomes easier to understand why the second hypothesis is imperfect in its application.

The third hypothesis may be differently perceived by different people.

7. Conclusion

There is clearly a metaphysical dimension to the hypothesis, and the line that I have taken will not be acceptable to all. In effect, we are presented with two basic choices: either human wisdom resembles divine wisdom because it is derived from it, whether through revelation or some other means, or divine wisdom resembles human wisdom because it is derived from it, whether through projection, magnification or some other means. While not denying the possibility of a genuine divine wisdom, I am inclined to take the line espoused by negative theology and assume that it is likely to be something beyond our comprehension and our language. What we call and know as divine wisdom, on the other hand, is a human construct. On this view, the gulf between human and divine wisdom is also a human construct and emerges when the divine is credited with more than we can achieve.

Finally, with regard to the fourth hypothesis and the best way in which wisdom is to be approached, I am heartened to find myself on the same side as Aristotle. In *Nicomachean Ethics* (1140a) he wrote:

> On the subject of wisdom, we may get what we need once we have considered who it is that we call 'wise'. (Aristotle 2002, p. 179)

It is clear from what has gone before that there was no universal agreement as to who should or should not be called 'wise', and the different lists of Seven Sages are perhaps testimony to that. On the other hand, some names just refuse to go away. Because people are different, wise people are different. In studying wise people we study wisdom in its concrete manifestations, just as the ancient Egyptians would give many different concrete examples of what living in accordance with *maat* was. Various professions became associated with wisdom for various reasons, and people associated with these professions clearly benefited from this. Myth, legend and history might provide ideal-types for these professions, while a number of them explicitly claimed to be dealing in the god-given. Wisdom literature has been given its place in the discussion, but I believe that the place it has been given, at the end rather than at the beginning, is the place where it belongs.

As I explained in the preface, because the subject of wisdom in the ancient world has turned out to be so vast, this book has to leave many areas open for further study and research. I hope enough has been said to indicate that such study and research will be both interesting and worthwhile. And I hope this book provides a useful introduction to the subject.

Bibliography

This bibliography contains information on the works cited in the text. A handful of others have been added that have been more or less directly drawn on even if not actually cited. For those unfamiliar with them, the titles of most works are sufficiently reliable guides to their contents. I have marked with an asterisk (*) some that may prove of particular interest. Translations of the works of ancient authors are listed under those authors' names.

Adkins, Lesley and Adkins, Roy A. (1996) *Dictionary of Roman Religion*. New York: Facts on File.

Alexander, Philip S. (1998) 'From son of Adam to second God: transformations of the Biblical Enoch' in Michael E. Stone and Theodore A. Bergren (eds) (1998), *Biblical Figures Outside the Bible*. Harrisburg: Trinity Press International, pp. 87-122.

Alster, Bendt (1974) *The Instructions of Suruppak: a Sumerian proverb collection*. Copenhagen: Akademisk Forlag.

Alster, Bendt (1997). *Proverbs of Ancient Sumer: the world's earliest proverb collections*, vol. 1. Bethesda, MD: CDL Press.

*Anderson, Graham (1994) *Saint, Sage and Sophist: holy men and their associates in the Early Roman Empire*. London: Routledge.

Apollonius of Rhodes (1959) *The Voyage of Argo* (tr. Rieu). Harmondsworth: Penguin.

Apuleius (1950) *The Golden Ass* (tr. Graves). Harmondsworth: Penguin.

Aristophanes (1970) *Plays*, vol. 1 (tr. Dickinson). Oxford: Oxford University Press.

Aristotle (1998) *Politics* (trans. Reeve). Indianapolis: Hackett.

Aristotle (2002) *Nicomachean Ethics* (tr. Rowe). Oxford: Oxford University Press.

Artemidorus (1975) *The Interpretation of Dreams* (tr. White). Park Ridge: Noyes Press.

Ascalone, Enrico (2005) *Mesopotamia: Assyrians, Sumerians, Babylonians* (tr. Giammanco Frongia). Berkeley: University of California Press.

Assmann, Jan (1989) *Maât, l'Égypte pharaonique et l'idée de justice sociale*. Paris: Julliard.

Athanasius of Alexandria (2003) *The Life of Antony* (tr. Vivian and Athanassakis). Kalamazoo: Cistercian Publications.

Augustine (2002) *On the Trinity* (tr. Matthews). Cambridge: Cambridge University Press.

Aune, David E. (1983) *Prophecy in Early Christianity and the Ancient Mediterranean World*. Grand Rapids: Eerdmans.

Baigent, Michael (1994) *From the Omens of Mesopotamia: astrology and ancient Mesopotamia*. London: Arkana.

Barnes, Jonathan (1987) *Early Greek Philosophy*. Harmondsworth: Penguin.

Becker, Udo (1994) *The Continuum Encyclopaedia of Symbols*. London: Continuum.

Bernal, Martin (1991) *Black Athena: the Afro-Asiatic roots of Classical civilization*. London: Vintage.

Bibliography

Bertman, Stephen (2003) *Handbook to Life in Ancient Mesopotamia*. New York: Facts on File.

Beyerlin, Walter (1978) *Near Eastern Religious Texts Relating to the Old Testament* (tr. Bowden). London: SCM.

Bienkowski, Piotr and Millard, Alan (2000) *Dictionary of the Ancient Near East*. London: British Museum Press.

Booth, Charlotte (2006) *People of Ancient Egypt*. Stroud: Tempus.

*Bottéro, Jean (1992) *Mesopotamia: writing, reasoning and the gods* (tr. Bahrani and Van de Mieroop). Chicago: Chicago University Press.

Bowen, James (1972) *A History of Western Education*, vol. 1: *The Ancient World: Orient and Mediterranean*. London: Methuen.

Boyce, Mary (1984) *Zoroastrians: their religious beliefs and practices*. London: Routledge and Kegan Paul.

*Brown, Peter (1982) *Society and the Holy in Late Antiquity*. London: Faber and Faber.

Browne, Thomas (1965) *Religio Medici and Other Writings*. London: Dent.

Burkert, Walter (1987) *Ancient Mystery Cults*. Cambridge, MA: Harvard University Press.

Burkert, Walter (2004). *Babylon, Memphis, Persepolis: Eastern contexts of Greek culture*. Cambridge, MA: Harvard University Press.

Cartledge, Paul (2002) *The Spartans: an epic history*. London: Pan.

Cartlidge, David R. and Dungan, David L. (1980) *Documents for the Study of the Gospels*. Cleveland: Collins.

Chadwick, Henry (1959). *The Sentences of Sextus: a contribution to the history of early Christian ethics*. Cambridge: Cambridge University Press.

Charlesworth, James H. (2003) 'Lady Wisdom and Johannine Christology' in James H. Charlesworth and Michael A. Daise (eds) (2003) *Light in a Spotless Mirror: reflections on wisdom traditions in Judaism and early Christianity*. Harrisburg: Trinity Press International, pp. 92-133.

Charlesworth, James H. (ed.) (1983) *The Old Testament Pseudepigrapha*, vol 1. London: Darton, Longman and Todd.

Charlesworth, James H. (ed.) (1985) *The Old Testament Pseudepigrapha*, vol. 2. London: Darton, Longman and Todd.

Charlesworth, James H. and Daise, Michael A. (eds) (2003) *Light in a Spotless Mirror: reflections on wisdom traditions in Judaism and early Christianity*. Harrisburg: Trinity Press International.

Cicero (1945) *Tusculan Disputations* (tr. King). London: Heinemann.

Cicero (1972) *On the Nature of the Gods* (tr. McGregor). Harmondsworth: Penguin.

Cicero (2001) *On Moral Ends* (tr. Woolf). Cambridge: Cambridge University Press.

Cicero (2006) *On Divination* book I (tr. Wardle). Oxford: Clarendon Press.

Clayton, Peter A. (1994) *Chronicle of the Pharaohs*. London: Thames and Hudson.

Clifford, Richard J. (1998). *The Wisdom Literature*. Nashville: Abingdon Press.

Cohen, S. Marc, Curd, Patricia and Reeve, C.D.C. (eds) (1995) *Readings in Ancient Greek Philosophy from Thales to Aristotle*. Indianapolis: Hackett.

Colless, Brian E. (1970) 'Divine Education', *Numen* 17 (2), pp. 118-42.

Cook, Edward M. (1994) *Solving the Mysteries of the Dead Sea Scrolls*. Carlisle: Paternoster Press.

Cook, J.M. (1999) *The Persians*. London: The Folio Society.

Cornford, F.M. (1957) *From Religion to Philosophy*. New York: Harper Brothers.

Crabbe, Lester L. (2003) *Wisdom of Solomon*. London: T&T Clark.

Crenshaw, James (1998) *Old Testament Wisdom: an introduction* (revised and enlarged edn). Louisville: Westminster John Knox Press.

Curnow, Trevor (1999) *Wisdom, Intuition and Ethics*. Aldershot: Ashgate.

Curnow, Trevor (2004) *The Oracles of the Ancient World*. London: Duckworth.

Curnow, Trevor (2006a) *Ancient Philosophy and Everyday Life*. Newcastle: Cambridge Scholars Press.

Curnow, Trevor (2006b) *The Philosophers of the Ancient World: an A-Z guide*. London: Duckworth.

Curnow, Trevor (2008) 'Were the Sophists Philosophers?' in Patricia O'Grady (ed.) (2008) *The Sophists: an introduction*. London: Duckworth, pp. 185-93.

Dalley, Stephanie (ed.) (2000) *Myths from Mesopotamia: Creation, The Flood, Gilgamesh, and others* (tr. Dalley, revised edn). Oxford: Oxford University Press.

Davies, A. Powell (1956) *The Meaning of the Dead Sea Scrolls*. New York: Mentor.

Davies, Stevan (2006) *The Secret Book of John*. London: Darton, Longman and Todd.

Dell, Katherine (2000). *'Get Wisdom, get Insight': an introduction to Israel's wisdom literature*. London: Darton, Longman & Todd.

Diakonoff, I. M. (ed.) (1991) *Early Antiquity* (tr. A. Kirjanov). Chicago: University of Chicago Press.

Dillon, John (2003) *The Heirs of Plato*. Oxford: Clarendon Press.

Dillon, John and Gerson, Lloyd P. (2004) *Neoplatonic Philosophy: introductory readings*. Indianapolis: Hackett.

Diogenes Laertius (1931) *Lives of Eminent Philosophers,* vol. 2 (tr. Hicks). Cambridge, MA: Harvard University Press.

Diogenes Laertius (1972) *Lives of Eminent Philosophers,* vol. 1 (tr. Hicks). Cambridge, MA: Harvard University Press.

Dodds, E.R. (1951) *The Greeks and the Irrational*. Berkeley: University of California Press.

Dudley, Donald R. (1967) *A History of Cynicism from Diogenes to the Sixth Century AD*. Hildesheim: Georg Olms Verlagsbuchhandlung.

Dumézil, Georges (1996a) *Archaic Roman Religion* (tr. Krapp) vol. 1. Baltimore: Johns Hopkins University Press.

Dumézil, Georges (1996b) *Archaic Roman Religion* (tr. Krapp) vol. 2. Baltimore: Johns Hopkins University Press.

Dunand, Françoise, and Zivie-Coche, Christiane (2004) *Gods and Men in Egypt: 3000 BCE to 395 CE*. Ithaca: Cornell University Press.

Edelstein, Emma J. and Edelstein, Ludwig (1975) *Asclepius: a collection and interpretation of the testimonies*. New York: Arno Press (a reprint of the two volumes of the 1945 edition in one book).

Edwards, Richard A. and Wild, Robert A. (eds) (1981) *The Sentences of Sextus*. Chico: Scholars Press.

Erskine, Andrew (ed.) *A Companion to the Hellenistic World*, Oxford, Blackwell, 2003.

Eusebius (2002a) *Preparation for the Gospel* vol. 1 (tr. Gifford). Eugene: Wipf and Stock (a reprint of the 1903 Clarendon Press edition).

Eusebius (2002b) *Preparation for the Gospel* vol. 2 (tr. Gifford). Eugene: Wipf and Stock (a reprint of the 1903 Clarendon Press edition).

Faulkner, R.O. (1985) *The Ancient Egyptian Book of the Dead* (revised edn). London: British Museum Press.

Ferguson, John (1970) *The Religions of the Roman Empire*. London: Thames and Hudson.

Festugière, A.J. (1950) *Contemplation et Vie Contemplative selon Platon* (2nd edn). Paris: J. Vrin.

185

Fideler, David (ed.) (1998) *The Pythagorean Sourcebook and Library*. Grand Rapids: Phanes.

Frankfort, Henri, et al. (1949) *Before Philosophy*. Harmondsworth: Penguin.

*Fowden, Garth (1986) *The Egyptian Hermes*. Cambridge: Cambridge University Press.

Frankfurther, David (1998) *Religion in Roman Egypt*. Princeton: Princeton University Press.

Gagarin, Michael and Woodruff, Paul (eds) (1995) *Early Greek Political Thought from Homer to the Sophists*. Cambridge: Cambridge University Press.

Gammie, John G. (1990) 'The Sage in Hellenistic Royal Courts', in John G. Gammie and Leo G. Perdue (eds) (1990) *The Sage in Israel and the Ancient Near East*. Winona Lake: Eisenbrauns, pp. 147-53.

*Gammie, John G. and Perdue, Leo G. (eds) (1990) *The Sage in Israel and the Ancient Near East*. Winona Lake: Eisenbrauns.

Gardiner, Alan H. (1947) *Ancient Egyptian Onomastica* (Text, vol. I). Oxford: Oxford University Press.

Gaster, Theodore H. (1964) *The Dead Sea Scriptures*. New York: Anchor.

Geffcken, Johannes (1978) *The Last Days of Greco-Roman Paganism* (tr. MacCormack). Amsterdam: North-Holland Publishing Company.

Goldin, Judah (1957) *The Living Talmud: The Wisdom of the Fathers*. New York: Mentor.

*Gordon, A.R. (1958) 'Wisdom', in James Hastings (ed.) (1958) *Encyclopaedia of Religion and Ethics*, vol. 12. Edinburgh: T&T Clark, pp. 742-7.

Gottschalk, H.B. (1980) *Heraclides of Pontus*. Oxford: Clarendon Press.

Gray, V.J. (2005) 'Xenophon and Isocrates' in Christopher Rowe and Malcolm Schofield (eds) (2005) *The Cambridge History of Greek and Roman Political Thought*. Cambridge: Cambridge University Press, pp. 142-54.

Grimal, Pierre (1991) *Penguin Dictionary of Classical Mythology* (tr. Maxwell-Hyslop, ed. Kershaw). Harmondsworth: Penguin.

Gutas, Dimitri (1975) *Greek Wisdom Literature in Arabic Translation*. New Haven: American Oriental Society.

Halliday, W.R (1913) *Greek Divination*. London: Macmillan.

Harrington, Daniel J. (1996) *Wisdom Texts from Qumran*. London: Routledge.

Heaton, E.W. (1956) *The Book of Daniel*. London: SCM Press.

Hengel, Martin (1974). *Judaism and Hellenism: studies in their encounter in Palestine during the early Hellenistic period*, vol. 1 (tr. Bowden). London: SCM Press.

Herodotus (1965) *The Histories* (tr. de Sélincourt). Harmondsworth: Penguin.

Hertzler, Joyce O. (1975) *The Social Thought of the Ancient Civilizations*. New York: Gordon Press.

Hesiod (1973) 'Works and Days' in *Hesiod and Theognis* (tr. Wender). Harmondsworth: Penguin.

Hodges, E. Richmond (1876) *Cory's Ancient Fragments of the Phoenician, Carthaginian, Babylonian, Egyptian and other authors*. London: Reeves and Turner.

Holmyard, E.J. (1957) *Alchemy*. Harmondsworth: Penguin.

Holy Bible (revised standard version). New York: Collins.

Homer (1950) *The Iliad* (tr. Rieu). Harmondsworth: Penguin.

How, W.W. and Wells, J. (1912) *A Commentary on Herodotus*, vol. 1. Oxford: Clarendon Press.

How, W.W. and Wells, J. (1928) *A Commentary on Herodotus*, vol. 2. Oxford: Clarendon Press.

Bibliography

Hultgren, Arland J. and Haggmark, Steven A. (eds) (1996) *The First Christian Heretics: readings from their opponents*. Minneapolis: Fortress Press.

Humphrey, Caroline, and Vitebsky, Piers (1997) *Sacred Architecture*. Boston: Little, Brown and Co.

Iamblichus (1989) *On the Pythagorean Life* (tr. Clark). Liverpool: Liverpool University Press.

Inwood, Brad and Gerson, L.P. (1997) *Hellenistic Philosophy: introductory readings* (2nd edn). Indianapolis: Hackett.

Jasnow, Richard (1992) *A Late Period Hieratic Wisdom Text (P. Brooklyn 47.218.135)*. Chicago: Oriental Institute of the University of Chicago.

Jonas, Hans (1963) *The Gnostic Religion* (2nd edn) Boston: Beacon Press.

Kahn, Charles H. (2001) *Pythagoras and the Pythagoreans: a brief history*. Indianapolis: Hackett.

Kaster, Joseph (1968) *The Literature and Mythology of Ancient Egypt*. London: Allen Lane.

Kerferd, G.B. (1981) *The Sophistic Movement*. Cambridge: Cambridge University Press.

Kingsley, Peter (1995) *Ancient Philosophy, Mystery and Magic*. Oxford: Clarendon Press.

Kirk, G.S and Raven, J.E. (1971) *The Presocratic Philosophers*. Cambridge: Cambridge University Press.

Klauck, Hans-Josef (2000) *The Religious Context of Early Christianity* (tr. McNeil). Edinburgh: T&T Clark.

Kramer, Samuel Noah (1963) *The Sumerians: their history, character and culture*. Chicago: University of Chicago Press.

Lactantius (1965) *The Minor Works*. Washington: Catholic University of America Press.

Lambert, W.G. (1996) *Babylonian Wisdom Literature*. Winona Lake, Indiana, Eisenbrauns (reprint of the 1960 OUP edition).

Lamy, Lucie (1981) *Egyptian Mysteries* (tr. Lawlor). London: Thames and Hudson.

Lawrence, T.E. (1962) *Seven Pillars of Wisdom*. Harmondsworth: Penguin.

Layton, Bentley (1987) *The Gnostic Scriptures*. London: SCM.

Leclant, J. et al. (1963). *Les Sagesses du proche-orient ancien*. Paris: Presses universitaires de France.

Leick, Gwendolyn (1999) *Who's Who in the Ancient Near East*. London: Routledge.

Leick, Gwendolyn (2001) *Mesopotamia: the invention of the city*. London: Penguin.

Levin, Flora R. (1994) *The Manual of Harmonics of Nicomachus the Pythagorean*. Grand Rapids: Phanes Press.

Lewis, John David (2007) *Early Greek Lawgivers*. London: Bristol Classical Press.

Lewy, Hans (1956) *Chaldaean Oracles and Theurgy*. Cairo: L'Institut Français d'Archeologie Orientale.

Lichtheim, Miriam (1975) *Ancient Egyptian Literature: a book of readings*, vol. 1. Berkeley: University of California Press.

Lichtheim, Miriam (1983). *Late Egyptian Wisdom Literature in the International Context: a study of demotic inscriptions*. Freiburg: Universitätsverlag.

Lindblom, J. (1963) *Prophecy in Ancient Israel*. Oxford: Blackwell.

Livy (1960) *The Early History of Rome* (tr. de Selincourt). Harmondsworth: Penguin.

Lloyd, G.E.R (ed.) (1978) *Hippocratic Writings*. Harmondsworth: Penguin.

*Lloyd, G.E.R. (1989) *The Revolutions of Wisdom*. Berkeley: University of California Press.

Bibliography

Lloyd, Seton (1984) *The Archaeology of Mesopotamia* (revised edn). London: Thames and Hudson.

Long, A.A. and Sedley, D.N. (1987) *The Hellenistic Philosophers*, vol. 1. Cambridge: Cambridge University Press.

Lucretius (2001) *On the Nature of Things* (tr. Smith). Indianapolis: Hackett.

Lundquist, John M. (1993) *The Temple: meeting place of heaven and earth*. London: Thames and Hudson.

Mack, Burton L. (1993) *The Lost Gospel: the Book of Q and Christian Origins*. Shaftesbury: Element.

Mack-Fisher, Loren R. (1990a) 'A survey and reading guide to the didactic literature of Ugarit: prolegomenon to a study of the sage' in John G. Gammie and Leo G. Perdue (eds) (1990) *The Sage in Israel and the Ancient Near East*. Winona Lake: Eisenbrauns, pp. 67-80.

Mack-Fisher, Loren R. (1990b) 'The scribe (and sage) in the royal court at Ugarit' in John G. Gammie and Leo G. Perdue (eds) (1990) *The Sage in Israel and the Ancient Near East*. Winona Lake: Eisenbrauns, pp. 109-15.

Marshall, Peter (2001) *The Philosopher's Stone*. London: Pan.

Martindale, J.R. (ed.) (1992) *Prosopography of the Later Roman Empire,* vol. 3. Cambridge: Cambridge University Press.

McGinn, Bernard, Collins, John J. and Stein, Stephen J. (eds) (2003) *The Continuum History of Apocalypticism*, New York: Continuum.

McKane, William (1970). *Proverbs: a new approach*. London: SCM Press.

Metzger, Bruce M. and Coogan, Michael D. (eds) (1993) *The Oxford Companion to the Bible*. New York: Oxford University Press.

Meyer, Marvin (2003) *Secret Gospels*. Harrisburg: Trinity Press International.

Meyer, Marvin (2005) *The Gnostic Discoveries: The Impact of the Nag Hammadi Library*. New York: HarperOne.

Nemet-Nejat, Karen Rhea (1998). *Daily Life in Ancient Mesopotamia*. Westport: Greenwood Press.

Neusner, Jacob (ed.) (1968). *Religions in Antiquity: essays in memory of Erwin Ramsdell Goodenough*. Leiden: Brill.

Nicomachus the Pythagorean (1994) *The Manual of Harmonics* (tr. Levin). Grand Rapids: Phanes.

Nightingale, Andrea Wilson (2004) Theoria *in its Cultural Context*. Cambridge: Cambridge University Press.

Nilsson, Martin P. (1972) *Greek Folk Religion*. Philadelphia: University of Pennsylvania Press.

O'Grady, Patricia (ed.) (2008) *The Sophists: an introduction*. London: Duckworth.

O'Grady, Patricia F. (2002) *Thales of Miletus*. Aldershot: Ashgate.

O'Meara, John J. (1959) *Porphyry's Philosophy from Oracles in Augustine*. Paris: Études Augustiniennes.

Oakes, Lorna and Gahlin, Lucia (2007) *Ancient Egypt*. London: Hermes House.

Ogden, Daniel (2002) *Magic, Witchcraft, and Ghosts in the Greek and Roman Worlds*. New York: Oxford University Press.

Oppenheim, A. Leo (1956) *The Interpretation of Dreams in the Ancient Near East*. Philadelphia: American Philosophical Society (Transactions of the American Philosophical Society, vol. 46, pt. 3).

Pausanias (1971a) *Guide to Greece*, vol. 1 (tr. Levi). Harmondsworth: Penguin.

Pausanias (1971b) *Guide to Greece*, vol. 2 (tr. Levi). Harmondsworth: Penguin.

Pelikan, Jaroslav (2005) *Jesus through the Centuries. Mary through the Centuries*. New York: History Book Club.

Bibliography

Philostratus (1970) *Life of Apollonius* (tr. Jones). Harmondsworth: Penguin.

Plato (1956) *Protagoras* and *Meno* (tr. Guthrie). Harmondsworth: Penguin.

Plato (1969) *The Last Days of Socrates* (tr. Treddennick). Harmondsworth: Penguin.

Plato (1970) *The Dialogues of Plato* vol. 2 (tr. Jowett). London: Sphere.

Plato (1992) *Republic* (tr. Grube). Indianapolis: Hackett.

Plutarch (1960) *The Rise and Fall of Athens* (tr. Scott-Kilvert). Harmondsworth: Penguin.

Pollard, John (1965) *Seers, Shrines and Sirens*. London: George Allen and Unwin.

Price, Simon and Kearns, Emily (eds) (2003) *The Oxford Dictionary of Classical Myth and Religion*. Oxford: Oxford University Press.

Pritchard, James B. (ed.) (1969) *Ancient Near Eastern Texts relating to the Old Testament* (3rd edn with supplement). Princeton: Princeton University Press.

Raaflaub, Kurt A. (2005) 'Poets, lawgivers, and the beginnings of political reflection in archaic Greece' in Christopher Rowe and Malcolm Schofield (eds) (2005) *The Cambridge History of Greek and Roman Political Thought*. Cambridge: Cambridge University Press, pp. 23-59.

Rad, Gerhard von (1972) *Wisdom in Israel*. London: SCM Press.

Reiner, Erica (1995) *Astral Magic in Babylonia*. Philadelphia: American Philosophical Society.

Reitzenstein, Richard (1978) *Hellenistic Mystery-Religions: their basic ideas and significance* (tr. Steely). Pittsburgh: Pickwick Press.

Rice, Michael (2002) *Who's Who in Ancient Egypt*. London: Routledge.

Robinson, James M. (ed.) (1977) *The Nag Hammadi Library in English*. Leiden: Brill.

*Rochberg, Francesca (2004) *The Heavenly Writing: divination, horoscopy and astronomy is Mesopotamian culture*. Cambridge: Cambridge University Press.

Rohl, David (1998) *Legend: the genesis of civilization*. London: Random House.

Rowe, Christopher and Schofield, Malcolm (eds) (2005) *The Cambridge History of Greek and Roman Political Thought*. Cambridge: Cambridge University Press.

Rudolph, Kurt (1983) *Gnosis: the nature and history of Gnosticism* (tr. Wilson). Edinburgh: T&T Clark.

*Rudolph, Kurt (1987) 'Wisdom', in M. Eliade (ed.) *The Encyclopaedia of Religion*, vol. 15. New York: Macmillan, pp. 393-401.

Russell, James R. (1990a) 'The Sage in Ancient Iranian Literature' in John G. Gammie and Leo G. Perdue (eds) (1990) *The Sage in Israel and the Ancient Near East*. Winona Lake: Eisenbrauns, pp. 81-92.

Saggs, H.W.F. (1965) *Everyday Life in Babylonia and Assyria*. London/New York: Batsford/Putnam.

*Saggs, H.W.F. (1978) *The Encounter with the Divine in Mesopotamia and Israel*. London: Athlone Press.

Samuelson, Norbert M. (2003) *Jewish Philosophy: an introduction*. London: Continuum.

Schipflinger, Thomas (1998) *Sophia-Maria: a holistic vision of creation*. York Beach: Samuel Weiser.

Scott, Martin (1992) *Sophia and the Johannine Jesus*. Sheffield: JSOT Press.

Scott, Walter (1992) *Hermetica*. np: Solos Press.

Seneca (1969) *Letters from a Stoic* (tr. Campbell). Harmondsworth: Penguin.

Shaw, Ian and Nicholson, Christopher (2003) *The Dictionary of Ancient Egypt*. New York: Harry N. Abrams.

Bibliography

Soden, Wolfram von (1994) *The Ancient Orient: an introduction to the study of the ancient Ear East*. Grand Rapids: Eerdmans.

Sprague, Rosamond Kent (ed.) (2001) *The Older Sophists*. Indianapolis: Hackett.

Strack, H. L. and Stemberger, G. (1991). *Introduction to the Talmud and Midrash* (tr. Bockmuehl). Edinburgh: T&T Clark.

Stroker, William D. (1989) *Extracanonical Sayings of Jesus*. Atlanta: Scholars Press.

Sweet, Ronald F.G. (1990a) 'The Sage in Akkadian Literature: a philological study', in John G Gammie and Leo G. Perdue (eds) (1990) *The Sage in Israel and the Ancient Near East*. Winona Lake: Eisenbrauns, pp. 45-65.

Sweet, Ronald F.G. (1990b) 'The Sage in Mesopotamian Palaces and Royal Courts', in John G. Gammie and Leo G. Perdue (eds) (1990) *The Sage in Israel and the Ancient Near East*. Winona Lake: Eisenbrauns, pp. 99-107.

Temple, Robert (1992) 'Consulting the Oracles; the classic systems of Greece and Rome', in John Matthews (ed.) (1992) *The World Atlas of Divination*. London: Headline, pp. 65-73.

Tripolitis, Antonia (2002) *Religions of the Hellenistic-Roman Age*. Grand Rapids: Eerdmans.

Turcan, Robert (1996) *The Cults of the Roman Empire* (tr. Nevill). Oxford: Blackwell.

Urbach, Ephraim E. (1979). *The Sages: their concepts and beliefs* vol. 1 (tr. Abrahams). Jerusalem: Magnes Press.

Valantasis, Richard (2006) *Gnosticism: and other vanished Christianities*. New York: Doubleday.

Valantasis, Richard (ed.) (2000) *Religions of Late Antiquity in Practice*. Princeton: Princeton University Press.

Vermes, Geza (1995) *The Dead Sea Scrolls in English* (4th edn). Sheffield: Sheffield Academic Press.

Vernant, J-P. et al. (1974). *Divination et Rationalité*. Paris, Éditions de Seuil.

Vitruvius (1960) *The Ten Books of Architecture* (tr. Morgan). New York: Dover.

Voegelin, Eric (1956) *Order and History* vol. 1 (Israel and Revelation). Louisiana State University Press.

Voegelin, Eric (1957) *Order and History* vol. 2 (The World of the Polis). Louisiana State University Press.

Weeks, Stuart (1994) *Ancient Israelite Wisdom*. Oxford: Clarendon Press.

Wellard, James (1973) *The Search for the Etruscans*. London: Sphere.

West, M.L. (1971). *Early Greek Philosophy and the Orient*. Oxford: Clarendon Press.

Westermann, Claus (1995) *Roots of Wisdom*. Edinburgh: T&T Clark.

Wilkins, Eliza (1979) *'Know Thyself' in Greek and Latin Literature*. New York: Garland.

Wilkinson, Richard H. (2003) *The Complete Gods and Goddesses of Ancient Egypt*. London: Thames and Hudson.

Williams, Ronald J. (1990a) 'The sage in Egyptian literature', in John G. Gammie and Leo G. Perdue (eds) (1990) *The Sage in Israel and the Ancient Near East*. Winona Lake: Eisenbrauns, pp. 19-30.

Williams, Ronald J. (1990b) 'The functions of the sage in the Egyptian royal court', in John G. Gammie and Leo G. Perdue (eds) (1990) *The Sage in Israel and the Ancient Near East*. Winona Lake: Eisenbrauns, pp. 95-8.

Wilson, Robert R. (1977) *Genealogy and History in the Biblical World*. New Haven: Yale University Press.

Winton, Alan P. (1990). *The Proverbs of Jesus*. Sheffield: JOST Press.

Bibliography

Witt, R.E. (1971) *Isis in the Graeco-Roman World*. London: Thames and Hudson.

*Witherington, Ben (1994) *Jesus the Sage: the pilgrimage of wisdom*. Edinburgh: T&T Clark.

Wittgenstein, Ludwig (1972) *Philosophical Investigations* (tr. Anscombe). Oxford: Basil Blackwell.

Wood, James (1967) *Wisdom Literature*. London: Duckworth.

Yamauchi, Edwin M. (1973) *Pre-Christian Gnosticism: a survey of the proposed evidences*. London: Tyndale.

Zaidman, Louise Bruit and Pantel, Pauline Schmitt (1992) *Religion in the Ancient Greek City* (tr. Cartledge). Cambridge: Cambridge University Press.

Index of Places

This index refers to the place names on the maps on pp. xii-xvii.

Abdera, xiii
Arbela, xvii
Argos, xii
Ashur, xvii
Athens, xii

Babylon, xvii
Bithynia, xv
Borysthenes, xiii

Canopus, xiv
Chalcedon, xv
Chalcis, xvii
Clazomenae, xv
Corinth, xii
Cos, xv
Crete, xii
Croton, xvi
Cumae, xvi
Cyclades, xii
Cyrene, xiii

Delos, xii
Delphi, xii
Didyma, xv

Ebla, xvii
Ecbatana, xiv
Edom, xvii
Elea, xvi
Eleusis, xii
Elis, xii
Ephesus, xv
Eridu, xvii

Gerasa, xvii

Heliopolis, xiv

Hermione, xii
Hermopolis, xiv
Hybla Geleatis, xvi

Isin, xvii

Lampsacus, xv
Leontini, xvi
Lesbos, xv
Locri, xvi

Madaura, xiii
Mari, xvii
Megara, xii
Megiddo, xvii
Mendes, xiv
Messene, xii
Metapontum, xvi
Miletus, xv
Mount Etna, xvi
Mount Olympus, xiii
Mytilene, xv

Nag Hammadi, xiv
Nineveh, xvii
Naples, xvi

Olympia, xii

Piacenza, xvi
Piraeus, xii
Plataea, xii
Priene, xv
Proconnessus, xv

Qumran, xvii

Index of Places

Rhegium, xvi
Rhodes, xv
Rome, xvi

Samos, xv
Saqqara, xiv
Scythia, xiii
Shuruppak, xvii
Sicily, xvi
Sile, xiv
Sinope, xiii
Smyrna, xv
Soknopaiou Nesos, xiv
Sparta, xii

Syros, xii

Tagaste, xiii
Tekoa, xvii
Telanissus, xvii

Telmessus, xv
Thebes (Egypt), xiv
Thebes (Greece), xii
Thrace, xv
Thurium, xvi

Ugarit, xvii
Ur, xvii

Index of Personal Names

Abaris the Hyperborean, 75-6
Abzu, *see* Apsu
Acusilaus, 6, 7
Adad (Hadad), 17
Adadshumuusur, 59
Adam, 42
Adapa, 39, 40, 56, 179
Aenesidemus, 103
Agathocles, 130
Ahab, 62
Ahiqar (Ahikar), 2, 147, 155
Aholiab, 61, 132
Ahriman, 31
Ahura Mazda, 30-1
Akkullannu, 59
Albinus, 175
Alexander Polyhistor, 60
Alexander the Great, 161
Amaziah, 63
Amenemhet I, 110, 117, 152-3
Amenemope, 153
Amenhotep III, 46
Amenhotep, son of Hapu, 46, 49, 51,
    54, 61, 95, 117
Amenope, 54, 149
Ameretat, 31
Amnon, 61
Amos, 63
Amphiarus, 47
Amphidamas, 137
Amphilochus, 47
Amun, 136
Anacharsis, 6, 7, 29, 101
Anaxagoras, 7, 74, 79, 86, 88, 98-9
Anaximander, 81-3
Anaximenes, 10, 81-2, 85, 94
Androdamus of Rhegium, 72
Anementus, 40
Anenlilda, 40

Angra Mainyu, 31
Ankhsheshonqy, 150, 154-5
Annedotus, 40
Anodaphus, 40
Antigonus of Carystus, 103
Antigonus of Soko, 65
Antiochus IV Epiphanes, 163
Antiochus, 74
Antisthenes of Athens, 101-2
Antony of Egypt, 77-8, 95
Anuabuter, 60
Any, 154
Aphrodite, 22, 80
Apollo, 13, 16, 27-9, 47, 49, 73-5, 78,
    87, 90-1, 95, 105, 118, 143, 173
Apollonius of Rhodes, 47
Apollonius of Tyana, 2, 76-7, 83, 170
Apsu (Abzu), 14, 16, 40
Apuleius of Madaura, 26
Aqhat, 44
Ares, 80
Aristeas of Proconnessus, 75-6
Aristeas, 1
Aristippus, 104
Aristobulus, 1, 60, 84
Aristodemus, 7, 8
Aristophanes, 75, 87-8, 90, 127
Aristotle, 1, 7, 49, 70-2, 76, 78, 93-4,
    97, 99, 122, 136, 177-9, 181
Armaiti, 31
Artabanus, 121, 122
Artemidorus, 84, 122-4
Asclepius, 28-9, 46, 48, 121, 132, 141
Asha Vahista, 31
Asherah, 34
Ashur (Assur), 14
Ashurbanipal, 56, 59, 60, 109, 110,
    121, 139, 177
Asqudum, 59, 119

195

Astarte, 22, 34
Atargatis, 22
Athanasius of Alexandria, 77
Athena, 22, 29, 30, 37, 48, 71
Atrahasis, 41-2, 44
Attius Navius, 74
Augustine of Hippo, 2, 106, 173
Avtalyon, 65
Azariah, 44
Azi, 56

Baia, 120
Balasi, 59
Bastet, 22
Belitabisha, 120
Belona, 22
Ben Sira, 66, 159, 160
Berossus, 39, 40
Bes, 121
Bezalel, 61, 132
Bias, 6, 7, 8, 9
Bion of Borysthenes, 102
Bolus of Mendes, 86, 170

Caesonia, 143
Cain, 42
Calcol, 61
Caligula, 143
Cassandra, 47
Cato the Censor, 106, 129
Cato the Younger, 106-7
Ceres, 22
Chaerephon, 87
Charondas, 71-2
Chilon, 6, 7, 9
Cicero, 91, 99, 100, 104, 107, 125, 130
Cincinnatus, Lucius Quinctius, 106
Claudius, 51
Cleanthes, 98
Clement of Alexandria, 124
Cleobolus, 6, 7, 8
Croesus, 72, 120
Cybele, 22, 25-7
Cyprian of Antioch, 77
Cyrus the Great, 128

Daedalus, 47

Daiaukku, *see* Deioces
Damascius, 173
Danel, 44
Daniel, 43-4, 47
Darda, 61
David, 61-2
Deborah, 63
Deioces, 72-3, 78
Demeter, 22, 25-7, 77
Demetrius of Phalerum, 130
Democritus, 86-8, 138
Diana, 22
Dicaearchus of Messene, 7, 10
Dictynnis, 22
Diocletian, 76, 125
Diogenes Laertius, 6, 9, 10, 65, 72, 79,
    82, 88, 93, 96, 100, 103-4
Diogenes of Sinope, 101-2, 104
Diogenes the Sophist, 131
Dionysus, 25, 27
Diopeithes, 75
Djedkare-Isesi, 53
Djoser, 45
Dunnashaamur, 59

Ea (Enki), 14-16, 29, 39-42, 178, 180
Ehlitesub, 56
Elijah, 62
Ellil, *see* Enlil
Empedocles of Acragas, 78-80, 83-4, 89
Eneubolus, 40
Eneugamus, 40
Enki, *see* Ea
Enlil (Ellil), 16, 58
Enmebulugga, 40
Enmeduga, 40
Enmegalamma, 40
Enoch, 42-3, 51, 64, 177
Epicharmus, 7, 9
Epicurus, 95, 99, 100, 104
Epimenides, 7, 8, 71, 76
Esarhaddon, 60, 120, 147
Ethan the Ezrahite, 61
Euclides, 104
Euedocus, 40
Euphorbus, 83
Eupolemus, 60, 84

Eupolis, 88
Eusebius, 60, 76, 173
Ezekiel, 134-5
Ezra, 160

Fabius Verrucosus, 74

Gad, 62
Gaius Marius, 74
Galen, 139
Gorgias of Leontini, 89, 90
Grannus, 28
Gregory the Wonderworker, 78

Hadad, *see* Adad
Hades, 174
Hammurabi, 58, 109, 112, 119, 120,
    177-8
Hananiah, 44
Hardjedef, 52-4, 150
Hathor, 22
Hatshepsut, 54
Haurvatat, 31
Hecate, 22, 173
Hegesistratus, 74
Heka, 142, 144, 170
Helen, 22
Heman, 61
Hephaestus, 19, 80
Hera, 22, 47
Heraclitus, 85, 93
Heras, 131
Hermes (Trismegistus), 18, 23, 25, 43,
    169, 170-1, 174
Hermippus of Smyrna, 6
Hermotimus, 76, 79
Herodotus, 72, 74-5, 120-1, 125
Herostratus, 137
Hesiod, 88, 137, 164
Hestia, 22
Hierocles, 75
Hillel, 65
Hippias of Elis, 88-90
Hippobotus, 7
Hippocrates, 28, 139, 140
Hippodamus of Miletus, 136
Hiram, 133

Homer, 28, 48, 88
Husanu, 56
Huy, 117

Iamblichus, 84, 104-5, 173-4
Iltahmu, 56
Ilumalku, 56
Ilussaamur, 59
Imhotep, 45, 46, 49, 51-3, 61, 95, 117,
    132, 139, 177
Irenaeus, 35
Ishmaia, 56
Isidore of Seville, 28
Isis, 2, 22, 23, 25-7, 29, 33-5, 37, 161
Ishtar, 34, 41, 120
Ishtarlatashiat, 120
Isocrates, 73

Jacob, 61
Janus, 50
Jared, 42
Jason, 8
Jeremiah, 63
Jesus of Nazareth, 35, 36, 67-9, 76,
    102
Job, 43, 158
Jonadab, 61, 179
Jose ben Jochanan, 65
Jose ben Joezer, 65
Joseph, 60-1, 122, 131
Joshua ben Perachyah, 65
Judah, 61
Judah of Tabbai, 65
Julian the Chaldaean, 173-4
Julian the Theurgist, 173
Julius Caesar, 107
Juno, 22
Jupiter Optimus Maximus, 27
Justinian, vii

Kabtiilanimarduk, 59
Kagemni, 150
Kairis, 52
Karranu, 56
Kenhirkshepsef, 117, 122
Khaemwaset, 54
Khakheperre-sonb, 52-3

Khety, 52-3, 116-17
Khufu, 53
Kore, 22
Kothar, 47
Kshatra Varya, 31

Lactantius, 125
Ladagalili, 120
Lampon, 74
Lasus, 7, 8
Leophantus, 7-8
Leto, 22
Leucippus, 86
Linus, 7, 8
Lipit-Ishtar, 56, 58, 178
Livy, 73
Lucilius, 98
Lucretius, 99
Lycurgus, 49-51, 69, 71, 112

Maat, 19-22, 34-5, 98, 111, 142
Machaon, 48
Manto, 47
Marcus Aurelius, 173
Marduk, 14-16, 41-2, 56, 58, 135, 147
Mary (mother of Jesus), 35
Matthew, 44-5
Melampus, 47
Menander, 167
Menoeceus, 100
Mentor, 48
Mentuhotep IV, 152
Mercury, 174
Merikare, 151-3
Methuselah, 43
Minerva, 22, 29-30, 37
Minos, 48
Mishael, 44
Mithras, 25-7, 77
Montanus, 77
Mopsus, 47
Moses, 60, 64-5, 67, 135
Musaeus, 71, 76
Myson, 6-8, 87

Naamrasap, 56
Nabonidus, 17, 56, 128, 131

Nabu (Nebo), 16, 17, 41, 56
Nabuahheeriba, 59
Nabuzuqupkena, 59
Nanshe, 17
Nathan, 62
Nebneretu, 130
Nebo, *see* Nabu
Nebuchadnezzar, 17
Nedjemusonbe, 55
Neferseshemre, 19, 20
Neferti, 52-3
Nemesis, 22
Nergaletir, 59
Nero, 141, 164
Nestor, 47-8
Nicias, 74
Nicomachus of Gerasa, 84
Ningal, 17
Nisaba (Nidaba), 16, 17, 42
Nittai of Arbel, 65
Noah, 42-4
Numa, 50, 51, 73
Numenius of Apamea, 60, 175
Nut, 22

Odysseus, 48
Ohrmazd, 31
Onomacritus, 71, 125
Orpheus, 7, 8, 71, 76
Osiris, 22
Osorkon II, 130
Ostanes, 86

Palamedes, 46, 51
Pamphilus, 7, 8
Parmenides, 78, 85-8, 90, 94
Pausanias, 74, 124
Pepi, 116, 117
Peregrinus Proteus, 77
Periander, 7, 8, 10
Pericles, 74-5, 86
Phaedo, 104
Phaleas of Chalcedon, 72
Pherecydes, 7, 8, 10
Philo of Alexandria, 35, 67
Philocrates, 1
Philolaus of Corinth, 72

Philostratus, 2, 76-7, 83
Phocylides, 166
Photius, 103
Pindar, 8
Pittacus, 6-8, 72
Plato, 6, 9, 12, 49, 60, 70, 73, 87, 90-7,
    99, 104-5, 142, 161, 174
Plotinus, 104-5
Plutarch of Athens, 173
Plutarch, 10, 50, 74-5
Podalirius, 48
Porphyry, 22, 83-4, 105, 173-4
Priam, 47
Proclus, 173
Prometheus, 48, 50
Proserpina, 22, 26
Protagoras, 88-90
Psyche, 173
Ptah, 18, 19, 21-2, 29, 136
Ptahemdjedhuti, 52
Ptahhotep, 52-3, 150, 151
Ptolemy I, 130
Ptolemy III, 130
Ptolemy IV, 130
Ptolemy VIII, 46
Pyrrho of Elis, 101, 103-4
Pyrrhus, 83
Pythagoras, 2, 5, 7, 8, 50, 60, 67, 71,
    75-6, 78, 82-5, 87-8, 105

Queen of Sheba, 64

Ramesses II, 54, 136
Ramose, 117
Re (Ra), 25, 54, 136
Rekhmire, 53
Renetutet, 22
Rhadamanthus, 48, 49, 69, 71
Rimute-allate, 120
Romulus, 50, 73, 135

Samuel, 62
Sapsumalku, 56
Sarapis (or Serapis), 23, 25, 29
Sargon the Great, 114
Saul, 62, 143
Sekhmet, 139, 142

Seneca, 1, 98
Sennacherib, 120
Senusret II, 110
Seth, 42
Sextus, 167
Shamash, 17, 27, 120-1
Shammai, 65
Sharrishtakal, 59
Shemaiah, 65
Shulgi, 56
Shuruppak, 2, 42, 146
Silvanus, 168
Simeon I, 65
Simeon II, 65
Simeon ben Shattach, 65
Simeon the Just (or the Righteous),
    65, 67
Simeon the Stylite, 77, 78, 95
Sinqishamur, 59
Siptinarum, 56
Snefru, 53
Sobek, 121
Socrates, 5, 12, 87-8, 90-2, 95, 99, 102,
    131
Solomon, 60-1, 64, 109-10, 112, 133,
    158, 161, 177-9
Solon, 6-8, 10, 49, 69, 70-1, 111-12
Sosibius, 130
Sossianus Hierocles, 76
Sothis, 22
Sotion, 65
Spenta Mainyu, 31
Stilbides, 74
Suetonius, 143
Syrianus, 173

Tages, 124
Talos, 47
Tarquin Priscus, 74
Tashmit, 16
Tat, 171
Teacher of Righteousness, 66, 67
Tellias, 74
Terra, 22
Thales, vii, 6-8, 10, 11, 71, 80-2, 84-5,
    94, 96, 98, 105, 137-8, 177-8
Thaletas, 71

Themis, 22
Theophrastus, 130
Thessalus of Tralles, 141
Thoth, 18, 25, 37, 42-3, 54, 169
Thrasybulus, 74
Three Wise Men, 44
Thuty, 54
Tiamat, 14
Tiresias, 47
Tisamenus, 74
Titus, 51, 131
Trajan, 173
Tuthmosis III, 53
Tyrtaeus, 70, 71

Uan, 39, 40, 116
Uanduga, 40
Uradgula, 59
Utnapishtim, 41, 42
Utuabzu, 40

Venus, 22

Vespasian, 131
Vitruvius (Marcus Vitruvius Pollio),
    133-4, 137
Vohu Manah, 31

Wisdom (personified/goddess), 22,
    32-7, 66-7, 69, 158, 160

Xenophon, 73
Xerxes, 121-2, 125, 127

Yasiranu, 56

Zaleucus of Locri, 71
Zalmoxis, 75, 76
Zeno of Citium, 95-8, 104
Zerah, 61
Zeus, 47-8
Zimri, 61
Ziusudra, 41-2
Zoroaster, 30

Index of Modern Authors

Alexander, Philip S., 43
Assmann, Jan, 19, 21

Bernal, Martin, 81, 149
Bertman, Stephen, 115
Bottéro, Jean, 15, 58, 116
Boyce, Mary, 30
Brown, Peter, 78, 132
Browne, Sir Thomas, 137
Bultmann, Rudolf, 68

Cartledge, Paul, 49
Chadwick, Henry, 167
Charlesworth, James H., 37
Crenshaw, James L.

Dalley, Stephanie, 42, 116
Dell, Katherine, 147
Dodds, E.R., 78, 80

Ferguson, John, 22, 77
Festugière, A.J., 95

Gammie, John G., 130
Gardiner, Alan, 149

Halliday, W.R., 124
Hengel, Martin, 160

Kerferd, G.B., 70
Kingsley, Peter, 78

Lambert, W.G., 145
Lawrence, T.E., x
Lewis, John David, 112
Lichtheim, Miriam, 111, 151, 153, 154, 155
Lindblom, J., 63
Lloyd, G.E.R., 138

Mack-Fisher, Loren R., 56
McKane, William, 151

Pelikan, Jaroslav, 68
Pope, Alexander, 3

Raaflaub, Kurt A., 70, 111, 112

Saggs, H.W.F., 113, 115, 129
Scott, Walter, 35
Soden, Wolfram von, 40, 149
Stroker, William, 68
Sweet, Ronald F.G., 3, 58, 179

Temple, Robert, 124

Valantasis, Richard, 36

Wellard, James, 125
Wilkinson, Richard H., 21, 22
Williams, Ronald J., 54, 130
Wittgenstein, Ludwig, 10
Wood, James, 158